DISTORTED DESCENT

DISTORTED DESCENT

White Claims to Indigenous Identity

DARRYL LEROUX

UNIVERSITY OF MANITOBA PRESS

Distorted Descent: White Claims to Indigenous Identity
© Darryl Leroux 2019

23 22 21 20 19   1 2 3 4 5

All rights reserved. No part of this publication may be reproduced or transmitted in any form or by any means, or stored in a database and retrieval system in Canada, without the prior written permission of the publisher, or, in the case of photocopying or any other reprographic copying, a licence from Access Copyright, www.accesscopyright.ca, 1-800-893-5777.

University of Manitoba Press
Winnipeg, Manitoba, Canada
Treaty 1 Territory
uofmpress.ca

Cataloguing data available from Library and Archives Canada
ISBN 978-0-88755-846-7 (PAPER)
ISBN 978-0-88755-596-1 (PDF)
ISBN 978-0-88755-594-1 (EPUB)

Cover design by David Drummond
Interior design by Jess Koroscil

This book has been published with the help of a grant from the Federation for the Humanities and Social Sciences, through the Awards to Scholarly Publications Program, using funds provided by the Social Sciences and Humanities Research Council of Canada.

The University of Manitoba Press acknowledges the financial support for its publication program provided by the Government of Canada through the Canada Book Fund, the Canada Council for the Arts, the Manitoba Department of Sport, Culture, and Heritage, the Manitoba Arts Council, and the Manitoba Book Publishing Tax Credit.

CONTENTS

Introduction
SELF-INDIGENIZATION IN THE TWENTY-FIRST CENTURY   1

PART ONE: THE MECHANICS OF DESCENT

Chapter One
LINEAL DESCENT AND THE POLITICAL USE OF INDIGENOUS WOMEN ANCESTORS   41

Chapter Two
ASPIRATIONAL DESCENT: CREATING INDIGENOUS WOMEN ANCESTORS   73

Chapter Three
LATERAL DESCENT: REMAKING FAMILY IN THE PAST   103

PART TWO: RACE SHIFTING AS ANTI-INDIGENOUS POLITICS

Chapter Four
AFTER POWLEY: ANTI-INDIGENOUS ACTIVISM AND BECOMING "MÉTIS" IN TWO REGIONS OF QUEBEC   135

Chapter Five
THE LARGEST SELF-IDENTIFIED "MÉTIS" ORGANIZATION IN QUEBEC: THE MÉTIS NATION OF THE RISING SUN   177

Conclusion
WHITE CLAIMS TO INDIGENOUS IDENTITY   214

ACKNOWLEDGEMENTS   221
APPENDIX   223
NOTES   239
BIBLIOGRAPHY   257
INDEX   273

Introduction

Self-Indigenization in the Twenty-First Century

This book examines the specifics of a social phenomenon that has been in full flight since the turn of the twenty-first century: the shifting of otherwise white, French descendants in Canada (and the United States) into an Indigenous identity. This type of phenomenon is not entirely new, as many scholars who have explored similar processes occurring in the United States since the 1970s have demonstrated. Nevertheless, research into the issue in Canada is more recent, as is the phenomenon itself. To be clear from the outset, this study is not about individuals who have been dispossessed by colonial policies—the Indian Act, residential schools, the Sixties Scoop, and still others—or their attempts to reconnect with their kin, family, and community. The impacts of the insidious efforts by settler governments to destroy Indigenous political capacity through attacks on the structure and integrity of families continue to reverberate through Indigenous lifeways in the twenty-first century. Countless individuals have sought to reconnect in ways that are complicated by the colonial legacies at work. I am especially attentive to ongoing practices in the child welfare and youth criminal justice systems that remove a hugely disproportionate number of Indigenous youth from their families and communities. My arguments may evoke some discomfort in readers, particularly among those who are reconnecting with Indigenous kin and/or reclaiming an Indigenous identity, but this book is not about the multi-generational efforts at reconnection that take place as a response to government policies and laws.

No, this study is concerned with an altogether different set of problematics, one that involves white French-descendant people using an

Indigenous ancestor born between 300 and 375 years ago as the basis for a contemporary "Indigenous" identity. Contrary to popular belief, only a small number of Indigenous women married French settler men during the first few decades of the French regime. Historical demographer Hubert Charbonneau confirms as much in an interview entitled "Myth or Reality: The Aboriginal Origins of the Québécois," when he explains that only thirteen Aboriginal women are recorded in the marriage registries in New France prior to 1680 (out of a population of nearly 3,700 other "founders").[1] Nonetheless, five decades of historical demographic research has shown that the small size of the French settlements in New France in the first two-thirds of the seventeenth century combined with a 350-year pattern of distant consanguinity (i.e., marriage between distant kin such as fourth cousins) has led to a situation today in which a significant majority of the descendants of the earliest French colonists have some limited (less than 1 percent on average) Indigenous ancestry.[2] Several recent studies by genetic scientists using state-of-the-art molecular technologies have confirmed the same findings.[3] Given that well over 10 million French descendants live in Canada today (primarily in Quebec, Ontario, and the Maritime provinces) and over 5 million live in the United States (primarily in New England, parts of the Midwest, and Louisiana), then upwards of 10 million white French descendants likely share the same small number of Indigenous women ancestors born primarily in the 1600s. Only a tiny proportion of these French descendants—at most 200,000—currently use this specific ancestral substance to formally claim an Indigenous identity. The large majority of those who claim an Indigenous identity through a tenuous genealogical relation with a long-ago ancestor have done so in the past decade and a half. This study examines the specific social process that has led much fewer than 5 percent of French descendants to take the plunge and shift into an Indigenous identity.

First, I do so through identifying and explaining the genealogical mechanics underwriting these recent claims to an Indigenous identity on a series of online genealogy forums. My observations about the multiple practices of descent—that is, which ancestors are reclaimed and in which ways—on these forums present a rich tapestry through which to observe contemporary identity formation: Indigenous ancestors are invariably sought, though not always found; several French women ancestors from the seventeenth century are reconstructed into Indigenous women, only to return to their previous French identity; and famous Indigenous people are remade as family, absent any direct ancestral relationship. Second, once I establish the common genealogical practices facilitating self-indigenization, I discuss two of the most prominent self-identified "métis" organizations currently operating in Quebec. Both organizations have their origins in a committed opposition to Indigenous land and territorial negotiations and encourage the use of the genealogical practices that I identify on the online forums. In this sense, the first part of the book hones in on the specific practices that lead French descendants to claim an Indigenous identity. The second part then explores how these claims are used politically to *oppose* actual, living Indigenous peoples.

The very nature of this study in questions of identity, ancestry, family, kinship, and belonging means that it is taking a path strewn with obstacles. What's more, its direct challenge to the nascent identity claims of tens of thousands of individuals ensures that for some it may be a path best left untaken. I have sought to remain sensitive to the emotional and/or intellectual roadblocks that might present themselves, including crucially to readers, by diving into my own family history. As a French descendant with multiple long-ago Indigenous ancestors, including at least three of the same seventeenth-century ancestors who are used to become "Indigenous" in this study, my own genealogical profile offers a generative means through which to understand the phenomenon in question. However, this is not a study that is primarily concerned with the individual motivations or intentions of social actors. Results from the past ten to twenty years of the Canadian census illuminate the social process under study, as the rate of increase in persons identifying as "métis" in Quebec, Nova Scotia, and New Brunswick has far outstripped the increase in those self-identifying as Métis nationally.[4] Combined with the appearance of dozens of organizations representing self-identified "métis" people in these provinces (and also in Ontario during the same period), many of which have either unsuccessfully mounted court cases to obtain legal recognition of their Aboriginal rights or are currently in the process of doing so, this phenomenon continues to be ascendant among French descendants.

As much as this study may appear principally to involve research into indigeneity, Indigenous identity, and/or Indigenous ancestry, it tells us much more about the shifting politics of whiteness, white privilege, and white supremacy. It closely follows a set of empirical material through the twists and turns that lead white people to switch their identity claims and to expand the boundaries of whiteness, in a way that was relatively inconceivable just twenty years ago. Still, several decades of Québécois and French-Canadian historiography and popular culture have set the stage for these emerging claims by arguing for the benevolence of French settler colonialism, often using the trope of "métissage" to do so.

MÉTIS, MÉTISSAGE, AND RACE

The idea of "métissage" has a specific lineage in French thought and linguistic practice that warrants some discussion before proceeding. According to historian Pierre Boulle, the term "race" entered into French usage sometime in the late fifteenth century, most likely borrowed from the Italian *razza*. "The term was first associated with lineage," Boulle argues, "rather than fixed, physically defined differentiation between broad human groups."[5] According to Boulle, the term itself was not neutral, since for much of its first century of circulation it referred to innate or inherited *character* traits, especially those associated with aristocratic rule. Historian Guillaume Aubert concurs with Boulle, explaining that by the second half of the sixteenth century, "the term 'race' began to be used interchangeably with 'blood' to express the notion of 'family' or lineage" in metropolitan France.[6] In Aubert's understanding, the main motivation for the development of the concept was to regulate *mésalliance*, or marriage between two people of different ranks in society. Aubert explains further: "According to early modern French aristocratic ideology, the most dreadful consequence of a mésalliance was the type of children it produced. In most French texts of the period, these children were designated by the term '*métis*,' defined in contemporary texts as the mixing of two different 'species.'"[7] In other words, in metropolitan France the term "métis" originated as a pejorative term that marked out the boundaries of social and political deviance along what resembles today's notions of "class" and "status."

Predating his European contemporaries by a couple of decades, French physician and intellectual François Bernier proposed an entirely different approach to understanding "races," one based primarily on physical characteristics, in 1684. Historian Siep Stuurman has called Bernier's work "the first attempt at a racial classification of the world's population," one that foreshadowed later anthropological understandings by more than a century.[8] Bernier's ideas were developed after extensive travel overseas, during which time he came to believe in "broad human categories characterized by distinct physical traits."[9] In particular, the colour of one's skin became *the* defining human characteristic of what he conceived of as five distinct racial groups.[10] His treatise, *Nouvelle division de la terre par les différentes espèces ou races qui l'habitent*, appeared in a major Parisian intellectual journal, but failed to catch on with the intelligentsia and remained rather limited in scope during his lifetime, given the deep metropolitan concern with status and rank. Consequently, up until at least the early eighteenth century, competing understandings of "race" circulated in metropolitan France. "Race" tended to be used to refer to differences accorded to social groups on the basis of lineage and descent, which were invariably linked to status and rank, reflecting the primary social concerns of aristocrats. Yet, increased travel overseas, combined with the development of an international political economy through the slave trade and European settler colonialism, meant that a shift toward a biological understanding of "race" was imminent.

The meanings of "métis" and "métissage" today do not translate easily into English, reflecting the concept's long and evolving history. In fact, there is likely no precise translation available in English. Historian Emmanuelle Saada's research into the more recent development of the term "métissage" is instructive. As she explains, her work focuses on "the constant semantic slippage between the biological concept of hybridity and the cultural implications of *métissage*."[11] It is crucial to discuss these dual, and at times competing, meanings of "métis/sage" now in order to set the stage for arguments throughout this book, since at times individuals or organizations using the French language display a rather open slippage between different meanings of the concept, fuelling the self-indigenization process.

The primary way in which the term "métis" is used in French today is in keeping with the legacy of Bernier's seventeenth-century biological understanding of human "races." Used in this sense, "métis" resembles the English-language concept "mixed-race," though in Canada, the term "métis" is used much more commonly in French than "mixed-race" is in English. Further, "métissage" (i.e., "mixing" in English) leads to a person who is "métis" (loosely, "mixed-race") in a biological sense, though in a departure from its English-language usage, it can also refer to any number of practices that in some way involve a mixture between two distinct entities, ideas, or forms. Thus, one can speak of "musical métissage" or "métis thinking" to refer to the cross-pollination of musical sounds or genres and ideas, respectively—a meaning that is altogether foreign to the English language.

As in the use of "mixed-race" in English, the term "métis" is itself imbued with the specificities of French colonial history and thus is used primarily in contexts involving "mixture" between racialized (e.g., African-descendant or Indigenous) and Euro-descendant people. As Saada argues, "both the notion [métis] and its ambiguities have roots in the long colonial history of France," and she shows "how the meanings that informed the concept of métissage, as with most concepts that refer to groups or social positions, were never static or clear cut."[12] For example, in places as diverse as Dakar, Paris, Montreal, and Fort-de-France, one normally uses the term "métis" to refer to an individual whose (biological) parents are categorized as "black" and "white," thus reinforcing notions of biological difference between "discrete" groups. Such usage is not normally pejorative, though it certainly can be.

Despite its complex origins in the cauldron of colonialism, if, in French, the term "métis" was limited to a parallel usage of mixed-race, most of the linguistic confusion jumping to English would be resolved. The main difficulty with the term "métis" in Canada is that it is also used to refer to an Indigenous *people* in French (and in English). Using the term "métis" to refer both to biological mixture between two individuals imagined to be of different "races" *and* to a distinct Indigenous people with a specific history, relations, and territories in the northern plains inevitably leads to some misunderstanding. This linguistic confusion is certainly not the sole or principal basis for debate and/or conflict, but it is worth noting given the tense deliberations about the nature of indigeneity currently brought forward by the self-indigenization movement outlined in this book.

The term "métis," which in the history of New France was only rarely used to refer to mixed-race individuals (see next section), is increasingly being mobilized in French to refer to a distinct, rights-bearing "Indigenous" community based in different regions of Ontario, Quebec, New Brunswick, Nova Scotia, and even parts of northern New England. To add to any confusion, this specific usage of the term, which began to take off in earnest in the early 2000s, overlaps with its more conventional usage to signal a "mixed-race" individual, the latter of which has a much longer history. For instance, during my 2017–18 sabbatical year in Montreal, people around me at dinner parties or at public events used the term "métis" to refer to somebody in their entourage on a number of occasions: "Oh yeah, isn't she that métis woman from Rosemont?" In each case, they were referring to a person whose parents were African/Haitian and French-Québécois. At the same time, French-language media popularized the idea that there existed a "Quebec métis" or "Eastern métis" people who not only were Indigenous, but had existed since the dawn of the colony as "métis," regularly conflating its dual meaning: mixed-race *and* a distinct Indigenous people.

What this brief interlude in sociolinguistic practice has illustrated is that there are, at times, several competing uses of the term "métis" in French. In contrast, the use of the term "métis" in English usually refers to the post-contact Indigenous people whose origins are traced back to their homelands in the northern plains. In this book, I use "Métis" to refer to the people recognized as Indigenous by their Plains Cree, Saulteaux, Assiniboine, and Dene kin, most of whom still live in their historic territory in parts of present-day British Columbia, Alberta, Saskatchewan, Northwest Territories, Manitoba, North Dakota, Montana, and Ontario. I use "métis" to refer to individuals and/or organizations that have no connection to the Métis people yet are claiming a Métis identity.

Part of the reason that the creation of an "Eastern métis" identity has become common among French descendants is the circulation of a belief in the widespread nature of mixed-race unions in early New France that has only intensified in this age of reconciliation. Let us turn to recent historiography in French and English that challenges the conventional wisdom about the extent of "métissage" (race mixing) in early New France.

THE "CHIMERA OF MÉTISSAGE": FRENCHIFICATION AND ASSIMILATION IN NEW FRANCE

Generations of French-Canadian and French-Québécois historiography have cycled through a number of powerful narratives about relations between French settlers and Indigenous peoples. Patrice Groulx's analysis of 250 historical narratives written about the Battle of Long Sault (circa 1660) between 1660 and 1997 illustrates the incredible range of narrative uses to which Indigenous peoples have been put over the course of more than three centuries of historiography. The Battle of Long Sault involved a small group of French colonists and Algonquin and Huron-Wendat allies fighting a party of Haudenosaunee in May 1660 on the banks of the Ottawa River, about seventy-five kilometres upstream of Montreal. From a story that held up the religious order of things in New France in the seventeenth century to one that factored into the rise of Quebec forms of nationalism in the latter part of the twentieth century, Groulx demonstrates how historians, religious officials, politicians, and writers have reconstructed aspects of the battle—the role of Indigenous peoples, the play between civilization and barbarity, descriptions of the events leading up to and following the battle—in a manner that illustrates how "the symbolic image of Indigenous peoples is fundamentally involved in shaping Québécois identity."[13] Much of the recent historiography on the French regime has self-consciously sought to reconcile Indigenous peoples with French descendants through blurring the lines between whiteness and indigeneity,[14] mirroring a range of efforts in popular culture.[15] According to these new origin stories, early French colonists and the Indigenous peoples whom they encountered created a novel form of "intercultural reciprocity, better still, an ethnocultural synthesis—a fusion of horizons—in which Quebec emerges as an entirely new society," political scientist Daniel Salée has explained. "The image is a seductive one."[16]

What Adam Gaudry and I have called these "revisionist" narratives are saturated with heteronormative fantasies involving French settler men and Indigenous women in boundary-crossing sexual escapades.[17] While all available evidence from the French regime (1608–1763) suggests that Indigenous women only rarely married French settlers, scholarly research and popular culture have nonetheless turned the "myth of métissage" into a relatively uncontroversial truth in Quebec and (French) Canada. At its basis is a nationalist belief in the innate kindness of French settler colonialism in New France, especially as it relates to its British (and to a lesser extent, Spanish) counterparts. A growing body of scholarly literature in the past half-generation has nonetheless challenged this foundational myth, leading historians Christopher Hodson and Brett Rushforth—citing Gwendolyn Hall, the noted historian of the French Atlantic—to argue that "it has become clear that [Hall's] assertion that the French exhibited a unique 'openness to peoples of other race and cultures' [in the early contact zone] is no longer tenable."[18]

Along these lines, in the past half-generation a number of scholars have researched the changing racial and gender dynamics of seventeenth-century New France. For example, in his research on the first few decades of settlement in New France, historian Gilles Havard explains the logic of French colonial policy at the time: "The policy of métissage was based on a universalist logic of reduction and assimilation. The children of a French father and a Christianized Aboriginal mother did not become 'métis' in the sense of a new category with particular characteristics... but obedient, Catholic, and Frenchified subjects."[19] Here, we can see how notions of culture, and especially conduct, trump biology in the early colony, predating the later emergence of biological understandings of "race" in French metropolitan thinking. The early French approach to "métissage" operated in a manner meant to solidify its civilizational project.

Further, historian Dominique Deslandres's research on what she calls the "fiction of métissage" in historiography casts a light precisely on the types of hierarchical, patriarchal, and imperial dynamics that propelled French strategies in New France. According to Deslandres, the idea of a unified French-Indian people has been a "chimera" in Quebec historiography, because French colonial policy and religious instruction ensured that miscegenation occurred only in quite limited and circumscribed contexts and only when it suited French gender norms. She notes that patriarchal values played a foundational role in developing French understandings of "métissage," since, "in a colony settled primarily by French men, the intermediaries targeted in the blending of people were Indigenous women. But not just any women: the French needed to find *civilized, Frenchified* wives among Indigenous women."[20] Historian Karen Anderson's archival study of seventeenth-century Jesuit journals from New France also demonstrates how the subjugation of Indigenous women according to Euro-Christian values was a primary goal of colonial officials during the French regime. According to Anderson, one key concern among the Jesuits was the elimination of Indigenous women's political and sexual sovereignty.[21] The feminist historiographic tradition questioning the patriarchal nature of French settler colonialism in New France suggests that French men sought to gain a sense of mastery over their foreign surroundings by subjugating Indigenous women to Eurocentric patriarchal norms. As an example, around 1635, the Jesuits, who were desperate for more converts, made the extraordinary decision to request formally that the Holy See allow marriages between French men and non-Christian Indigenous women, arguing that "this would oblige the natives to love the French as their brothers."[22] The request was denied, and as Peter Cook demonstrates, "the literal side of the French project of becoming 'one people' with the Native nations of the region lost steam toward the end of the 1630s."[23]

Drawing on documents from the early seventeenth century, Havard describes a situation in which the French expressed a determined belief in their fundamental civilizational superiority, even during the early integrative period: "Métissage is not conceived as an equal mixture since, due to education, its Indian element is meant to disappear in favour of its European element. Ethnic fusion must serve the religious and cultural unity of the Franco-Indian colony."[24] In this fashion, the early colonial policy on miscegenation was rooted in a broad Frenchification project, not simply enlightened benevolence or a desire to foster a new people. Rather than envisioning a cultural unification that was in large part Indigenous, early policy in New France saw intermarriage as part of a broader strategy to expand the French population base. Crucially, métissage during this period, currently imagined in evocatively romantic terms as the origin-point of the myth of métissage, occurred on a radically unequal colonial playing field where Frenchification and the eventual elimination of Indigenous peoples as Indigenous were the end goal. Both Havard and historian Saliha Belmessous, in keeping with Cook and historian Mairi Cowan's more recent research, recognize that early French policy in New France, which lasted no more than a few decades, was certainly frayed by the time the colony came under royal charter in 1663.²⁵

So few Indigenous women elected to marry French men that prior to the arrival of the first shipment of *filles du roi* (the approximately 700 young French women sent to New France by the king of France in order to produce French, Catholic colonists) in 1663, Louis XIV offered 150 livres to the families of Indigenous women who married French settlers. For a short time, the king even favoured paying Indigenous women's dowries over those of French women, as a way to incentivize mixed-race unions. Nevertheless, as late as 12 November 1682, a leading bureaucrat in New France complained to the Foreign Ministry that even though several Indigenous women were educated *à la française* by the Ursulines, too few of them elected to marry Frenchmen.²⁶ Notwithstanding the relatively small number of Indigenous women who married French men in the early colonial period, the chimera of métissage has dominated representations of French colonialism in scholarly literature.²⁷

By the turn of the eighteenth century, well after the arrival of the *filles du roi*, a considerably different approach had emerged. No longer necessary, and increasingly frowned upon by colonial officials, social and political unions with Indigenous women became even more unusual than they had been prior to 1663. Sexual unions continued to occur, but mixed-race children were, for the most part, reared by Indigenous women in Indigenous communities and were racially stigmatized and excluded by French colonial society.²⁸ As Belmessous explains, "At the beginning of the eighteenth century, French administrators started articulating a new ideology that reconsidered the terms of membership in civil and political society: first, miscegenation was discouraged and intermarriage prohibited (at least discursively) for political and biological reasons—the confusion of both terms was a crucial step in the construction of the new ideology; second, native policy was now firmly grounded on exploitation."²⁹ The hardening of racial divisions followed the pattern in the broader European imperial world—as France became a key player in the capture, enslavement, and trade in African peoples, culminating with its brutal slave colonies in the Antilles. The beginning of the eighteenth century also coincided with the formal legalization of slavery in New France, in which the main colonial centres (Montreal, Quebec City, and Trois-Rivières) saw an influx of both enslaved African and Indigenous peoples.[30]

Laying the broad intellectual groundwork for the self-indigenization phenomenon, the chimera of métissage posits a grand narrative of friendly cohabitation and mutual respect between early French settlers and the Indigenous peoples they encountered. At the centre of this narrative is an erasure of the patriarchal disposition of French colonialism in New France, which sought to subjugate Indigenous women's sovereignty and self-determination to Euro-Christian patriarchal norms. Even more, the chimera presents the nightmare of colonialism—death and disease brought on by the French presence—as a tale of French men's virility and Indigenous women's promiscuousness. Historians of the period have nonetheless pushed back at this fanciful narrative, encouraging us to reconsider our understanding of the early colonial period in New France.

A GENEALOGIST'S PARADISE: THE STRENGTH OF GENEALOGY IN QUEBEC

Another key site of scholarly research that has exposed the chimeric nature of métissage in early New France has been the field of genealogy, which has a long history in French Canada. Cyprien Tanguay, author of the monumental seven-volume, 4,400-page *Dictionnaire généalogique des familles canadiennes depuis la fondation de la colonie jusqu'à nos jours*, published from 1871 to 1890, is often held up as the "father of genealogy" in Quebec and/or French Canada. It is no coincidence that a former priest carries such a title, since the Catholic Church's commitment to record and archive all aspects of its flock's religious lives led to the strength of the genealogical records in the first place. That a large part of the Church's commitment to record marriages in particular arose from its desire to regulate consanguinity to more than three generations often goes unnoticed today.

French descendants are certainly not the only people with a well-developed genealogical sector,[31] nor are they the only one whose genealogical project cuts across contemporary national boundaries (i.e., the U.S. and Canada). Yet, it has long been common for historians and genealogists to argue for the *unique* place of genealogy in Quebec. For instance, historian

Leslie Choquette argued that France "transformed the colony into a kind of laboratory of state-of-the-art social practices. Administrators and Catholic reform clerics extended their authority into every domain of social life; hence, the plethora of ecclesiastical, administrative, notarial, and judicial records that are such a boon to demographers and historians."[32] René Jetté, Quebec's most decorated twentieth-century genealogist, goes so far as to call the province a "genealogist's paradise":

> The advent of a genealogy market in the first half of the twentieth century and especially, its constant growth since the 1960s, are in reality symptoms of a much deeper phenomenon: genealogy has become the *pastime*—or passion—of not only a few dozen scholars ... but for tens of thousands of fans who go hunting for their ancestors during their leisure time.... The recent growth of genealogy in Québec is ... related to specific factors that ascribe to Québec the enviable qualifier of a 'genealogist's paradise': the quality of its *sources*, whether in terms of content or preservation, as well as the production and distribution of numerous *research instruments*.[33]

The strength of the genealogical sector has led to a number of high-profile research projects and collaborations, such as the Project de recherche démographique historique (PRDH) at the Université de Montréal (1966–present), which have supported the development of the academic discipline of historical demography in Quebec. Besides the PRDH, BALSAC, a genealogy-based research project, was founded in 1971 by perhaps the most well-known scholar in Quebec, Gérard Bouchard, and has gone on to receive tens of millions of dollars of mostly public funding since its inception, more than any other research project in the social sciences and humanities in Canadian history.[34] Thus, genealogy is not simply the purview of community-based historians and hobbyists in Quebec, since its university system has also developed formidable genealogical infrastructure.

Over the past five decades, two of Quebec's most renowned historical demographers—Hubert Charbonneau and Bertrand Desjardins—have both argued persuasively and consistently that under the French regime ethnic *and* racial homogeneity were quite pronounced in New France. In his later work, Desjardins explicitly locates his argument as a response to a "myth of diversity" that focused on a small minority of non-French root ancestors in New France that was amplified by several Québécois historians in the mid- to late 1980s. Analyzing the marriage contracts signed during the French regime, he deduced that French (mostly Norman, western France, and Parisian metropolitan) ethnicities made up 97.6 percent of the overall ethnic composition of the population of New France by the end of the French regime.[35] While "country" marriages between French men and Indigenous women would not have been officially recorded, and therefore would not show up in Desjardins's "ethnic" reconstruction of the French settler population, his work and that of his colleagues in historical demography confirm one key dimension of French settlement: early French settlers were by and large an ethnically homogenous group.[36] To be clear, Desjardins's research does not deny French-Indigenous unions, but it does offer compelling evidence of their relative *absence*. As he asserts, "all 'old stock' Québécois probably have at least one Aboriginal person in their family tree, but the actual importance of the phenomenon remains negligible."[37] After all, as Desjardins seemed to recognize three decades ago, there is a substantive difference between finding limited Indigenous ancestry in one's family tree over three centuries ago and being an Indigenous person today.

Not only was the particular phenomenon of French-Indigenous unions negligible in New France, but, according to Desjardins, English and other European ethnicities together made up almost quintuple the percentage of the Indigenous component of the ethnic composition of French settlers at the time of the British Conquest (1.9 percent versus 0.4 percent, respectively). In other words, if it is *probable* that every "old stock" Québécois has at least one Aboriginal ancestor, it is much *more likely* that they have several English, Belgian, German, Swiss, Irish, and/or Portuguese ancestors.

Given Desjardins's and Charbonneau's well-known and extensive research, one might reasonably ask: why is there not a much louder and bolder Québécois-as-Euro (-as-German, -as-Portuguese, or dare I say, -as-English) campaign? Together with more recent scholarly literature on the chimera of métissage, historical demographic work based in the rich genealogical records available to researchers certainly challenges the common-sense understanding of the contact zone in New France. What we learn is that despite considerable present-day efforts to tell us otherwise, French settlers were much more likely to marry and have children with other Europeans than with Indigenous people, regardless of initial differences in language and religion. By and large, Indigenous women, and by association, Indigenous communities, resisted fusion with the French.

SELF-INDIGENIZATION, RACE SHIFTING, AND BECOMING INDIAN

The white desire to be Indigenous has been expressed in a number of different guises, not least of which is the pattern of marketing Indigenous names and caricatures as sport, corporate, and military symbols, as several scholars in the United States have examined.[38] These efforts have not been limited to the U.S., as recent critiques of the use of Indigenous symbolism during Olympic Games in Canada make plain.[39] There is a long history of white settlers "playing Indian," as historian Phillip Deloria has skillfully outlined in his study that spanned the Boston Tea Party to the advent of the "new age" movement in the United States.[40] There have also been several notorious cases of Euro-settler individuals feigning an "Indigenous" identity in Canada, perhaps the most infamous being Englishman Archibald ("Archie") Belaney as Grey Owl.[41] The public controversy over prominent author Joseph Boyden's shifting claims to indigeneity in 2016 also raised difficult questions about Indigenous identity that remain hot-button issues.[42]

Throughout the 1990s several scholars in the field of Native American Studies/American Indian Studies concerned with the pernicious phenomenon of white scholars claiming an "Indigenous" identity pushed back at what they called "ethnic fraud" in higher education.[43] Cornel Pewewardy defined ethnic fraud as "the inaccurate self-identification of race by persons applying for faculty positions at mainstream colleges and universities, or for admissions into special programs, and for research consideration."[44] Efforts to expose the dynamics of ethnic fraud in academia appear to have waned, but have been reinvigorated by recent writing in the United States and Canada.[45]

A number of important studies in anthropology, sociology, and Indigenous Studies/Native American Studies have emerged in the same period covered in this book (2000–2018) that examine the broader phenomenon of white settler self-indigenization.[46] It appears that efforts to become "Indigenous" are not confined to any specific geographical space in Canada or in the United States. What these efforts have in common is the relatively recent development of a desire for an otherwise white settler population to become "Indigenous" in a manner that is largely opposed by existing Indigenous peoples.

Indigenization and Race Shifting in the United States
Stephen Pearson's "The Last Bastion of Colonialism" opens up some space to think through contemporary efforts at self-indigenization through an empirical analysis of white settler indigenization in Appalachia. Pearson outlines how white Appalachians have been involved in indigenization efforts since the 1970s, largely supported by liberal Appalachian studies scholars in the region. An important component of this process has been the creation of a form of *white indigeneity* for settler Appalachians: "In the wake of the global decolonization movements, Appalachians asserted their indigeneity—with its attendant anticolonial orientation and resistance—to critique coal mining industries."[47] Pearson explains that the current movement is linked directly to the opposition to mountaintop removal (MTR) among local residents, who have reinvented themselves as Indigenous mountaineers who have lived in Appalachia "since the beginning," in a region being called the "last bastion of colonialism" or the "Appalachian Reservation" among its most vocal proponents.[48] In this version of history, traditional mountain culture (or hillbilly culture) is what Pearson calls a "decolonizing site of resistance" for the local population, who are struggling against the invasion of the coal mining industry since the late 1800s. Pearson suggests that Appalachian settlers "employ indigenization in late settler-colonial contexts in order to negotiate land claims and other inequalities among White settlers."[49] They thus construct the entire region "as the rightful possession and homeland of one group of settlers (but not another)" in a manner that "forbids the land restoration and repatriation that Indigenous theories of justice and decolonization"

entail.⁵⁰ Pearson employs a settler colonial analytic in his critique of indigenization among white Appalachians, one that places whiteness at its centre. In her book *Becoming Melungeon*, anthropologist Melissa Schrift explains a similar process among a group of mixed-race Appalachian people long associated with a county in northeastern Tennessee. She explains that among the people who have identified as Melungeon since the 1960s (and especially since the 1990s), a small minority self-identifies as Indigenous, while the large majority identifies as white (often with unspecified "Mediterranean" ancestry).⁵¹ In either case, African ancestry has been forcefully elided. These claims to white settler forms of indigeneity in Appalachia—despite a lack of documented Indigenous ancestry—parallel the case of the neo-Chumash in present-day southern California.

Anthropologists Brian Haley and Larry Wilcoxon have published two articles that focus on the ethnogenesis of the "neo-Chumash" community in the Santa Barbara area that emerged in the context of the U.S. Bureau of Indian Affairs' (BIA) settlement of California land claims in the 1960s.⁵² Haley and Wilcoxon illustrate how the indigenization of identity, as they call it, arises in conjunction with nation-state policies that provide settler populations with the motivation to become Indigenous. They use the term "neo-Chumash" to refer to the descendants of some of the first settlers from Mexico (circa 1769 to 1820)—not to be confused with the Chumash communities in Santa Ynez, Santa Barbara, and Ventura, "who are descended from contact-era villages and who have maintained a continuous identity."⁵³ Over the course of nearly two centuries of census data under the aegis of Mexico and then the United States, the ancestors of today's neo-Chumash underwent several significant identity changes. They were eventually identified as *Español* by the late nineteenth century, at a time when anti-Mexican prejudice was preponderant following the end of the U.S.-Mexican War in 1848.

Between 1850 and 1930, all of the neo-Chumash ancestors that Haley and Wilcoxon identified in the archives were recorded as white in U.S. and California censuses.⁵⁴ Nonetheless, several of their descendants in Santa Barbara sought a settlement share in the BIA's land claims process by claiming to have California Indigenous ancestry. Repeated efforts by regional genealogists to document either California Indigenous or Chumash ancestry failed, until one of them re-categorized a woman ancestor from the late eighteenth century as Indigenous to California. According to Haley and Wilcoxon, this genealogist was the first authority to "classify [the] 'neo-Chumash' as Indians and to assert that [the] neo-Chumash have California Indian ancestry," despite the fact that their ancestors are otherwise identified as non-Indigenous in the archives. "It appears likely," Haley and Wilcoxon argue, "that most of the Santa Barbara Spanish or Californio families that subsequently became neo-Chumash got their initial spark from [this one genealogist's] research."[55]

Despite the facts that no evidence of California Indigenous or Chumash ancestry was found among the neo-Chumash's ancestors and that they were subsequently denied BIA recognition for the purpose of the land claims, these descendants of some of the first Mexican settlers of California have nonetheless persisted in their claims to Native American (Chumash) identity, which has fuelled conflicts with Chumash people in the region. Eventually, as Haley and Wilcoxon explain, the neo-Chumash sought federal recognition as a Native American tribe: "Because federal acknowledgment requires political and social continuities, the process fostered claims that earlier generations 'had to hide their Indianness,' went 'underground,' or had 'passed as Mexican.'"[56] Their efforts at federal recognition ultimately failed; they ran out of money and a second genealogist confirmed that the neo-Chumash had no Chumash ancestry.

Notwithstanding their verified lack of Chumash ancestry or their failure to gain federal recognition, the neo-Chumash have been particularly successful at mobilizing the support of scholars and local governments to their cause. A number of officials and academics have repatriated human remains to them for reburial, promoted their claims to Chumash ancestry, and/or approached them for lessons on Chumash traditions.[57] The takeaway from Haley and Wilcoxon's work is that the truth about claims to indigeneity appears less important than what types of support these claims are able to mobilize among white settler power brokers: "Certainly, it is a revision of history from whole cloth, yet it also reflects the local social context in ascertainable ways. Clearly, people can create identities from whole cloth if they have access to appropriate knowledge and outside support, and if their identity fits local expectations."⁵⁸ The question of what regional white settlers expect of Indigenous peoples is particularly salient to this study.

Anthropologist Circe Sturm's book *Becoming Indian* is the most ambitious study analyzing the self-indigenization phenomenon in the United States. Sturm's analysis focuses on the widespread phenomenon of Cherokee identity claims since the 1970s. She points out that between 1970 and 2000, the number of individuals identifying as Cherokee on the U.S. Census increased by more than 1,000 percent, even though only a little more than one-third (35 percent) are federally recognized.⁵⁹ The remarkable increase in the number of organizations and individuals identifying as Cherokee led Sturm to develop the concept of race shifting. She illustrates how race shifting involves a diverse group of people—some have documented Indigenous ancestry although no personal history of being Indigenous, some aspire to identify Indigenous ancestors, and some rely on family stories of a Cherokee great-great-great-great-grandmother. "Despite their differences," Sturm explains, "these people share a firm belief that they have Indian blood and that this means something significant about who they are and how they should live their lives."⁶⁰ Contrary to the examples brought forward by Pearson and by Haley and Wilcoxon, a number of race shifters in Sturm's study may in fact have some Indigenous ancestry.

Importantly, Sturm identifies "symbolic inversion" as a key element of race-shifter strategies in the United States, defined as a social process "in which apparent whites are considered real Cherokees and apparent real Cherokees are made into something vaguely Euro-American," in keeping with race-shifter desires to become "Indigenous".⁶¹ Such a narrative strategy has been generative for race shifters, as it has allowed them to go one step further, by claiming that their authenticity as "Indigenous" people—preserved through generations by "hiding in plain sight" and refusing government intervention in their lives—has remained intact. "Not only are they *real* Cherokees," Sturm explains, "but also they are *better* Cherokees than anyone else."⁶² Through a bold narrative strategy, self-identified Cherokee often present themselves *and are accepted* by mainstream U.S. society as the only authentic Indigenous people in a given territory or location, erasing actual Indigenous peoples in the process. Her astute observations here tie back to Haley and Wilcoxon's argument about how neo-Chumash people have been received favourably by scholars and municipal leaders, who see in their claims an opportunity to advance their own political interests.

Sturm's research analyzing the self-identified Cherokee phenomenon in the United States is by far the most in-depth study focused on the phenomenon of white settler indigenization. While there are several notable differences between race shifting by self-identified Cherokee in Sturm's study and by French descendants in mine, there are many overlapping dimensions of the social phenomenon. When appropriate, I return to these three studies—especially Sturm's—to contrast with some of my analysis.

Self-Indigenization and Métissage in Canada
The academic study of self-indigenization in Canada is a relatively new field of inquiry, normally associated with the discipline of Indigenous studies, which has been concerned primarily with questions of indigeneity, Indigenous peoples, and, especially, Indigenous sovereignty and self-determination. Since self-indigenization in Canada usually involves claims to a "new Métis" identity, in many ways sociologist Chris Andersen's seminal book, *Métis: Race, Recognition, and the Struggle for Indigenous Peoplehood*, launched this field of inquiry by pushing back against the common belief in Canada that the defining feature of the Métis is their mixed-race lineage.[63] In a manner similar to that explained by Sturm about the Cherokee in the United States, the Métis have been imagined as *less* Indigenous than other Indigenous peoples, no doubt because their origins are at the nexus of the fur trade.[64] Throughout his study, however, Andersen articulates the specific cultural, social, economic, and historical basis for the existence of the Métis *people*, as an Indigenous people whose existence as such has its origins in kinship-based political alliances with the Cree, Saulteaux, and Assiniboine people of the northern plains in what is currently known as the United States (especially North Dakota and Montana) and Canada (especially Manitoba, Saskatchewan, Alberta, and parts of the Northwest Territories and British Columbia). Andersen was not the first scholar to articulate the grounds for Métis peoplehood,[65] but his work stands out because of his direct opposition to the contemporary challenges to Métis

peoplehood brought on by the contemporary race-shifting process, particularly among French descendants.

Since section 35 of the Constitution Act, 1982, recognized and affirmed the Aboriginal rights of the Métis, debates about Métis peoplehood have periodically erupted nationally. This has been especially true in the decade and a half since the 2003 *Powley* decision by the Supreme Court of Canada (SCC), which for the first time recognized a rights-bearing Métis community.[66] The case revolved around the father-son team of Steve and Roddy Powley, who shot a bull moose without a hunting licence near Sault Ste. Marie, Ontario, on the morning of 22 October 1993. A week later the pair was charged with hunting moose without a licence and unlawful possession of moose in contravention of Ontario's Game and Fish Act (1990). In 1998, a provincial trial judge dismissed the charges, and after a series of appeals by the Crown, both the Ontario Superior Court of Justice and the Ontario Court of Appeal confirmed the trial judge's decision. Ultimately, the SCC agreed with the three provincial court decisions, affirming that the Powleys had a constitutionally protected Aboriginal right to hunt moose as Métis people.

As part of its ruling, the SCC introduced a ten-part test, known as the *Powley* test, to define Métis rights and identify Métis rights holders. According to the SCC, to be recognized as Métis with Aboriginal rights under section 35 of the Constitution Act, 1982, an individual must self-identify as a member of a Métis community with an ongoing connection to a historic Métis community; prove an ancestral connection with a historic Métis community whose collective rights they are exercising; and prove acceptance by the contemporary community, which may include a Métis political organization, if its membership requirements and role in the Métis community are put into evidence. As scholar Chelsea Vowel and I have explained about the *Powley* test, "Beyond meeting the *Powley* test for identity, the exercise of section 35 Aboriginal rights also requires the claimant do the following: characterize the right (for instance, hunting for food); identify the historical timeframe of the practice; show whether the practice is integral to the culture of the claimant; demonstrate whether the contemporary community the claimant belongs to continues to engage in the practice; prove the right was not extinguished; show whether the right has been infringed upon and if so, show that the infringement was not justified."[67] Nonetheless, in following the "métis-as-mixed" framework widely critiqued by Métis scholars, within a few short years the *Powley* decision became a pivotal event that pushed tens of thousands of otherwise white French descendants to turn to a new "métis" identity in Quebec, New Brunswick, Ontario, and Nova Scotia. Notably, the ruling provided individuals opposing Indigenous land claims and political sovereignty with the second part of a new legal and political course of action, as I demonstrate in this study.

Andersen's explicit argument for Métis peoplehood combined with the development of a post-*Powley* social movement claiming an "Eastern métis" identity has contributed to the recent rise of scholarly work on settler self-indigenization in Canada. For instance, a special dossier in the journal *TOPIA* in fall 2016 highlighted the work of Métis scholars Andersen, Gaudry, Vowel, Zoe Todd, and Jennifer Adese in relation to debates about Métis identity.[68] In their contribution, Gaudry and Andersen use the concept of "self-indigenization" to refer to the twenty-first-century phenomenon of white settlers identifying as Indigenous (primarily as Métis) in order to claim Indigenous lands and rights as their own. They differentiate self-indigenization from practices of incorporating individuals who have been disconnected from their Indigenous polity by colonial policy, such as Indian Act provisions, residential schools, and the Sixties Scoop or other forms of child abduction. In their estimation, First Nations and Métis membership and citizenship codes include provisions to welcome such people that are widely accepted and broadly inclusive.[69]

Gaudry's more recent analysis of six so-called Eastern métis organizations develops a deeper understanding of the concept of self-indigenization. He identifies these new organizations' disregard for still-living Indigenous voices and political collectivities as centrally implicated in their rise. In fact, Gaudry explains that the post-*Powley* self-indigenization movement relies on "communing with the dead" in its reconstruction of indigeneity, arguing that "it is the discursive disregard of living Métis that locates the promise of Métis cultural revival in blood memory, genealogy, and lineal descent— connections to the dead—rather than a connection to the living culture of Métis communities."[70] By capitalizing on the enthusiasm for self-identification and "reconciliation" in Canada, these "new métis" organizations are ultimately able to find some support for their political claims. One similarity that Gaudry has found between organizations in eastern Canada and the self-identified Cherokee "tribes" that Sturm studied is their creation of a narrative of past victimization that led them to hide their true "Indigenous" identities—in this case, for over two centuries. Gaudry points out that in the organizational narratives he studied, these "hidden Métis" individuals are waiting for a more tolerant time, what he calls a "kind of new age," when they can reclaim their true selves.[71] The dawn of the twenty-first century seems to have offered such a moment.

Contrary to the process of indigenization in the United States, most of these "new métis" are not fabricating their Indigenous ancestry out of thin air, however; as Gaudry argues, "it is their orientation to their ancestors rather than [to] contemporary communities that makes 'new Métis' identity claims similar to New Age ones [in the United States]."[72] Ultimately, Gaudry finds fault in their lack of ongoing relationships with Indigenous peoples. On this last point, Métis historian Brenda Macdougall asserts that Métis peoplehood has been based in female-centred family networks that situate Métis families in dense relation to their First Nations kin. Macdougall demonstrates how these relations have been fostered through Cree-based practices of *wahkootowin*, or "the expression of a world view that laid out a system of social obligation and mutual responsibility between related individuals—between members of a family—as the foundational relationship for pursuing any economic, political, social, or cultural activities and alliances."[73] Métis scholars have pressed for an understanding of indigeneity in relation to Métis peoplehood that places kinship at its foundation.[74]

THEORIZING DESCENT: AT THE INTERSECTION OF INDIGENOUS STUDIES AND CRITICAL STUDIES OF GENEALOGY

Combining a focus on the centrality of kinship-making practices and citizenship orders to Indigenous identity and one on the politics of genealogical research and self-making in Western society, my conceptual framework is grounded in the specific mechanics of descent underwriting the race-shifting process.

In conversations with colleagues and in reviewing relevant literature, it became apparent that to some scholars, the reliance on a long-ago ancestor as the sole basis for an Indigenous identity appears to resemble the logic of hypodescent, popularized as the "one-drop" rule, that has been enforced in the United States since the dawn of slavery. For example, in the case of Sturm's research among self-declared Cherokee tribes, she explains the reliance on a single, long-ago ancestor to claim Cherokeeness in these terms: "Much like the laws and logic of hypodescent that have long been at work in African-American communities, it is almost as if there is a type of racial homeopathy at work here, such that a tiny fraction of blood, or better yet, Cherokee ancestral substance, has the power to remake one's entire racial, cultural, and social body."[75] I have sought to move away from hypodescent by instead building on Sturm's idea of "racial homeopathy" in order to develop an appropriate framework that speaks to the specific racial logics at work.

To critical race theorists familiar with strategies to solidify racial hierarchies in the United States and Canada, the logic of hypodescent not only reified a tiny fraction of African "blood," but, more critically, ensured that those fixed by this trace of biological inheritance were seen as inferior in a manner that constituted the anti-Black violence of white society. One of its primary functions was to entrench white men's control over black women's bodies, ensuring that children conceived through sexual violence remained the property of white slave-owners. Historian Winthrop Jordan has demonstrated that the psychological and social underpinnings for the one-drop rule were formed in the first several generations of life in what became the United States.[76] By the mid-1800s, the logic of hypodescent appeared in a variety of legal codes in the United States at a time when the white plantation order sought to defend its practice of racial slavery from increased political scrutiny. Later, the one-drop rule was eventually made (in)famous as part of the Jim Crow–era segregation of African Americans, an important component of which was the legal prohibition of interracial sex and/or marriage. In this sense, the idea of hypodescent has been crucial in ensuring white society's accumulation and distribution of wealth and resources.

In her study of Hawaiian identity in the wake of U.S. imperialism, anthropologist J. Kēhaulani Kauanui provides further clarification on the use of hypodescent in relation to indigeneity, sex, and reproduction, pointing out that "in settler societies, depending on the context, the so-called inferior racial stock is not always regarded as a pollutant."[77] In fact, Kauanui argues that at different times in settler colonial history "red" and "white" blood have been imagined as easy to blend, in keeping with the assimilationist logic at the basis of efforts to civilize Indigenous peoples.[78] In addition, "red" and "white" blood have been consistently imagined as resisting fusion with "black" blood. In other words, hypodescent does not capture the *specific* ways that "red" blood continues to circulate in white society and in fact might elide its *particular* force in regulating black subjectivity. As Kauanui argues, "We need to account for the contrasts between assimilative projects and boundary drawing 'antipollution' approaches to relationships understood as interracial and how they differed historically for American Indian and white mixes versus African American and white ones."[79]

The inverse of hypodescent—when mixed-race individuals are considered "white"—has also been theorized by scholars, but to a much lesser degree. For instance, in her work on the creation of the Mexican American "race," legal theorist Laura Gómez has argued that a "reverse one-drop rule" often applied to Mexican Americans in the Southwest, in which drops of Spanish blood made them "white" enough for certain rights. According to Gómez, this logic was used in the nineteenth century to grant Mexican Americans certain political and legal rights vis-à-vis African Americans and Native Americans, cementing an enduring racial hierarchy.[80] Similarly, geographer Reuben Allen has posited that the use of *blanqueamiento* in Puerto Rico has been influenced by the rules of hyperdescent, "whereby mixed-race offspring are often perceived as members of the socially dominant group."[81]

As an example, Allen explains that even though nationalist understandings of race celebrate the mixed African, Indigenous, and Spanish ancestry of the population, over 75 percent of Puerto Ricans identified as "white, alone" in the 2010 U.S. census.[82]

Besides a few examples from Spanish-descendant populations, most of the scholarly work on hyperdescent in the United States has focused on the mixture of "red" and "white" blood, in Kauanui's terms. For instance, sociologists Aaron Gullickson and Ann Morning note that "perhaps less well-known, but just as deeply rooted, is the historical convention whereby people of mixed white and American Indian ancestry have frequently been racially classified as white. In this hyperdescent regime, American Indian heritage is not considered to have the determining properties that African ancestry does, and so individuals who claim to have indigenous American origins can ... classify themselves as white."[83] While there continue to be instances of individuals with recent Indigenous ancestry identifying as "white," this study considers the opposite phenomenon, in which individuals with limited or no Indigenous ancestry identify as "Indigenous" in the United States and in Canada. In this sense, Kauanui's point remains: because it is imagined that "red" and "white" blood are easy to blend, there exists a degree of fluidity between the two that continues to push the boundaries of whiteness and indigeneity. In that sense, I heed Aileen Moreton-Robinson's recent call to Indigenous studies scholars to consider "how racialization works to produce Indigeneity through whiteness" by foregrounding the workings of whiteness and white supremacy in the self-indigenization process.[84]

In this study, we have a situation where a diverse population of white people sharing much of the same ancestry across a range of international and national borders is *choosing* to identify themselves as Indigenous through repurposing their long-ago ancestry with a few Indigenous (and/or at times French) women. The political choice exists in the first place because under the dominant racial frame indigeneity is always already imagined as a racial category, one that involves a great deal of overlap with whiteness, as Kauanui points out. That the choice to self-identify as "Indigenous" is opposed most often by the actual Indigenous people whose ancestry race shifters are using starkly outlines the political struggle at play. Neither hypodescent nor hyperdescent provided me with the precise tools to engage with self-indigenization because neither explains an attempted shift *away* from whiteness. The phenomenon presented a puzzle: How do we explain these efforts to assume an Indigenous identity by members of an otherwise socially dominant white racial group?

The unique ancestral history of French descendants provided the first clues to the puzzle. As I indicated previously, French descendants have unparalleled access to four centuries of ancestral information, meaning that genealogy has become an incredibly popular pastime and academic pursuit. Predictably, genealogical research is at the centre of the race-shifting process, as ancestors are invariably put to a variety of different social and political uses. Geographer Catherine Nash has considered how genealogy organizes social relations in a manner that is "at odds with non-western indigenous models of place and identity."[85] Given its increasing role in making identities, she has cautioned against the reification of genealogy as family: "Genealogy does not describe family. It is not equivalent to kinship. It is not an account of relatedness.... To think of genealogical relatedness, that is relatedness defined in terms of genealogical links alone, as standing for family and kinship is to exclude the flexible, elastic, and practiced nature of familial relatedness and kinship."[86] Nash continues by contrasting what she calls the "ongoing practice of kinship through which a range of family forms are continuously enacted" with a "strictly genealogical account" of relatedness that discounts the "significance of relationships shaped through social practice."[87] Genealogy often stands in problematically as the *only* (or at least, the principal) kinship-making practice among race shifters in this study, ensuring that blood is at the centre of the race-shifting process. As such, race shifters generally do not engage with or otherwise consider Indigenous forms of belonging and citizenship.

In order to understand how French-descendant race shifters move into an "Indigenous" identity, I quickly realized that I had to track the different ways that specific ancestors circulated in their narratives. A sustained focus on the precise mechanics of descent—which ancestors are reclaimed and in which ways—has allowed me to detail the shift away from white identity. In the following pages, I build on these empirical observations and understand descent as a *practice* that moves many of its practitioners to believe remarkable and at times heroic stories about a long-ago ancestor. Most of the time, though, one *does* descent—meaning one transforms one's ancestors—not as part of a heroic story about the past, but to imagine a future that further dispossesses Indigenous peoples of land, of sovereignty, and of identity.

Whatever the specific claim, these practices of descent support French-descendant mobility *away from* a settler identity toward that of an "Indigenous" people in a manner that solidifies existing colonial logics. French descendants are not held back by their discovery and subsequent mobilization of (Indigenous) ancestry. On the contrary, these same French descendants bring this particular "ancestral substance" to light in a number of public venues, including online genealogy forums, as a badge of pride. Here, we have a process more in keeping with Kauanui's theorization of the assimilationist logics at the basis of ongoing efforts to civilize Indigenous peoples. "White" and "red" blood mix easily, and, perhaps unsurprisingly, these new "Indigenous" people begin to imagine themselves as more "Indigenous" than actual Indigenous peoples. These practices of descent are a form of legitimization—through their self-recognition, race shifters claim a legitimacy to speak for and act as Indigenous peoples. Race shifters solidify colonial logics through transcending colonialism altogether, thereby evading responsibility in more than three centuries of colonial violence (including concurrent forms of anti-black racism) by retroactively claiming indigeneity. The boldness of this shift away from whiteness is even more remarkable since race shifters openly admit that they and their immediate families were not subject to the violence inherent in the laws and policies of the Canadian state (and its forebears) aimed at Indigenous peoples.

All of the attention paid to one's connection to a supposed Indigenous woman from long ago contravenes long-standing Indigenous conventions about citizenship and kinship. At the centre of these efforts to redefine indigeneity is the practice of self-identification, which sociologist Eva Marie Garroutte has critiqued for its emphasis on an individualism that undermines Indigenous sovereignty and self-determination.[88] Her study of Native American identity broadly documents many of the conflicts that arise when non-Indigenous people attempt to redefine the boundaries of Indigenous identity: "What all of these disputes about real Indianness demonstrate is that it is one thing to claim identity as an Indian person, and it is quite another for that claim to be received by others as legitimate."[89] In order for one's claim to be received, Garroutte focuses on outlining the importance of Indigenous kinship as "an ongoing practice or skill, an active relationship that must be maintained and that is not invariably tied to one's genealogical connections."[90] Garroutte explains that this type of kinship practice or skill involves a "responsibility to reciprocity" that, I argue throughout, contrasts with French-descendant efforts to redefine indigeneity through imaginative practices of descent, which elide contemporary relationships with Indigenous people and ultimately rely solely on blood (and, at times, genes). Professor of American Indian studies Joanne Barker has argued that a singular focus on blood has hidden the "complexities posed by Native customs and epistemologies—which offered alternative perspectives on belonging and kinship that would have included a generosity regarding intermarriage, adoption, and naturalization as well as alternative understandings of belonging and kinship that would have tied members back to their lands and governments as citizens with multiple kinds of responsibilities."[91] The remaking of indigeneity through a long-ago blood relation discovered through genealogy—as presented in this book—betrays how these efforts stand to benefit white people at the expense of Indigenous peoples.

Legal theorist Pamela Palmater's work on Mi'kmaw identity and belonging also focuses on the need to look beyond blood quantum to determine contemporary forms of Indigenous citizenship. Palmater outlines how the Indian Act has long sought to alter the Crown's legal relationship with sovereign Indigenous nations to one between Canada and individual "Indians." By racializing what are *political* entities through technologies such as blood quantum and the generational cut-off now used in the Indian Act, the Canadian government ensures its current and future access to Indigenous lands. In an effort to support the growth of a dynamic Mi'kmaw Nation well into the future, Palmater develops a citizenship code whose emphasis is on a number of social, political, legal, and cultural criteria—in addition to an ancestral connection—that build ongoing social relationships among the Mi'kmaw people.[92] In a similar analysis of Indigenous political citizenship, professor of American Indian studies Jill Doerfler insists that family and relationships based in Anishinaabe values are the most appropriate means by which to determine tribal citizenship. According to Doerfler, efforts at defining Anishinaabeg in present-day Minnesota solely in terms of blood have sought to undermine the United States' political obligations toward the Anishinaabeg.[93] Her work, then, is an effort to counter the construction of indigeneity in terms of biology and race with one that treats Indigenous peoples as belonging to sovereign political entities capable of self-determining who belongs, and that carry responsibilities to particular lands, in a manner that is echoed in Palmater's work[94] on the Mi'kmaq.[95] In many ways, Palmater's and Doerfler's efforts to intervene in race-based colonial legacies among the Mi'kmaq and Anishinaabeg mirror the efforts of Andersen, Gaudry, and Macdougall among the Métis.

Besides theoretical contributions pushing back at the various "blood logics" based in genealogy that are used to redefine Indigenous identity, there is also a growing body of scholarly research on "genetic genealogy," or what sociologist Alondra Nelson defines as "the use of DNA analysis for the purpose of inferring ethnic or racial background and aiding with family history research."[96] As an example, anthropologist Kim TallBear sensitively documents the transition from blood to genes in discourses about Native Americans. TallBear explains how the logic behind the search for "Native American DNA" in molecular science relies on the narrative that Indigenous peoples are bound to disappear in a "sea of admixture," and as a result, little room is provided, she argues, for change and transformation. "Notions of ancestral populations, the ordering and calculating of genetic markers and their associations, and the representation of living groups of individuals as reference populations," TallBear maintains, "all require the assumption that there was a moment, a human body, a marker, a population back there in space and time that was the biogeographical pinpoint of originality. This faith in originality would seem to be at odds with the doctrine of evolution, of change over time, of becoming."[97] Purity, it seems, continues to be the ghost haunting racial science, one that conveniently facilitates strategies that undermine Indigenous self-determination in the contemporary era, as we will see in this study. In fact, the legitimacy afforded its scientific (read: neutral and value-free) basis means that molecular technology such as DNA ancestry testing can intervene in complex political and social matters in ways that lead to unforeseen material consequences.

As such, "Native American DNA," to use TallBear's term, refers to "a material-semiotic object with power to influence indigenous livelihoods and sovereignties."[98] Increasingly, DNA ancestry testing is marketed as a means of discovering one's definitive molecular origins and thus is being used to redefine tribal and white settler identities in the United States and, as I demonstrate in this study, First Nation and Métis sovereignty in Canada, posing risks to Indigenous claims to land and life.

Through her research on the use of DNA ancestry testing in genealogical research, Nelson concluded that DNA evidence did not provide ancestry seekers with the finality that they may have been seeking. Instead, those who engaged in online genealogy forums, among other interrelated activities, integrated new knowledge about their ancestral past in a manner that *confirmed* their pre-existing beliefs about ancestry, race, and/or ethnicity. "Genetic genealogy testing may thus amplify possibilities for subject-formation and ancestral affiliation," Nelson argues, "rather than simply reducing them to genetic determinants." As such, she concludes that "genetic genealogy testing provides a locus at which 'race' and ethnicity are constituted at the nexus of genetic science, kinship aspirations, and strategic self-making."[99] Nelson's work puts into focus the aspirational basis for molecular technologies, one determined by the specific social and political contexts in which ancestry seekers find themselves. In contrast to Nelson's African American research subjects—who are seeking African ancestors to connect with a past that has been violently cut off by the Middle Passage and subsequent practices of white terror and violence, including plantation slavery and Jim Crow—many French descendants in this study turn their backs on their ancestors in the Old World, choosing instead to focus intently on their reconstruction of North American indigeneity. As such, race shifting operates as a form of strategic self-making, what sociologist Anne-Marie Kramer calls a "technology of belonging" that selectively centres Indigenous women ancestors as the basis for contemporary identity.[100]

Choosing which ancestor matters most is intimately linked to one's desired identity in contemporary genealogical practice. As sociologist Ashley Barnwell argues, "the reasons family history researchers choose to delve into their ancestry, and more specifically, the selective branches they choose to follow, reflect not only the desire to have an interesting origin story, but to have a story that affirms our desired identities. . . . Family history research, in this context, is a practice of self-authentication, but also a creative act of revisionist life writing."[101] In this sense, how one moves *beyond* descent tells us a great deal about the self-making project: "the imperative of veracity is eclipsed and the need to know one's family history or origin narrative rests on the desire for a contemporary social connection."[102] As is the case in this study, facts about long-ago ancestors are much less important to race shifters than are their current efforts to create the truth about their identity. Nonetheless, at the same time as their claims tell us a great deal more about their *political* objectives than the reality of their complex ancestral histories, race shifters are invariably obsessed with a specific (Indigenous) ancestor—often one out of more than 2,000 (1/2,000) at that genealogical depth—inasmuch as that one ancestor can hold the key to their contemporary social transformation. Exploring the tension between moving *beyond* and remaining *obsessed with* descent has been a productive feature of my analytical framework.

The conceptual framework developed herein, where specific practices of descent—how one transforms one's ancestors—lead to the race-shifting process, allows me to explain the mechanics through which white French descendants claim an Indigenous identity and some of the broader political purposes of those claims.

VIRTUAL ETHNOGRAPHY AND TEXTUAL ANALYSIS

As a way to capture the complexity of twenty-first-century race shifting, I have employed a range of research methods. Focusing on the use of genealogy has been crucial, since the unique genealogical infrastructure available to French descendants is the basis of contemporary race shifting. As such, the first part of the book involves an in-depth analysis of a series of online genealogy discussion forums through adopting Nelson's notion of "virtual ethnography."[103] Overall, I agree with her argument on the need to immerse oneself in online research, "since contemporary genealogical research is a substantially technological pursuit."[104] In addition to Nelson's path-breaking work, I have also sought to emulate TallBear's use of virtual ethnography in her study of a high-profile genetic genealogy listserv based in the United States.[105] The bulk of the empirical material in the first three chapters of this study corresponds to public posts and threads on five prominent French-descendant online genealogy forums (three in French, two in English) on topics such as Indigenous ancestry, Indigenous identity, and/or indigeneity. A research associate on the project—Diahara Traoré—and I spent countless hours surveying genealogy forums and collecting posts throughout 2016 and 2017. We amassed well over 400 pages of forum threads containing over 100,000 words. In order to alleviate privacy concerns we selected forum threads that are archived in the public realm. We did not participate in or join any of the forums, so as to avoid influencing the direction of online discussions.

We sharpened our focus on the general forums (i.e., those not specifically about indigeneity) by selecting threads that began with a title post related to Indigenous identity/ancestry or indigeneity. Representative samples include titles such as the following: "Indian blood in our maternal lineage?"; "Indian or not?"; "Aboriginal ancestor?"; "Is there Indigenous ancestry in my family?"; "I would like to know if I have métis ancestry or not"; and "Am I Mi'kmaq through my ancestors?" Overall, we analyzed sixty-eight threads (roughly 750 individual posts) spread out over the five forums for a period of twelve years, although the large majority of the threads took place between 2012 and 2017. Threads related to the themes of indigeneity and Indigenous identity/ancestry have become more common since 2010 on these forums.

When it came to methods of analysis, I treated the online threads as textual archives. I read through the entirety of the archive on five different occasions, each time looking for recurrent tropes, common fault lines, apparent contradictions, and repeated assertions. I also searched the database for key terms from the academic literature (e.g., "ancestors/try," "métis," "Indigenous," "genealogy," "status," "Indian," "Aboriginal"). I then identified several interrelated themes in the archive and selected representative excerpts. Despite a prior engagement with academic literature that spoke to the dynamic conversation about these matters online, I was nonetheless consistently surprised by the complexity of the debate on the forums. Once I had established the main themes, selected representative excerpts, and begun writing, three different practices of descent emerged.

Lineal descent involves identifying direct ancestors in one's ancestral history. In the case of race shifting, individuals rely on the presence of a long-ago Indigenous (woman) ancestor in their direct ancestral lineage to claim an "Indigenous" identity today. The second practice of descent is what I call *aspirational*, since it relies on the creation of an Indigenous (woman) ancestor at a time and in a place where one did not exist previously. The *indigenization* of a European woman who lived nearly 400 years ago involves a range of emotional and technological investments that notably build on *lineal* descent. The third practice of descent is what I call *lateral*, since it makes a direct ancestor's relation (great-aunt, fourth cousin, great-great-uncle) who happens to be Indigenous the basis for one's indigeneity in the present. In its search for and ultimate creation of a familial connection it resembles *aspirational* descent, but in this case, the chosen ancestor is nevertheless "related" to a direct ancestor, usually in an unspecified or opaque manner that creatively mobilizes the concept of descent and/or family. Ultimately, through using either *aspirational* or *lateral* descent, race shifters can become "Indigenous" without any actual Indigenous ancestry.

In addition to "virtual ethnography" and the subsequent textual analysis, I have become a genealogist as part of this study, in following the type of genealogical reconstruction that Heather Devine developed in her study of Métis history: "Genealogical reconstruction provides a framework for detailed study of families [and enables one] to identify kin groupings, to postulate sociopolitical alliances, to track the migrations of . . . individuals and extended families into different regions, to examine the socioeconomic status of these families over time, and to trace the process of acculturation as they responded to changing socioeconomic circumstances and adopted Indian, Métis, or Euro-Canadian modes of behaviour to survive."[106] In June 2017, I began compiling my own ancestral family tree using a range of online databases and sources. In the course of an intense three-month period during the summer of 2017, I spent several hundred hours entering birth, death, marriage, and other available details for over 1,700 direct ancestors going back thirteen generations. To facilitate the process, I purchased one of the many software programs available for these purposes (MacFamilyTree 8), which undeniably helped to organize the massive amount of information. Still, I was unable to identify a number of ancestral lines at that genealogical depth. To facilitate the complete genealogical reconstruction of my ancestry back to the arrival of Europeans in New France (and, it turns out, in New England), I hired a genealogist in February 2018 who identified the remaining ancestors in private genealogical archives. I have now identified 100 percent of my ancestry, or just over 2,500 ancestors, at an average depth of just over twelve generations. I turn to my own genealogy on a number of occasions in the first part of the book, as a way to bring to life French-descendant genealogical claims. I also reconstruct the genealogy of several individuals and/or families, especially in Chapters 1 and 3, to verify the claims of forum posters about their own ancestry.

Lastly, throughout 2017, I assembled a large archive with hundreds of documents that relate directly to two major court cases in Quebec. In the *Corneau* case, over twenty members of the Communauté métisse du Domaine-du-Roy et de la Seigneurie de Mingan (CMDRSM)—the self-identified métis organization headquartered in the city of Chicoutimi—have been in court since 2006 seeking the right to hunt, fish, and otherwise access Aboriginal rights in what amounts to roughly a third of the province.[107] Among the documents in that case are thirty-one semi-structured interviews with leaders and members of the CMDRSM from the summer and fall of 2007, as well as twenty-seven member genealogies. I made extensive use of the interview guide, which was included alongside the interviews, as a way to contextualize them. Given their interest in providing evidence for the existence of a historic Métis community, the interviewer stuck closely to the interview guide. I selected three main themes from the interview guide as a way to organize the analysis. First, I considered participant narratives about the origins of the organization and, relatedly, of their shift to an Indigenous identity. Second, I turned to participant explanations of their impressions of and/or relationships with local white French-Québécois people, as a way to concentrate on the racial dynamics at work. Third, I analyzed participant statements about local Indigenous people (Innu). A second research assistant—Geneviève Dick—and I each read through the 400-plus pages of transcribed interviews and selected hundreds of excerpts that touched directly on one of the three themes. From there, I read through the excerpts and selected those that most faithfully represented the themes above.

The second court case involves the Métis Nation of the Rising Sun (MNRS), located in New Richmond, on the Gaspé Peninsula in Quebec. I obtained the transcripts of the preliminary testimony of two of its founders in the *Parent* case, which involves a founding member of the organization seeking recognition as Métis under the Constitution in order to access Aboriginal rights. Transcripts of the testimony amount to about 700 pages combined. I followed a similar reading practice as above, in that I identified two main themes that touched upon the organization's development. First, I searched for relevant statements about the MNRS's origins. Second, I sought statements about the practices of descent encouraged through its membership policies. The same research assistant and I read the testimony several times and selected about fifty different excerpts from both transcripts that spoke to the themes. Given the rather limited structure of the court setting, the analysis was supplemented with a variety of documents produced by the MNRS up until 2015, including meeting minutes and online statements by some of its leaders.

ORGANIZATION OF THE BOOK

The book is organized into two parts. The first part (Chapters 1, 2, and 3) examines threads on five online genealogy forums, primarily between 2012 and 2017. In Chapter 1, I introduce an active debate about Indigenous identity on a multi-year thread. The debate outlines many of the most common themes on the genealogy forums and manifests practices related to *lineal* descent, in that a single Indigenous ancestor in the 1600s discovered through genealogical practice is used to claim an Indigenous identity today. Through researching the handful of Indigenous women ancestors who were mentioned on the forums, I illustrate how some of the same seventeenth-century Indigenous women are now being reclaimed by French-descendant people in places as diverse as Quebec, Nova Scotia, Ontario, Vermont, and New Hampshire as the basis for several *different* Indigenous identities. In Chapter 2, I examine three case studies involving four French women ancestors born prior to 1650 who are commonly reconstructed on the forums as Indigenous women. I develop the concept of *aspirational* descent to explain the efforts to reconstruct indigeneity in the past, often through molecular technologies. In Chapter 3, I continue an examination of the online genealogy forums by turning to an understanding of how French descendants reclaim certain family names (patronyms) that are associated with indigeneity—particularly Métis patronyms—as the basis for an Indigenous identity. I have developed the concept of *lateral* descent to explain these efforts to shift into an Indigenous identity with no direct Indigenous ancestry.

The second part of the book (Chapters 4 and 5) moves away from the online genealogy forums into an analysis of a range of documents produced by two of the largest self-identified métis organizations in Canada. Focusing specifically on member interviews and preliminary court testimony, I trace the origins of these two organizations in social movements actively opposing the political claims of actual Indigenous peoples. Organizational leaders come to know each other as white French descendants opposing land negotiations between Indigenous peoples and settler governments in their respective regions, eventually switching to an "Indigenous" identity after the Supreme Court of Canada's *Powley* decision (2003) offered them a potent legal strategy. These movements appeal especially to French-descendant men and have become the locus for the performance of dominant forms of masculinity in these regions. In Chapter 4, I focus on the creation of the CMDRSM in the contiguous Saguenay–Lac-Saint-Jean and Côte-Nord regions of Quebec—the first so-called métis organization in Quebec to go to court to claim Aboriginal rights under the *Powley* test in 2006. In Chapter 5, I turn to the MNRS in the Gaspésie region of Quebec across the St. Lawrence River from the CMDRSM. Founded eighteen months after its predecessor, in June 2006, the MNRS had become the second-largest self-identified métis organization in Canada by 2018, with over 20,000 registered members. While each organization has its own unique origins and subsequent development, I illustrate how they nonetheless share a number of crucial characteristics. Above all, they exist as organizations that consolidate forms of white power in their respective regions.

Part One

THE MECHANICS OF DESCENT

Chapter One

Lineal Descent and the Political Use of Indigenous Women Ancestors

Genealogy forums offer anyone with a computer and an internet connection an accessible way to piece together their family history. They also provide the type of social environment that leads individuals who may be aware of some distant Indigenous ancestry to move toward a claim of Indigenous identity. In my reading of these online discussions, I have striven to be respectful of individual "race-shifter" stories as they manifested themselves in the forums. More to the point, I have sought to express sensitivity about individual claims, given how white settler colonialism has led to the disenfranchisement and alienation of countless Indigenous people. Whether in the case of policies such as those that led to Indian residential schools and the Sixties Scoop, or those contained in the Indian Act, the Canadian government and its white citizenry have aimed to disconnect Indigenous peoples from kinship-based relationships for centuries. For many Indigenous people, then, sorting through an identity that was stolen from self and family is a messy business. With this in mind, the interpretation herein is not meant to foreclose the possibility of reconnection with Indigenous kin for those who have been dispossessed in such a manner.

Instead, I read the stories that I outline below as components of a much broader social phenomenon that deserves dedicated scholarly attention at this particular juncture—one in which white settler consciousness has embraced the language of reconciliation in a manner that anticipates no possibility for restitution or reparations.[1] In this context, settler self-indigenization *makes sense*, in that it provides white North American peoples with another avenue through which to avoid accountability in the ongoing violence of a system that we continue to benefit from almost exclusively. As we will see, most of these newfound claims to an Indigenous identity take the form of a mixed-race, "métis" identity, though in this chapter, parallel identity claims are explored as well. As Adam Gaudry has succinctly explained, "These [new] 'Métis' identities are described as a personal journey, rather than a connection to a historically continuous and still-living Métis community, making them relatively difficult to critique in settler societies that privilege self-identification in identity construction."[2] In order to explain the types of claims made on the genealogy forums, I have turned to broad concerns—expressed primarily by Indigenous scholars—related to governance and kinship. In particular is the concern that the continued racialization of Indigenous peoples' identities overrides the *political* basis for Indigenous peoples' relationships with the United States or Canada. Seen in this light, the wide variety of individual claims on the online genealogy forums are situated as part of a renewed strategy of white settler control—based in the mechanics of descent outlined herein—over the lands and lives of Indigenous peoples.

My use of the concepts of race shifting and race shifters has been inspired by Circe Sturm's extensive research on the phenomenon of white Americans becoming "Cherokee" in the United States. One of the key similarities between Sturm's findings and my own is that, in mine, only a small minority of those who are aware of their Indigenous ancestry actually go on to claim an Indigenous identity. As such, understanding what has pushed an increasing number of French descendants to claim an "Indigenous" identity in the past decade and a half is a priority in this book. Sturm explains that the social process through which an individual becomes aware of their ancestry determines whether or not they will eventually identify as Indigenous. In particular, she posits that the shift from gaining knowledge of one's Indigenous ancestry to claiming an Indigenous identity usually occurs after one is involved in "extended social contact with other race shifters."[3] In this sense, I read online genealogy forums as providing the type of social contact that is required to propel French descendants—whether they speak primarily French or English and live in Quebec, Ontario, Nova Scotia, New Brunswick, Maine, Vermont, or New Hampshire—to claim an "Indigenous" identity.

To be sure, while there are many apparent synergies between becoming Cherokee in the United States and becoming "Eastern métis" in Canada, there are also many clear differences. The most striking difference that I have found among French descendants is the interchangeability of Indigenous women ancestors. This study's analysis of genealogy forums uncovered a remarkable fact: some of the same seventeenth-century Indigenous women are now being reclaimed by French-descendant people as the sole basis for several *different* Indigenous identities. The interchangeability of Indigenous women ancestors and identities is in stark contrast to Sturm's work that focused specifically on the use of Cherokee identity, which tends to act as a container for race-shifter claims to indigeneity in the United States due to the tribe's history of exogamy (out-marriage) and cultural adaptation.[4] The claims below certainly call into question the legitimacy of self-indigenization and/or race shifting, especially in its disregard for, even opposition to, both past and existing forms of Indigenous identity based in kinship and citizenship.

Much of the upcoming analytical work is empirically based and, as such, focuses on the detailed mechanics of race shifting: not only do I focus on the broad arguments mobilized to claim an Indigenous identity, but I also identify the specific (Indigenous women) ancestors who are at the basis of these newfound claims.

In this moment, when individual self-fashioning is given primacy over social and political analysis, it has become common to accept self-identification as the main determinant of one's social identity. The next three chapters push back against self-identification as a primary mode of self-making, by casting a gaze on the social organization of self-identification on online genealogy forums. As Kramer has argued, reading genealogy as a "technology of belonging" allows us to be attentive to the labour that goes into *making* relations through the practice of genealogy.[5]

SETTING THE STAGE: FIVE KEY GENEALOGY FORUMS

Going forward, I examine several of the highest-profile and most-used online genealogy forums aimed at French descendants, as well as a couple of additional forums that emerged in preliminary research. Without a doubt, the Généalogie du Québec et d'Amérique française (GQAF) website is the most far-reaching of these sites. By mid-2017, the GQAF forum included well over 500 pages of material, representing more than 5,500 individual threads going back to 2007, each started by a site member with a single post. As with all forums that I encountered, one can become a contributing member of the GQAF forum by signing up for a free account, though one can read the publicly archived threads without being a member. In the period from July 2015 to July 2017, each thread included on average four replies, though a significant minority of posts (between 5 and 10 percent) received no replies, while others (again, 5 to 10 percent) received a dozen or more replies. All threads garnered at least a few readers, though the average number of views per thread numbers in the range of 300 to 400. Threads devoted to Indigenous identity and ancestry or indigeneity more broadly make up a small minority (1 to 2 percent) of the threads in the forum, but they attract significantly more replies and views than is the norm on the site. It is not uncommon for a year-old thread on indigeneity or Indigenous identity/ancestry to attract upwards of 1,000 views. Along with its forum, the GQAF website hosts one of the most in-depth and easily accessible French-descendant genealogy databases on the Web, which no doubt drives much of the traffic to the forum. The database contains hundreds of thousands of entries based primarily on information from marriage, birth, and death registries. It covers a period stretching from the first French colonist born in Quebec City in 1620—Hélène Desportes, who is my direct ancestor through four different family lines—to the latter part of the twentieth century. Using its database alone, I was able to determine in excess of 70 percent of my overall ancestry going back thirteen generations.

I also analyze four other popular online genealogy forums dealing largely with the descendants of French colonists. The Vos origines (VO) website is run by a few community-based genealogists who facilitate a broad range of genealogy forums, from which I selected the Aboriginal-themed forum.

The general forum of the Nation autochtone du Québec (NAQ) is the only one in my selection that is run by a self-identified Indigenous organization, the Alliance autochtone du Québec (AAQ). The AAQ adopted a broad-based membership policy that opened up membership to anybody with Indigenous ancestry after the *Powley* decision. The three criteria—more expansive than in *Powley*—are to be of Indigenous ancestry, to self-identify as Indigenous, and to be accepted by one's community.[6] The AAQ's most recent policy stands in contrast to that of its forebear, the Alliance laurentienne des Métis et Indiens hors reserve (1972–83), which adopted a strict four-generation cut-off in 1975 in order to limit the impacts of race shifting. The Ancestry Métis forum is run by a number of prominent French-descendant genealogists and is the most active forum in English. Last is the Rootsweb MetisGen-L forum, which is managed by an expert in Acadian genealogy. I analyzed these forums for a number of reasons. Both the VO and the NAQ forums, for instance, focus specifically on Indigenous identity/ancestry, and the Ancestry and Rootsweb forums are in English, which distinguishes them.

"THE WEAK DEGREE OF MÉTISSAGE IN QUEBEC": DEBATING RACE AND IDENTITY ONLINE

Mobilizing Long-Ago Ancestry

I was often surprised by the complexity of the conversations in the discussion forums. Indeed, my surprise betrays my own skepticism about genealogy's contemporary political uses. One lengthy thread on the VO forum highlights some of the conflict over the existence of the "Quebec métis" as a distinct Indigenous people. In a thread that was active for more than five months, beginning in early September 2013 and ending in late February 2014, at least eleven separate posters expressed their ideas and analyses of contemporary indigeneity in Quebec with quite a bit of passion and forthrightness. The thread began with an initial post titled "The weak degree of métissage in Quebec" by Anne-Marie, which included a link to a story in the French-language press featuring well-known historical demographer Hubert Charbonneau, who had affirmed the scholarly consensus that relatively few mixed-race individuals were born during the French regime (see Introduction). After a couple of posters expressed their incredulity ("Does that mean that the Métis don't exist?"),[7] Bernard, a frequent poster, followed up by differentiating between "real" Métis and those who identify with one of the many post-*Powley* organizations in Quebec: "Métis people exist, but not in the same manner as these organizations claim. . . . a large majority of today's Métis are on Indian reserves and are thus Aboriginal, and the others simply mixed with the rest of the population, they don't want any label. The real Métis have nothing to do with the organizations of the same name, where there's simply too much genealogical fraud."[8]

Denise, the forum administrator until the end of 2016, responded with the genealogical basis of her claim to a "métis" identity—a common forum occurrence. Denise's direct ancestor, Marie Olivier Manitouabouich (a.k.a. Marie Sylvestre), an Indigenous woman born around 1624, married Frenchman Martin Prévost (born about 1610) in 1644; Denise explained that this fact had come to her accidentally later in life. Quite a bit has been written about Sylvestre, since she figures prominently in the *Jesuit Relations*. Olivier LeTardif, a French colonist from Brittany who worked closely with the Jesuits in their missionary efforts, adopted Manitouabouich, which was when she was given the name Marie Sylvestre by Church officials. As part of French colonial efforts to civilize Indigenous peoples at the time, Marie Rollet, a Parisian woman among the earliest French settlers to Quebec City, was charged with raising two young Indigenous girls born in the 1620s to be French women. Thus, from the age of about seven, Marie Sylvestre and Euphrosine-Madeleine Nicolet—daughter of an unnamed Nipissing woman and French settler Jean Nicolet—were raised primarily in Rollet's home. Sylvestre went on to have eight children, half of whom died before reaching adulthood. Besides her eldest son, who was fifteen years old at the time of her passing, all of Sylvestre's surviving children were raised by a French-Canadian stepmother.

Support for Denise's position that one can be Indigenous today solely on the basis of the discovery of an ancestor born nearly 400 years ago was swift. A post by Lory represented the general response, one in which individual self-identification, supported by genealogical evidence, was sufficient to claim an Indigenous identity as Métis: "I deplore that some people treat

Métis status as a mish-mash [*de toute les sauces*]. But it's bad form to put those who have proudly rediscovered their Aboriginal roots in the same boat. No Métis person can deny their origins, if they have proof supporting their claim."[9] Shortly after, Denise agreed: "Sure Lory, there has certainly been some fraud and some people who shall remain nameless use it purely for their own financial benefit. Unfortunately, there have been many victims. As you said, there must be proof."[10] The fact that many organizations representing "Quebec métis" act fraudulently was a concern that found a general consensus among posters across all forums, regardless of their perspective on the existence of the so-called Eastern métis (or "Quebec métis").

Marco, a frequent poster on multiple websites and forums, openly expressed his disgust with efforts to undermine race-shifter claims in Quebec, such as those in previous posts by Anne-Marie and Bernard. Marco listed four marriages between French men and Indigenous women in mid-seventeenth-century New France, including the aforementioned Marie Sylvestre in 1644, as evidence of the deficit in Bernard's argument. Even more notably, Marco shared a common sentiment that no "pure" Indigenous people exist today; according to him, all Indigenous people are mixed-race (or "métis"). In this sense, Marco mobilized a discourse of blood in order to place all individuals with any Indigenous ancestry on an equal playing field, regardless of their cultural, political, or social lives—a discursive strategy that is also quite common among organizations representing the so-called Quebec métis. Needless to say, these biological imaginaries anticipate the disappearance of Indigenous peoples as sovereign, self-determining entities in a "sea of admixture," as TallBear has argued.[11]

When Anne-Marie responded by reiterating the 1 percent ancestry figure common in scholarly research in order to question whether the French Québécois can legitimately claim being Indigenous, Marco turned to an explicitly sexualized rendering of the contact zone: "I have a hard time believing this percentage, when I imagine the first (French) colonists arriving here and seeing gorgeous hairless Indian girls, bare-breasted and sexually promiscuous.... I don't believe they were abstinent."[12] As we can see, the erotics of the contact zone continue to generate useful fantasies for French-descendant men, which in this case coincided with a massive public outcry following media reports about sexual violence against Indigenous women by police officers in the northern resource town of Val d'Or.[13]

In fact, concerns about ongoing sexualized violence against Indigenous women in Quebec specifically and in Canada more generally exploded into a wide-reaching social movement led by Indigenous women and girls in cities as diverse as Vancouver, Saskatoon, Winnipeg, Thunder Bay, and Val d'Or in the past half-dozen years. Central to this movement has been an analysis of the foundational role that sexualized violence against Indigenous girls and women has played in the colonial project.[14] On this topic, Audra Simpson explains that "feminist scholars have argued that Native women's bodies were to the settler eye, like land, and as such in the settler mind, the Native woman is rendered 'unrapeable' (or, highly rapeable) because she was like land, matter to be extracted from, used, sullied, taken from, over and over again, something that is already violated and violatable in a great march to accumulate surplus, to so called 'production.'"[15] Central to Marco's highly sexualized fantasy of the contact zone is the recirculation of a favoured narrative of Indigenous women as always available to French male colonists. Fantasy here takes on a double meaning, since it is through the hypersexualization of Indigenous girls and women that the fantastical notion of French-descendant "indigeneity" is created in the first place. Even when the normative European male colonist gaze was explicitly on display in these genealogy forums, posters avoided raising questions about consent, exploitation, or politics in the early sexual economy. As I point out in the next section, the objectification of Indigenous women ancestors is common on the forums, since they create an online environment favourable to fantasizing about and ultimately creating novel forms of French-descendant "indigeneity" in the present that rely on a romanticized, heteronormative story of the contact zone.

While a firm belief in the trope of sexually available Indigenous girls and women prevails in the United States and Canada, ample evidence suggests that Indigenous women in New France were loath to marry French men. As I explained in the Introduction, French efforts at assimilating Indigenous peoples mostly failed throughout the seventeenth century, despite Crown incentives offered to Indigenous women. The fact that the same three or four Indigenous women married prior to 1660 are the primary basis for almost all of the claims to indigeneity on the forums certainly supports the scholarly consensus that only a small fraction of the thousands of Indigenous women (and girls) living near French missions and towns in New France (e.g., Trois-Rivières, Tadoussac, Montreal) at the time married French men. Besides, Métis scholars have long argued for the importance of placing Indigenous women—and not French men—at the centre of Métis ethnogenesis.[16] In a 2017 interview, Jennifer Adese explains the limits of an "Eastern métis" discourse that all but ignores the role of Indigenous women beyond sex and reproduction: "As a Métis woman, I find that claims made regarding Métis as 'originating in the East' or from the 'paternal homeland of Québec' are unforgivably sexist. [They] elide the rootedness of Métis in their maternal homeland—and thus in the language, kinship networks, and knowledge systems of maternal relations."[17] Nevertheless, Marco's sexually charged presentation of early French settlement, in which French men's desire for Indigenous girls and women propel the colony forward, is foundational to the genealogical search for indigeneity among French descendants, as other examples below make clear.

In response to Marco's post, Lory affirmed her Indigenous identity and agreed with his assertion that all existing Indigenous peoples in Quebec are in fact "métis," an argument that goes against the centuries-old existence of eleven distinct Indigenous peoples throughout the entire territory of Quebec: "I'll add that there are Métis people where I live, whatever one says. Fear, shame, and contempt taught the Métis to lower their heads and to be quiet. Now that our world has started to change, these Métis are learning to no longer be ashamed. They assert their Métis-ness. I am one.... In Quebec, it's not the Métis who don't exist, but pure Indians, as one says.... This will be my last comment on this thread. A descendant of François Pelletier and Françoise, *montagnaise* [Innu], I am and will remain Métis."[18] At the end of this post, Lory cites a marriage between Frenchman François Pelletier and an Anishinaabe woman named Françoise Ouechipichinokoue (whom she misidentifies as Innu) in the summer of 1677 as the sole basis of her identity as métis today. That specific Indigenous ancestors are publicly claimed in these forums is not an anomaly; on the contrary, due to the number of easily accessible genealogical databases and associated infrastructure, many of the same women from the seventeenth century come up over and over again. The very discovery of their name(s) in a marriage registry or genealogical database is enough to evoke a sense of awe and inspiration. As Sturm explains, "racial shifters tend to seize on particular ancestors, real or imagined, as touchstones when they rewrite their autobiographies."[19]

Without a doubt, Marie Sylvestre is the most common ancestor that comes up in online genealogy forums, though two other Indigenous women married prior to 1660 also appear regularly. Table 1 documents the number of descendants, per generation, of the three Indigenous women who appear most often on the genealogy forums.

TABLE 1. THREE INDIGENOUS WOMEN ANCESTORS IN QUEBEC AND THEIR DESCENDANTS, BY GENERATION

	1ST GENERATION	2ND GENERATION	3RD GENERATION	4TH GENERATION	5TH GENERATION
"Nipissing woman" (b. prior to 1615)	1 descendant (b. 1628)	4 descendants (b. 1652–73)	11 descendants (b. 1668–1711)	59 descendants (b. 1693–1751)	123 descendants (b. 1735–97)
Marie Sylvestre (b. about 1624)	4 descendants (b. 1651–65)	34 descendants (b. 1676–1728)	170 descendants (b. 1695–1734)	317 descendants (b. 1720–88)	1,349 descendants (b. 1745–1833)
Marie Miteouamegoukwe (b. about 1631)	6 descendants (b. 1659–73)	26 descendants (b. 1683–1726)	41 descendants (b. 1707–59)	103 descendants (b. 1733–93)	459 descendants (b. 1751–1816)

If we fully consider these early demographic records, the frequency with which Sylvestre appears in race-shifter genealogies can be explained. Her marriage to Martin Prévost in 1644 is the second union between a French man and Indigenous woman recorded in present-day Quebec. The first union (not a marriage), between Jean Nicolet and an unnamed Algonquin (Nipissing) woman, produced one child—Euphrosine-Madeleine Nicolet—in 1628. Euphrosine was eventually adopted by Marie Rollet, one of Samuel de Champlain's most trusted confidants, at a young age when the girl's father moved back to Quebec City after her mother apparently died. She eventually married Frenchman Elie Dussault in that town in 1663. While Euphrosine-Madeleine had four children, the second generation of her descendants in

New France (born between 1668 and 1711) included only eleven children, all of whom were well integrated into colonial society due to Euphrosine-Madeleine's upbringing in a French colonial household of some importance. In the case of Sylvestre—who was raised alongside Euphrosine-Madeleine by French women—the third generation of her progeny (born between 1695 and 1734), which overlaps with Euphrosine-Madeleine Nicolet's second generation, included 170 descendants, also fully integrated in colonial society. By the dawn of the nineteenth century, there were over 1,000 Sylvestre descendants in New France, far outstripping the number of Nicolet descendants, as well as the descendants of all of the other Indigenous woman who married French men prior to 1660 *combined*. I took my analysis further by using demographer Jacques Henripin's estimate for the rate of population increase among French Québécois between 1760 and 1850 and genealogist Daniel Fournier's for 1871 to 1961.[20] Using these figures, Sylvestre likely has just over 800,000 descendants to the thirteenth generation (mean year of birth = 1986) and Nicolet likely has just over 100,000 descendants to the thirteenth generation (mean year of birth = 1984). In other words, Sylvestre's earlier marriage (nineteen years before Euphrosine-Madeleine's) and the fact that her four children who lived to adulthood each had on average 8.5 children ensured that she is the Indigenous woman ancestor who appears most often in French-descendant genealogies today.

One striking difference from Sturm's observations about becoming Cherokee in the United States is that forum posters in my study relied on a much more interchangeable understanding of indigeneity with no apparent cultural or territorial grounding. In many ways, posters used what Nash calls the "genealogical model of identity in which identity is a direct function of genealogy and genealogical inheritance."[21] Nash argues that this model of identity contrasts with non-Western, Indigenous understandings of place and identity, but nonetheless "is a deeply appealing model of belonging because of its simplicity, security, and singularity."[22] In following Nash's theorization, genealogical evidence, when it is available, suffices for race shifters, as in the case of Sylvestre's present-day descendants, many of whom are claiming one ancestral line going back twelve or thirteen generations (as few as 1 in 8,192 ancestors, or 0.00012 percent) as the basis for their Indigenous identity today.

If At First You Don't Succeed . . . :
White Settlers Using Indigenous Women

In an Ancestry forum thread titled "manitouabeouich/ outchibahabanoukoueou" that was active for nearly nine years (from November 2008 to July 2017), about twenty posters discussed how to use their ancestry with Sylvestre to obtain Métis "status." Since the forum is in English, it attracts French descendants from all corners of the United States and Canada, most of whom do not necessarily associate their identities with their French (ethnic) ancestry. Robert, a U.S. resident, shared his recent discovery of Sylvestre among his long-ago ancestors, in a September 2011 post: "I also am able to trace my ancesters [sic] back to these 2 people as the parents of Marie-Oliver-Sylvestre Manithabehick who married Martin Prévost [in 1644]. I always felt I was missing something and had a feeling there was native in my background. So, can I claim status [for me] and my children and who and where do we go?"[23] Robert received several instructive responses, all anticipating his self-identification as métis. For instance, a frequent poster, Silverrose, explained that the Métis Nation of Ontario (MNO) does not accept new members on the basis of Manitouabeouich's 400-year-old line, while pointing Robert (and the three or four other posters searching for a means to obtain formal recognition) to alternative organizations. According to Silverrose, "You said [that] you contacted the Metis Nation, do you mean the Ontario Metis Nation [sic], if so you will never get a card from them. [. . .] If your [sic] near Ottawa you can also contact the [Communauté Métis autochtone de Maniwaki]—for this one you will need to translate it if you cannot speak French. Both are excellent places and you will have no trouble getting your status."[24] Several other posters offered advice similar to Silverrose's, pointing to other organizations in Quebec accepting the Sylvestre "line," such as the American Metis Aboriginal Association Lodge and the AAQ.

In a post much later in the thread (January 2016), Lise explained her process for considering membership given the MNO's more restrictive policy: "I also wanted to add that [the Communauté Métis autochtone de] Maniwaki does accept the [Sylvestre] line as long as you have all the marriages/baptisms to prove your relationship and your claim. For those applying in Quebec, please do your due diligence as some organizations are recognized in terms of applying for scholarships (such as Indspire) and others are not. Quebec is fighting to be recognized within [*sic*] the federal government as part of [the] Metis Nation, but it will take time."²⁵ In these cases, posters circumvented the Métis Nation's citizenship policy (via the MNO), openly casting doubt on the legitimacy of Métis sovereignty and self-determination along the way. In fact, many of the posters expressed open contempt for the political institutions governing the Métis Nation, inasmuch as they are seen as an impediment to claiming their own form of indigeneity. One such poster on a previous thread on the Ancestry forum in September 2005 even went so far as to argue that the post-*Powley* citizenship policy of the Métis National Council (MNC) "would cut off Louis Riel from being a Metis, since he was born in Quebec!"²⁶ Such reactionary arguments—Louis Riel was born in the Red River Settlement (near present-day Winnipeg, Manitoba) and would certainly be considered Métis by the MNC—betray a fundamental opposition to the Métis as an Indigenous *people* with the inherent right to determine its citizenship.

In his incisive critique of self-identification through genealogy, Gaudry provides a useful counterpoint for understanding Métis peoplehood by arguing that "contemporary notions of citizenship practiced in Métis communities are not just maintained by abstract relationships to one's ancestors, but also by practicing proper social conduct in everyday relationships with fellow community members, a practice in which many First Nations people are also linked through to Métis communities through generations of intermarriage."²⁷ In their singular focus on abstract relationships to long-ago ancestors, forum posters manifest a biology-based understanding of Métis-ness that runs counter to the understandings of Métis peoplehood that Métis scholars (and community members) have developed over generations. As opposed to this genealogical model of identity, Brenda Macdougall's theorization of *wahkootowin* "as a system of social obligation and mutual responsibility between related individuals—between members of a family" encapsulates the basis for what she calls a Métis "style of life."²⁸

Given the near-universal lack of precision about tribal origins on display in "Eastern métis" claims and the slippage at work between Métis and mixed-race, Marie Sylvestre is used as the basis for a number of other Indigenous identities in the vicinity of Quebec, including in some circumstances to an "Algonquin" (Anishinaabe) identity in Ontario. For example, a frequent poster introduced the idea of becoming "Algonquin" through Sylvestre to those whose métis claim has been rejected in Ontario, displaying a form of interchangeability between Indigenous identities that diverges considerably from Sturm's work in the United States. It seems important to note here that throughout the thread, Sylvestre's parents are alternatively reclaimed as Abenaki and Huron (Wendat), Algonquin and Abenaki, or Algonquin and Huron (Wendat). Yet, how Sylvestre is ultimately reimagined (métis or simply Algonquin) mostly did not correspond with her parents' identities.

Irene, for instance, first introduced the "Algonquin" option for formal recognition in a post on the same Ancestry thread that began in late 2008, several years after the *Powley* decision: "I have that Roch [Sylvestre's father] was Huron and [his] wife [was] Abenakis, the daughter [Marie Sylvestre] is an Algonquin living amongst the Huron Reserve.... Groups like Mattawa/North Bay Algonquins have now accepted this lineage to be Algonquin as of November 2008, as a genealogist I have just heard that two of my clients have now been accepted as Algonquin descendants."[29] Irene's post led to an energetic discussion during which a number of posters asked pointed questions about how they could obtain either Métis or Algonquin "status" through their lineal connection to Sylvestre. Irene replied to the thread nearly three years later, in September 2011, explaining that one could "either be a Metis or a Descendant of an Algonquin and register yourself with [the] Mattawa/North Bay, [Algonquin] First Nation"; she then encouraged forum members to call the Mattawa-based organization to become a member.[30] In an earlier thread on the same forum, well-known genealogist Johan advised people to consider moving away from recognition as métis by the MNO in favour of recognition as "Algonquin," in a May 2008 post: "If you have [an] Algonkin [*sic*] ancestor, it is possible that you could register with the Bonnechere Algonquin [First Nation] as a Metis.... I know they accept out of province members.... [Y]ou will need to get in contact with them."[31] These two posts by Johan and Irene—and the responses that followed confirming some posters' new membership in what seemed to be Algonquin organizations—cast a light on the multiple ways that the same Indigenous woman could be used by race shifters. It would seem, through research provided by the Algonquin Nation Secretariat (ANS), the political arm of the Algonquin Nation Tribal Council, that the efforts of Irene, Johan, some other posters, and other French descendants living in south-central Ontario to reconstruct themselves as "Algonquin" were quite successful.

To be clear, the ANS opposes the use of "root ancestors" such as Sylvestre as the basis for Algonquin identity, as does the only federally recognized Algonquin community in Ontario (Algonquins of Pikwàkanagàn First Nation [APFN]). Algonquin concerns that individuals are being offered membership by organizations representing non-status Algonquins solely on the basis of these so-called root ancestors extend to the fact that in 2016 these new "Algonquins" were provided with the ability to vote on a comprehensive land claim with the federal and provincial governments. In other words, settler governments are deciding which organizations can define who is an Algonquin, often against the wishes of actual Algonquin people, in land claims processes that lead to the extinguishment of Algonquin rights and title.[32] In this sense, the Algonquins of Ontario (AOO)—the organization tasked with adjudicating Algonquin identity for the purpose of the land claim process—is but the latest incarnation in a long history of settler governments defining who counts as Indigenous, with all the resulting consequences. In its report on individuals who were recognized as Algonquin by the federal and provincial governments for the purpose of the comprehensive land claim, the ANS writes,

> In the process of review, we identified a very large number of individuals who have relied on root ancestors whose only connection to the Algonquins or Nipissings appears to date back to the 1600's or early 1700's. It appears that these root ancestors relocated to New France during that period, and were entirely absent from the territory until their descendants moved back to the Ottawa Valley as French Canadian or Franco-Ontarien settlers in the mid-1800's. In other cases, these "root ancestors" are actually descended from Abenakis, not from Algonquins or Nipissings. It also appears that the "Algonquins" who are relying on these root ancestors have had no intermarriage with anyone of Algonquin or Nipissing ancestry for at least 200, and in some cases, more than 300 years.[33]

The ANS consistently expressed concerns with the AOO treaty process and, especially, its creation of new "Algonquin" people on the basis of the genealogical model of identity. The ANS's analysis above also matches my own family history almost exactly. Three of the Algonquin women eventually added to the government-sanctioned AOO Master Schedule of Algonquin Ancestors are my direct ancestors. All three had children with French colonists, and two were married and lived out their lives in New France: Euphrosine-Madeline's mother died shortly after giving birth in Nipissing territory, just outside of the proposed AOO claim territory, in 1628; and Marie Miteouamegoukwe was born in 1631, baptized in Montreal in 1650, and died in Trois-Rivières, where she spent the majority of her life, in 1699. We know much less about Marguerite Pigarouiche, who was baptized in 1646 and married in 1671. The three women had children who show up in my ancestral history, born between 1664 and 1672.

Allow me to follow the thread of Pigarouiche's descendants in order to provide further analysis of the ANS report. Pigarouiche's descendants end up in my maternal great-grandfather Brabant's ancestral line. In following her descendants who are my direct ancestors through time, one notices that the first four generations are women who marry French descendants. These women, born between 1672 and 1764, all lived in and around Montreal, especially near Lac des Deux-Montagnes, which in 1721 became the location of a large Sulpician mission with hundreds of Algonquin, Mohawk, and Nipissing residents as well as a neighbouring French military garrison. For these four generations, it appears that Pigarouiche's female descendants lived in proximity to Indigenous people living at the mission, while marrying French descendants who were associated with the garrison. This pattern changes with the birth in 1794 of a Brabant son, who settled in a small French-Canadian town near the border with Ontario. He married a French settler woman whose root ancestors (five generations at this point, or thirty-two people) were *all* born in France in the late 1500s or early 1600s. The next three generations of Brabant men follow the same pattern, though they show up in records in Ontario from time to time, as when one of them married a French-Canadian woman right across the border in Ontario in 1858. It appears through census records that the Brabant family ultimately settled in the Sudbury, Ontario, area in the late 1800s, about fifty kilometres northwest of traditional Algonquin territory in the Ottawa River (Kichi Sibi, Algonquin for "great river") watershed. Prior to the family's migration west to Ontario, the Legislative Assembly of Ontario passed into law the Free Grants and Homestead Act in 1868, which guaranteed that men over eighteen years old could claim 100 acres of land (up to 200 acres under some conditions) and receive title to the land if they built a small cabin, cleared at least two acres per year for five years, and lived on the land. The act was signed into law between the signing of the Robinson-Huron Treaty (1850) and the adoption of the Indian Act (1876), which together paved the way for the dispossession and displacement of Anishinabek[34] people in the Sudbury area. Combined with the construction of the railway through north-central Ontario in the 1880s and the scarcity of arable farm land in rural Quebec due to the system of land tenure, French descendants from Lower Canada (Quebec) resettled in the region, including several of my great-great-grandparents.

Incredibly, of the 115 ancestors I have managed to trace back to Pigarouiche's generation (or further in a couple of cases in which European settlers were born prior to her in New France) in the Brabant line, 112 or 97.4 percent of them were born in France. The only non-French ancestors other than Pigarouiche are two ancestors born in England. It is certainly the case, therefore, in following the ANS's conclusion, that had I (or any of my forty or so relatives who grew up and live in Algonquin territory) opted to register as an elector and beneficiary by the AOO's deadline, I would have done so *despite* the fact that there has been no intermarriage in my lineage with anyone of Indigenous ancestry for about 350 years, nor does there appear to have been any significant and sustained social relationships with Indigenous people for *at minimum* 230 years.

Clearly, not everyone who matched the specific genealogical profile outlined in the ANS report joined one of the new organizations created for the purpose of the AOO's land claims process. Nevertheless, such individuals ended up representing a significant number of AOO electors and beneficiaries. As an example, according to the ANS's analysis of the final AOO voter list (December 2015), 53 percent of the Mattawa/North Bay organization's membership (or nearly 2,000 people) fell into this category, while about 39 percent of the nearly 8,000 people eligible to vote in the

2016 comprehensive land claim relied solely on one of these same seventeenth-century "root ancestors" for membership.

Besides these remarkable statistics, the ANS problematizes whether six of the eleven available "root ancestors" in the government-sanctioned AOO's membership roll were actually Algonquin to begin with, alerting us to the ultimate malleability of indigeneity through genealogy. The work of genealogy, it seems, can create indigeneity as much as describe it, in following Barnwell's observations about contemporary genealogical research: "While genealogy seemingly represents a linear narrative of historical truths collated from events and identities of the past, in reality it is just as reflective of the desires of the present. At a certain point, veracity ceases to be the basis of identification and the desire for identification itself becomes a surprisingly powerful basis for veracity."[35] The fact that thousands of French descendants chose to become new "Algonquins" using the genealogical model of identity suggests that the desire for identification played a crucial role in their self-understanding.

The ANS's own research on Sylvestre, for instance, eventually concluded that she was most likely Abenaki. What's more, although the AOO's addition of Sylvestre to the Master Schedule of Algonquin Ancestors used to identify electors and beneficiaries of the land claim on 21 November 2008 brought protests by representatives of the APFN, the Ontario Superior Court judge tasked with finalizing the membership list upheld her inclusion.[36] Notably, Irene raised the possibility of joining an AOO-affiliated organization via Sylvestre on the forums only days after the contested AOO decision. Irene explained that Sylvestre's parents were Wendat and Abenaki, but nonetheless declared that their child was Algonquin. Irene's statement about Sylvestre being Algonquin appears to flow directly from the work of several noted genealogists who sought to have her included in the AOO's Master Schedule of Algonquin Ancestors despite the disapproval of Algonquin people.

Another example of the inclusion of a contested ancestor concerns Thomas Laguarde *dit* St-Jean. The most common root ancestor named in the ANS report—my analysis found him used as a root ancestor by over 1,005 new "Algonquins"—St-Jean was first included on the Preliminary List of Algonquin Ancestors in March 1999. An appeal by the APFN in

January 2000 led to Laguarde *dit* St-Jean's removal as a root ancestor. At a hearing less than four months later, Laguarde was re-included on the AOO's list of root ancestors. Finally, at a hearing in March 2013, the same retired Ontario Superior Court judge charged with overseeing the proceedings rejected an appeal by the APFN, affirming that "on the balance of probabilities" Laguarde had Algonquin ancestry. The decision hinged on a letter written by a priest in June 1845 that claimed Laguarde was descended from Algonquins, despite the fact that the APFN presented a range of documentary evidence over six decades that refuted this claim.[37]

Further demonstrating Indigenous opposition to these genealogy-based claims to an Indigenous identity, the ratification vote that took place in early 2016 exposed the political cleavage between APFN and the broader AOO. Of the 3,323 AOO electors who voted on the land claim, 95.6 percent voted in favour of ratification. In contrast, electors who are citizens of the APFN voted 56.1 percent *against* ratification in their own referendum.[38] As an APTN news report on the election results outlines, much of the opposition in Pikwàkanagàn was due to the use of "root ancestors" from over 300 years ago as the basis of membership in the AOO: a significant majority of pre-AOO Algonquins simply disagreed that a long-ago Indigenous ancestor in the 1600s makes one Algonquin (or, more generally, Indigenous) today.[39] Accordingly, whether today's French descendants are claiming so-called métis *or* Algonquin identity through their nearly 400-year-old lineal connection to Sylvestre or a few other Indigenous women born in the first half of the 1600s, one thing that remains constant is the organized opposition to these claims by actual Métis and Algonquin peoples.

Given the interchangeability of Indigenous women ancestors, as indicated above, Sylvestre's presence in the family tree of generations of French descendants has led to her being used to validate a third "Indigenous" identity: besides standing in as the sole basis for either a "Métis" or "Algonquin" identity, Sylvestre is also reclaimed as a root ancestor for a number of members of the principal self-identified Abenaki organizations in Vermont, New Hampshire, and Quebec. Four so-called Abenaki tribes have been granted state recognition in Vermont since 2011, despite the fact that the two existing Abenaki First Nations in Quebec (Conseil des Abénakis d'Odanak and Conseil des Abénakis de Wolinak) have largely opposed such moves. The increase in state recognition in the United States since the 1980s has created a range of conflicts over Indigenous sovereignty. Sturm has explained that many states (e.g., Vermont) have few guidelines or procedures for state recognition at all, often making it "pure politics."[40]

Denise Watso, citizen of Odanak in south-central Quebec and long-time resident of Albany, New York, has documented the Abenaki opposition to the Vermont state-recognition process in some detail. For instance, she points to how the Vermont Senate Committee on Economic Development, Housing and General Affairs invited four Odanak citizens, including two elected Odanak councillors, to testify at the hearing into the recognition of the first two "Abenaki" tribes in January 2011. Two days before the hearing, the four Odanak citizens were uninvited, on the grounds that none were Vermont residents. Watso explains, "This attempt to silence the Abenaki people is in direct opposition to Abenaki history and to our aboriginal rights. Some of us have our primary residence in Vermont, and many others live in Quebec, New York, Massachusetts, Connecticut, New Hampshire and elsewhere. However, Vermont has been part of our homeland for thousands of years. We will not abandon our nationhood—something much larger than one state—because legislators are scared to hear from the true indigenous people of the Champlain Valley, the Green Mountains, the Connecticut River and the shores of Lake Memphramagog."[41] Consistent efforts to oppose the state-recognition process by Abenaki individuals and political organizations have been rebuffed by using the same international boundary that dispossessed the Abenaki people in the first place.

There are now several self-identified "Abenaki" tribes throughout New England and in southern Quebec, and much as in the case of "Eastern métis" organizations in Quebec, Ontario, Nova Scotia, New Brunswick, and Maine, a documented connection to a seventeenth-century ancestor is all it takes to become "Abenaki." In his PhD dissertation on the topic of Abenaki sociality in New England, anthropologist Christopher A. Roy makes a clear distinction between self-identified Abenaki tribes and Abenaki people whose unambiguous Abenaki ancestry has been established until at least the late nineteenth century: "[There] are ... a number of self-identified Abenaki groups currently operating in New England and Quebec. Such groups claim Abenaki ancestry (and rights based on aboriginal ties to territory) despite a lack of evidence linking organizations and members to historically known aboriginal groups and ancestors. Many of my informants oppose—a few actively—these organizations; some are supportive of them. The vast majority of Abenaki people seem agnostic about the issue, their skepticism tempered by the limits of their own historical knowledge and the support self-identified Abenaki receive from some scholars, technocrats, and politicians."[42] My own archival research—including of the Odanak community newsletter *W8banaki Pilaskw*, several dozen Odanak council letters to self-identified tribes and state or federal authorities, and a variety of documents circulated by Vermont state legislators—confirms some of Roy's conclusions, though I would specify that Abenaki political institutions, such as the council at Odanak and the Grand Council of the Waban-Aki Nation, have consistently opposed self-identified "Abenaki" organizations in Quebec and New England for at least two decades.

As one example, in March 2003, the Chief of the Conseil des Abénakis d'Odanak, Gilles O'Bomsawin, provided testimony to the Standing Committee on Aboriginal Affairs, Northern Development, and Natural Resources (Government of Canada) about the proliferation of so-called "Abenaki" groups in Quebec and in New England. He stated in his testimony, "There was a day when nobody wanted to be an Indian. Now everybody wants to be an Indian.... We have information since the 1700s or 1800s on the backgrounds of the back families, the O'Bomsawins, the Panadis, the Wawanolets and everybody else. The priests left backgrounds on the activities and everything else, so we know our people. [Now] Indians are coming out of every branch of every tree in the province of Quebec and the states of New England."[43] For the most part, self-identified Abenaki tribes in New England have actively opposed all efforts by Odanak and Wolinak citizens and political institutions to question their "Abenaki" identities, perhaps because many members of the self-identified tribes highlighted in Roy's work trace their genealogy back to Sylvestre in New France, or to other Indigenous women from the seventeenth century who were Huron (Wendat), Mi'kmaq, Algonquin, or Abenaki, as I observed in some of their publicly available organizational records. All of these new "tribes" operate according to membership policies that accept members on the basis of any purported Indigenous ancestry at any time or place within their lineage.

An ancestral connection with Sylvestre has become the basis for membership in a remarkably diverse number of organizations in the United States and Canada, as well as for claims to *at least* three distinct Indigenous identities. These efforts to redefine indigeneity stand in contrast to the work of scholars, such as Leanne Betasamosake Simpson, who have called for Indigenous political resurgence drawing on land-based pedagogies and ongoing kinship relations.[44] In the case of French-descendant race shifters in this study, I have seen neither any evidence of kinship relations with living Indigenous peoples, nor any effort to articulate the specific territorial basis for their indigeneity. Instead, as in the case of Sylvestre, a long-ago Indigenous woman's identity is transformed in such a way that today's race shifters claim that a genealogical link to her leads one to be "Indigenous" to anywhere they happen to live.

Returning to my own genealogy, I count Marie Miteouamegoukwe as one of my maternal great-grandmother's (Quesnel family) direct ancestors. Miteouamegoukwe is likely the second-most well-known Indigenous ancestor in French-descendant genealogical circles today, after Sylvestre. She married Pierre Couc in Trois-Rivières, the site of a mission with a large Algonquin community, in 1657. Theirs is the fourth recorded marriage between an Indigenous woman and male French colonist in New France. In another extraordinary display of the remaking of indigeneity and the misuse of Indigenous women ancestors by French descendants, Miteouamegoukwe, who is clearly identified in all available historical records as Algonquin, is commonly used in claims to "Abenaki" identity throughout New England. For instance, of the 918 members enrolled in the Cowasuck Band of the Pennacook Abenaki (based in Alton, New Hampshire) in 2008, at least 14 percent of those who listed a root ancestor listed only Miteouamegoukwe—the third-largest number overall. Miteouamegoukwe also happens to be on the AOO's Master Schedule of Algonquin Ancestors, ensuring that a large number of French settlers claiming an Algonquin identity in Ontario are doing so on the strength of her presence in their genealogy.

TABLE 2. COMMON ROOT ANCESTORS IN MEMBERSHIP LISTS IN NEW HAMPSHIRE, QUEBEC, AND ONTARIO

	COWASUCK ABENAKI NEW HAMPSHIRE (2008) SAMPLE = 918	MANIWAKI MÉTIS QUEBEC (2016) SAMPLE = 1,906	ALGONQUINS OF ONTARIO (2015)* SAMPLE = 2,957	SAGUENAY MÉTIS QUEBEC (2007) SAMPLE = 27
Marie Sylvestre (m. 1644)	17.2% (#2)	13.7% (#1)	30.5% (#2)	8.6% (#5)
Marie Miteouamegoukwe (m. 1656)	14.4% (#3)	8.5% (#6)	23.4% (#3)	0
Marguerite Pigarouiche (m. 1670)	0	2.2% (#13)	4.2% (#6)	0
Nipissing Woman (d. 1628)	0	4.8% (#8)	10% (#4)	2.9% (#7)

* The sample for Ontario is from the Algonquin Nation Secretariat's analysis, which includes only AOO members who are reclaiming an ancestor from the seventeenth century or who were otherwise contested (about 40 percent of members).

Table 2 presents some of the data that I collected on four Indigenous women who were born prior to 1650, lived entirely in the seventeenth century, and are now used as root ancestors in the membership records of *at least* two separate organizations representing "Algonquin," "Abenaki," and/ or "Métis" members. As you can see, Sylvestre and Miteouamegoukwe are reclaimed as root ancestors in the records of at least three separate organizations, in which individuals are claiming to be "Abenaki" in New Hampshire, "Métis" in Quebec, and "Algonquin" in Ontario. Together, they came up over 2,100 times in the 5,245 membership genealogies. Sylvestre is easily the single root ancestor who appears the most often in the membership records that I have obtained (23.4 percent overall), mirroring her appearance on the genealogy forums.

Wherever the use of long-time ancestry and the accompanying blood logic manifests itself, Indigenous peoples vigorously oppose it. Whether we turn to Métis scholars, the ANS and the APFN, or Abenaki First Nations at Odanak and Wolinak, Indigenous peoples insist that it is their prerogative to govern the parameters of citizenship and recognition. Unfortunately, Marie Sylvestre and Marie Miteouamegoukwe are but two examples of women who married at least 360 years ago upon whose shoulders otherwise diverse French descendants (Canadian, Québécois, American/English-speaking and French-speaking) are reconstructing the basis of indigeneity, all while openly opposing those whom they now claim as part of their kin, as I will demonstrate in some detail in Chapters 4 and 5. While they are the two women who popped up most often in threads on genealogy forums, a few other seventeenth-century Indigenous women, such as Euphrosine-Madeleine Nicolet and Marguerite Pigarouiche, also turned up repeatedly.

Lineal Descent and the Remaking of Indigeneity: The Political Use of Indigenous Women

That a diversity of Indigenous identities can be linked to the same single ancestor born in the early 1600s may certainly seem odd in the context of Sturm's conclusions about racial homeopathy tied specifically to *Cherokee* ancestral substance in the United States. Nonetheless, the remaking of indigeneity by French descendants is made possible by "a tiny fraction of blood" in a wide region straddling northeast North America. My conception of race shifting as involving genealogical practices that *move beyond* and *are obsessed with* specific (Indigenous) ancestors provides an explanation of these observations.

First, participants on a range of French-language and English-language genealogy forums regularly search for, discover, and/or discuss their ancestral connection to a small number of seventeenth-century Indigenous women. The intense devotion that accompanies the focus on a handful of these women—notably, Marie Sylvestre and Marie Miteouamegoukwe—dramatically inflates their overall contribution to French-descendant ancestry. As a reminder, in the case of either Sylvestre or Miteouamegoukwe, forum posters are focusing on their lineal connection to one ancestor among more than *at least* 2,000 at that depth of time (at least twelve generations). This type of devotion is part and parcel of the logic of race shifting; without it, the claims that I explore on the forums would not be possible. These practices of descent *work*—meaning, they move thousands of French descendants to claim to be "Indigenous"—because individual race shifters are willing and able to spend hour upon hour poring over historical records and engaging in debate about a given seventeenth-century woman. Notably, only on rare occasions do any of the posters who discuss one of these women ever discuss aspects of these women's lives, or, for that matter, any of their children's or grandchildren's lives. These practices of lineal descent, then, are tied up in a genealogical model of identity, with all of the deep political and social meanings that such an identity confers.

Second, forum posters display a belief in the power of lineal descent that accords with J. Kēhaulani Kauanui's argument that "red" and "white" blood have been imagined as easy to blend. As part of this logic, reclaiming a long-ago ancestor and then *using* her in a manner that fits white French-descendant desires in the present becomes commonplace. The multiple examples from the forums of posters identifying with a specific Indigenous woman who lived in the 1600s only to reclaim an Indigenous identity today that does not match their ancestor's actual identity exemplifies how these practices move *beyond* descent. For the most part, we are not witnessing a benign desire to identify with indigeneity that is divorced from politics. On the contrary, race shifters are emboldened to join a number of nascent organizations as a way to have their identity claims legitimized in the sociopolitical world. One aspect of the race-shifting process that manifests itself over and over again on the forums is how it facilitates French-descendant opposition to Indigenous forms of belonging and identity. Whether in the multiple statements about the MNC's "exclusionist" citizenship policy or in the promotion of the AOO's definition of who counts as Algonquin, race shifters inevitably wade into political territory that supports the status quo colonial order of things. This move away from descent into the political realm is justified through a belief that race shifters are transcending settler colonialism and its legacies altogether. Through encouraging a deep obsession with specific Indigenous ancestors that facilitates opposition to Indigenous peoples in the present, these practices of descent lay the groundwork for the race-shifting process.

Nevertheless, I was encouraged to observe that on some of the forum threads (especially those in French), the self-indigenization of the French-descendant population was contested. To return to the first thread from the VO forum, a poster called Bernard pushed back at the position that genealogy could be the sole basis of Indigenous identity and, especially, at the idea expressed in the forum that a long-ago Indigenous ancestor makes one Indigenous today:

> You're not understanding, it's not métissage that is being questioned, but these alleged métis communities.... having one or two Indigenous ancestors 10, 11, or 12 generations ago doesn't make us métis, having ancestors whose origins and parents are unknown doesn't make us métis, having ancestors who did business with Indigenous peoples doesn't make us métis.... [These people] want all the alleged privileges hitherto accorded without the flip side that Indigenous peoples have experienced since forever.... By falsely pretending to be Aboriginal people for several years now, these so-called métis organizations have done a lot of damage to Aboriginal people. [The Department of] Indian and Northern Affairs Canada even remade more secure Indian status cards because of the fake cards being issued by these supposed métis organizations. The wrongdoing by these so-called communities is much more widespread then [sic] we think.[45]

Bernard's response was a rather direct result of his previously frustrated efforts to challenge forum participants in their reconstruction of indigeneity. His position is expressly against the use of long-ago ancestry as the means to reformulate indigeneity. In direct response to Bernard, Denise reiterated her ancestral connection to Marie Sylvestre by posting the entire twelve generations of that specific ancestral line, before doubling down on Marco's previous sexually charged claims about the contact zone, writing, "The French arrived here mostly single, and the only residents here at the origins of the colony were Indigenous peoples, so clearly many of them united with these Indigenous peoples, which built our country ... from there, Métis ancestors."[46] When pushed, forum participants such as Denise often named a specific ancestor in the seventeenth century as a way to legitimize their claims, all the while eliding the long history of colonial violence against Indigenous girls and women that would undermine their romantic vision of the past.

Still, in September 2013, in her ongoing effort to push back at the belief in purely genealogical sources of indigeneity, Anne-Marie again cited

Hubert Charbonneau's well-known research: "Whether it pleases one or not, the facts are there, uncompromising as they are: in genealogical terms, French-Québécois ancestors lived in isolation during ten to twelve generations; it follows that by the mid-twentieth century at least, this [group] was undeniably not métis but almost exclusively of French origins."[47] Among those individuals who pushed back at race shifting, Indigenous identity was more than simply a question of blood. Yet, these same posters had difficulty describing what would be a more legitimate basis for Indigenous identity. As Barker's analysis suggests, the discussion on the forums revolved singularly around blood, manifesting a general lack of understanding of Indigenous belonging and kinship that "would have tied members back to their lands and governments as citizens with multiple kinds of responsibilities."[48] In these cases, where ideas of racial mixedness and the concomitant devaluation of indigeneity oversaturate the discursive field, Indigenous ontologies offer a corrective to centuries of Euro-settler colonialism. Gaudry points out that "it is the discursive disregard of living Métis that locates the promise of Métis cultural revival in blood memory, genealogy, and lineal descent— connections to the dead—rather than a connection to the living culture of Métis communities."[49] Gaudry's argument applies to the social practices associated with lineal descent that I have presented in this chapter, in which race shifters all but erase living Indigenous polities in favour of their newly constituted identities. After all, it is far easier to develop a so-called métis identity through genealogy than it is to re-establish relations (if and where they exist) in a matrix of accountability to Indigenous peoples. In the next section the analysis of the use of lineal descent continues, through examples of forum posters who openly opposed efforts at self-indigenization.

"Why Are You Doing This Research?":
When Posters Challenge Race Shifting

A second lengthy thread, this time on the GQAF general forum, further supports my previous observations about the repurposing of lineal descent among French descendants. In a post entitled "Métis Ancestry," a relatively new member, Nathalie, posted the birthdates and marriage details of her parents, grandparents, and great-grandparents accompanied by the following request: "I would like to know if I have métis ancestry or not."[50] Within four hours of her post, Renée, a frequent poster to the forum, posted twice with Web links leading Nathalie to a particular website containing her ancestral tree, affirming that these lines showed no Indigenous ancestry. In a later exchange on the forum that lasted for over an hour, Renée openly challenged Nathalie's motivations:

> RENÉE: I have a question for you. Please tell me, why are you doing this research?
>
> NATHALIE: Simply by curiosity. . . . [M]y partner is métis and he has his card. I'm simply trying to see if by chance I may be as well.
>
> RENÉE: And what does one get with this card??? Why do you want one?? I don't understand . . . sorry.
>
> NATHALIE: It's mostly for the kids, because with this card, they can apply for post-secondary scholarships offered by [the Government of] Canada via the Indspire program.
>
> RENÉE: Since when?
>
> NATHALIE: [pasted a Web link] My kids [have received it] the past two years because before that they were in high school and weren't eligible. My daughter received a scholarship worth $1,000 and my son nearly $4,800.[51]

This passage features the most explicit statement on the forums linking one's desire to (self-) indigenize with economic motivations. I found little evidence supporting the common belief that race shifting is motivated primarily by the perceived economic advantages conferred on Indigenous peoples, which is in keeping with Sturm's research in the United States. The pushback to Nathalie's statement suggests that seeking out an Indigenous identity for economic purposes is generally frowned upon. Dominique, a frequent forum poster and professional genealogist, pushed even further, arguing that "Métis cards produced by these self-identified 'communities' or 'Aboriginal' organizations [in Quebec] confer absolutely no status to their holders."[52] Forum administrator Denise then introduced her support for the so-called Quebec métis in no uncertain terms: "Personally, I cannot turn my back on my origins or the fact that I am a descendant of a métis couple [in the early seventeenth century]. There's no point arguing about my profound values."[53]

By personalizing comments that were not aimed at any particular individual, Denise is able to return the discussion to the more comfortable sphere of self-identification: having a seventeenth-century Indigenous woman as an ancestor is part of her value system and is therefore unimpeachable. Framing race shifting and its associated practices as part of a personal value system ("I value self-identification above all other forms of identification") or individual right ("I have a right to be who I want to be") are two common defensive strategies onto which forum posters fall back in order to resituate debates about the social phenomenon of race shifting. Garroutte usefully explains how the power of self-identification rests principally on "rules that systematically direct attention away from questions of law, blood, or culture. They concentrate, instead, upon the individual's understanding of herself as she expresses it in a personal profession of identity. Under these definitions, Indians are simply those who *say* that they are Indian."[54] In the current social environment, pregnant with the possibilities offered by dominant reconciliation discourses, lineal descent becomes synonymous with Indigenous identity. Despite the currency of self-identification in society, Garroutte nonetheless maintains that "the fact that anyone can assert an identity does not mean that all such identifications are accepted as meaningful."[55]

On this point, Indigenous (studies) scholars have been clear over the past generation that self-identification must not be accepted as the sole basis for claims to Indigenous identity. In 1993, the Association of American Indian and Alaska Native Professors (AIANP) adopted a statement against ethnic fraud in academia that aimed to "recognize the importance of American Indian/Alaska Native nations/tribes in upholding their sovereign and legal right as nations to determine citizenship."[56] The AIANP also made a range of recommendations to staunch the flow of race shifters among student, faculty, staff, and administrators on campus. More recently, the Council of the Native American and Indigenous Studies Association adopted a "Statement on Indigenous Identity Fraud" in 2015. The statement explains, "Belonging does not arise simply from individual feelings—it is not simply who you claim to be, but also who claims you. When someone articulates connections to a particular people, the measure of truth cannot simply be a person's belief but must come from relationships with Indigenous people, recognizing that there may be disagreements among Indigenous people over the legitimacy of a particular person's or group's claims. According to the UN Permanent Forum on Indigenous Issues' statement on Indigenous identity, the test is 'Self-identification as indigenous peoples at the individual level and acceptance by the community as their member.'"[57] Self-identification as the sole source of Indigenous identity continues to be opposed by Indigenous scholars on a number of fronts.

In keeping with this line of thought, instead of turning away from the apparent conflict, Dominique leaned into it: "The simple fact of having one Indigenous ancestor twelve generations ago ... does not make us Métis, even if some organizations accept you in their ranks simply on the presentation of a genealogy. ... To be Métis also involves practicing a culture distinct from that of Europeans and First Nations (or a mixture of both), transmitted from generation to generation continuously over a long period of time."[58] In the hundreds of forum posts that I have read, Dominique was the clearest in challenging race shifting through identifying some of the basis of Métis peoplehood. In short, she presented a concise overview of the limits of the common-sense use of lineal descent on the forums, while also sketching out the beginnings of how an alternative understanding of Indigenous identity might work. In some ways, Dominique echoes Andersen's, Palmater's, and Doerfler's work on the Métis, Mi'kmaq, and Anishinaabe, respectively. Before signing off, Dominique responded with an interpretation of her own ancestral history: "It's not a question of 'turning my back on my origins.' I also have Indigenous ancestry, [a]s does nearly 50% of Québécois (or French Canadians) or Acadians. My Indigenous ancestry has been verified and documented. All of these ancestors are very far down my tree, at the eleventh or twelfth generation, as they are for a good proportion of Québécois. However, they represent less than 2% of my genealogy, which is very diverse: French and Acadian, English and German."[59]

From the scholarly material that I present throughout this study, as well as from my own genealogical reconstruction, Dominique shares the ancestral history of the average French descendant. Notably, what struck me most during the process of creating hundreds of individual genealogical

Lineal Descent and the Political Use of Indigenous Women Ancestors | 71

files during my own genealogical research (besides the repetitive strain injury I picked up) was the sheer number of people born in France among my direct ancestors. Of the over 1,200 root ancestors (i.e., born in late sixteenth and early seventeenth centuries) that I identified using genealogical records, 95.1 percent were born in France, 2.1 percent were born in England, 1.8 percent were born in Switzerland, 0.3 percent were born in Belgium, 0.3 percent were Algonquin, 0.1 percent were born in Germany, and 0.1 percent were born in Ireland. In addition, two Euro-descendant ancestors were adopted into Mohawk communities in the early eighteenth century (see Chapter 3). In other words, much like the average among French descendants today, Indigenous people figure into less than 1 percent of my ancestral genealogy overall. If we return to Desjardins's figures from the previous chapter, my genealogical profile more or less matches that of the average French descendant.[60]

TABLE 3. APPROXIMATE RECONSTRUCTION OF LEROUX/BRABANT GENEALOGY, BY RACE/ETHNICITY

	FRENCH	ENGLISH	OTHER EUROPEAN	INDIGENOUS
Average French descendant genealogy	97.6%	0.9%	1%	0.4%
Author genealogy	95.1%	2.1%	2.3%	0.5%

To her credit, Nathalie, the original poster, graciously thanked Dominique for her efforts before asking a few more questions about the whereabouts of specific French-descendant ancestors.

Inspired by the path-breaking work of Alondra Nelson and Kim TallBear, I identified and collected data from five of the most well-used online genealogy forums geared toward French descendants. Virtual ethnography allowed me to explore the richness of the online forum space through placing the voices of participants at the forefront. It turns out that participants held at times diametrically opposed positions, which certainly speaks to the lively debate about the use of lineal descent in contemporary race-shifting efforts. According to the practices of *lineal* descent, one claims an Indigenous ancestor in one's direct lineage ten generations ago or more as the sole basis for an "Indigenous" identity today. The large majority of these types of claims among French descendants in Canada and the United States involve a remarkably small number of Indigenous women from the seventeenth century.

One of the most surprising dimensions of my research on the forums was how it led me to discover that some of the same Indigenous women at the basis of the race-shifting process are used in multiple U.S. states and Canadian provinces to claim significantly different Indigenous identities (Métis, Abenaki, Algonquin). This discovery in turn led me to seek a way to explain the interchangeability of one Indigenous woman/identity for another. Ultimately, the strength of lineal descent—its simplicity and singularity—facilitates an interchangeable understanding of indigeneity, and provides the groundwork for the process of race shifting, as observed on the forums. I contrasted the reliance on lineal descent—based in a heteronormative, patrilineal understanding of the contact zone that eroticizes and objectifies Indigenous women—with existing Indigenous ontologies that reject blood as the *sole* basis for belonging. Significantly, the racialization of Indigenous polities through biology has a long history in the United States and Canada, as do Indigenous efforts to resist such efforts. Near the end of the chapter, I began to sketch out how race shifting undermines Indigenous sovereignty and self-determination. This is an element of my argument that weaves its way through the next two chapters (2 and 3), which analyzes genealogy forums, and becomes especially prominent in the final two chapters (4 and 5), which examine the work of two self-identified métis organizations in three regions of Quebec.

Chapter Two

Aspirational Descent: Creating Indigenous Women Ancestors

While examining the genealogy forums in mid-2017, I identified another way that descent is reconstructed. Forum participants not only sought out a long-ago female Indigenous ancestor, but many also actively participated in transforming a French ancestor in the 1600s into an "Indigenous" woman. This second practice of descent is not quite as common as the first, but it nevertheless involves a degree of commitment to research and deliberation that can be significantly more substantial. I have since discovered an entire infrastructure among today's French descendants that supports the creation of "Indigenous" ancestors. The practice often involves a turn to genetic genealogy and the use of DNA ancestry testing.

For the purpose of the analysis below, I have called this second practice of descent *aspirational* descent. It differs from lineal descent in that the actual indigeneity of the "root" ancestor at the basis of one's claim to an Indigenous identity today is largely contested. We find a parallel with Haley and Wilcoxon's observations about the emergence in southern California of the neo-Chumash, whose identity is based on the transformation of one ancestor in the mid-nineteenth century from mestizo/español to Chumash.[1] The practice of aspirational descent that I document—focusing as it does on transforming the identities of a small number of French women ancestors— is an example of what Barnwell calls a "practice of self-authentication [and] also a creative act of revisionist life writing."[2] More than the two other forms that I identify in this first part of the book, aspirational descent illuminates the creative thrust pushing French-descendant race shifters forward.

DESIRE-FOR-INDIGENEITY: GENEALOGY AS TECHNOLOGY OF SELF-MAKING

"What Makes You Think That You Have Indigenous Ancestry?":
Self-Identification and the Desire to Be Indigenous

In the majority of cases on the forums, a general desire to discover Indigenous ancestry seemed to propel posters forward in their search. In cases where posters shared information about (potential) ancestors, forum administrators or long-time forum members often pushed back against this desire with vigour. For example, in a thread titled "Métis ancestry" in the GQAF forum in July 2017, new member Sophie shared the names of her paternal great-great- and great-great-great-grandparents and then asked, "It seems that [my great-great-great-grandmother] Sylvie-Anne is Indigenous. How do I go about finding out if this is true and if there are documents that can prove it?"[3] Two frequent posters responded to Sophie's request. First, Yves provided her with three separate Web links to genealogical databases and census documents from the period in question, pointing out that none of the documentation supports her theory about her ancestor Sylvie-Anne. Second, in a post thirty minutes later, Renée reviewed the available genealogical database(s) and answered Sophie's question unequivocally: "Often oral history is a very creative source. We can see [the family line] repeated three times here ... sometimes cousins get married and it creates such an oral history. In thirty-five years of volunteering at the local [genealogical] society, I've received hundreds of oral histories that do not support what everybody seems to want to believe."[4] Without a doubt, the overwhelming majority of these general searches for Indigenous ancestry ended with the poster being told that they did not have Indigenous ancestry (at least not where they were looking for it).

For the moment, let us examine additional examples, on other forums, of the desire-for-indigeneity. In March 2016 on the VO forum, new member Sarcelle started a thread with the statement "I would like to know if I have métis ancestry or not."[5] After listing three generations of ancestors to aid in follow-up research, a prolific poster replied with Web links to Sarcelle's ancestral genealogy and the following comment: "I don't understand what makes you think that you have Indigenous ancestry."[6] Sarcelle responded that she was "simply trying to find out. I'm a beginner at genealogy."[7] Four days after that post, one of the most prominent site administrators responded matter of factly: "I verified the marriage registries for each [one of the ancestors that you provided] and there's no reason to believe that a close or distant family member is Aboriginal."[8] With that, the thread came to an end, but not before Sarcelle had illustrated that indigeneity, in the form of a long-ago ancestor, held some form of value to her.

A month later on a thread called "Requests for Métis cards and information," we found out a bit more about Sarcelle's motivation for discovering Indigenous ancestry when she posted that the rest of her immediate family are members of a prominent self-identified métis organization in Quebec, the Nation Métis Contemporaine (NMC). Sarcelle explained, "My partner and two children are members of this association and unfortunately, I noticed that the métis line upon which the card was issued is false. . . . Here is [the NMC president's] answer about this specific ancestry: 'Your ancestor Jeanne Denis is a Mi'kmaw Indian who is also Maliseet, because the Viger Maliseets come from New Brunswick just like the Mi'kmaq they're the same race.' After verification on several sites, [I discovered that Denis] was actually born in France, so she's not Aboriginal. I'm a bit disappointed."[9] In this case, a new passion for genealogy led Sarcelle to an uncomfortable discovery about her husband's purported Indigenous ancestry. Besides the troubling racialization of the Mi'kmaq and Maliseet above (these nations are part of the same *political* confederacy, not the same *race*), Denise agreed that the woman in question was born in France and that all of Sarcelle's husband's ancestors in that same line were French: "I really don't know why they said that Jeanne Denis was Mi'kmaq."[10] The remaking of a French woman into an Indigenous woman (Mi'kmaq in this case) by a prominent organization is an example of the practice of aspirational descent that I develop in this chapter.

In a second example, this time from the Nation autochtone du Québec (NAQ) main forum, Amoratio started a thread titled "Great-great grandmother is Ojibway?" in May 2017.[11] In it, Amoratio provided the forum with relevant details of their great-great-grandmother's genealogical profile (born 1839) and claimed that their family tree identified her as Ojibway. The site's main administrator, Abitawis, who also seems to act as a public registrar for the organization, provided a Web link to Amoratio's genealogy going back a further four generations to the mid-eighteenth century. Abitawis explained, "According to this genealogy, at first glance and without any errors, her ancestors all seem to be of European origins, especially French ... hence the difficulty in 'proving' that she was Ojibway or of another Indigenous nation."[12] Perhaps reflecting that the NAQ forum is managed by the Alliance autochtone du Québec, an organization that grants membership to those who can document any Indigenous ancestry, forum administrators drew the clearest boundaries around Indigenous identity, even though they advocated for a broad, race-based vision of "métis."

The NAQ forum also consistently featured the most detailed and complex discussion of DNA ancestry testing of the five forums. It was in this sense that Abitawis continued his response to Amoratio: "Not only can we retrace most of her ancestors all the way to Europe, but from her few female ancestors whose origins are said to be 'unknown' and could be Indigenous, genealogists have been able to demonstrate through DNA ancestry testing (mtDNA) on many of her descendants (your cousins), that they were, in all probability, of European origins."[13] In the same vein, a month earlier, in April 2017, Abitawis stated to a first-time poster searching for Indigenous ancestry that "if you only want to know if you have 'Aboriginal' ancestors without knowing their names or their Nations, a commercial DNA ancestry test might provide you with answers," before providing an in-depth overview of the limits of DNA-based technologies.[14] Two days later, the original poster responded in a manner that focused on the source of her interest: "In my family, there were general claims about being Métis.... I had the privilege of attending an Indigenous ceremony in Natashquan [an Innu community on the north shore of the St. Lawrence River]. When I heard the sound of the big caribou-skin drum (reserved for a few insiders only), I started to cry and cry. And the next day too. In the tent, there were Aboriginals and whites and I was the only one crying. So, I have a taste for knowledge."[15] This poster's focus on what could broadly be called the "spiritual" basis of her interest in indigeneity was actually quite rare on the forums. Contrary to Sturm's research and the activist work of such organizations as New Age Frauds and Plastic Shamans in the United States, race shifting among French descendants seems rarely to have its origins in spiritual or metaphysical transformation, at least not on these specific forums. Given the relative strength of the genealogical records, it appears that French-descendant race shifters centre on blood (or genes) in contrast to spiritual connection in their coming-out narratives.

Returning to the NAQ's site, in an earlier thread on its forum, in December 2012, Abitawis challenged another effort to indigenize a French ancestor. After a poster began a thread titled "Françoise Morel – an Indigenous woman??," Abitawis seemed impatient: "A certified genealogist on this site has already informed you that [Morel's] parents were French... and that this so-called 'Aboriginal' line was an invention."[16] Abitawis then provided the poster with Web-based resources that included copies of the original marriage records from the seventeenth century confirming the French origins of the person in question. Before signing off, Abitawis reiterated his position and tied it to broader concerns: "In my humble opinion, if a person gets any kind of Aboriginal certificate based on the pretense that *Françoise Morel*... was Aboriginal... then it's FRAUD... that not only damages the reputation of all Aboriginal people and their organizations but is itself a crime.... So, the so-called genealogist who prepared this genealogy for your family must immediately retract it and any Aboriginal certificate issued on the basis of this false information must be returned with an explanation."[17] The NAQ forum illustrates the complex politics of indigeneity at work among French descendants. Not only are we dealing with a situation in which individuals are reclaiming long-ago ancestors as the sole basis for an Indigenous identity today, but the actual indigeneity of some of these ancestors is itself often in question.

At least a dozen different threads on the genealogy forums ended up with the same conclusion as immediately above—the suspected "Indigenous" ancestor turned out to be a woman born in France. Morel, for instance, came up on four separate occasions in three different forums, as did another French woman in the seventeenth-century Laurentian Valley, Françoise Grenier, while a third French woman in Acadia, Catherine Lejeune, figured into conversations on six separate occasions on four different forums. In this charged political context, disagreement is common on the forums. For example, at the very end of 2012, a poster named Mr. Richer, identifying himself as a professional genealogist, challenged the NAQ's own membership policy: "Unfortunately, through my experience on the web and in private practice . . . when people do genealogy for the sake of supposed Métis/Aboriginal origins and privileges . . . 98.9% of their requests are based on unfounded family histories and rumours, and thus, the proof is simply not there (it's not, as we say, written in stone)."[18] Despite his own role in disproving some of these same genealogical claims, Abitawis responded firmly to Mr. Richer that everybody with Indigenous ancestry has the fundamental right to self-identify as they see fit:

> It is my humble opinion that a mixed-race person [*personne métissée*], regardless of the number of generations back, should be free to choose their identity and to become a member of the community of their choice, whether Inuit, Indian, Métis, or non-Aboriginal. Isn't this a fundamental right guaranteed by the *Canadian Constitution* and by international law? . . . To deny the identity and Aboriginal rights of Aboriginal organizations in Québec or elsewhere and, consequently, of all of their legitimate Aboriginal members because of the fraudulent conduct of a small or *even a large number* of imposters who have infiltrated their ranks, is not, in my opinion, very respectful of others, constructive, nor does it encourage dialogue and the recognition of the identity and rights of the Aboriginal minority in our beautiful country.[19]

Here, Abitawis expresses the common-sense logic of lineal descent, as displayed on the online genealogy forums: claims to indigeneity are mediated by the individual rights regime codified by the colonial state apparatus, which includes above all the right to self-identification. The use of lineal descent to become Indigenous is repeatedly protected from scrutiny by forum posters, who fall back on comfortable liberal rights talk to defend it. We might ask, following the work of Doerfler and Barker, what is the place of Indigenous self-determination, including notably an Indigenous people's right and responsibility to govern its own citizenship orders and kinship practices? Abitawis politely explained the marginal place of Indigenous peoples as political agents in their own vision of the recognition process: "Respectfully and without any bad will whatsoever, it is totally unacceptable for Inuit, Indian, Métis or certified genealogists to deny folks their legitimate identities and rights."[20] In Abitawis's opinion, Indigenous *peoples* are of the same order as certified genealogists, in what represents a clear rebuke of Indigenous self-determination. In his argument, the bio-racialization of Indigenous identity (through ancestry or descent) ensures the continued subjugation of the political agency of Indigenous peoples. The only "right" recognized by the lead administrator of the only genealogy forum administered by a supposed Indigenous organization (Alliance autochtone du Québec) is an individual's right to self-identify as they see fit. Indigenous peoples and certified genealogists, inasmuch as they represent official obstacles to self-identification, must be stripped of any legal and/or political legitimacy that they might hold.

Sturm's research on self-identified Cherokee race shifters in the United States provides a productive counterpoint to consider the ultimate reliance on self-identification among French descendants: "Race shifters refuse such notions of genealogical distance and quantification of racial kinship, in no small measure because such logic would surely work against them.... They focus on the shared belief that if they have any degree of [Indigenous] blood, then this is all that matters—they are [Indigenous], end of story."[21] This shared belief is actually a rallying point for forum posters, providing (some of) them with a sense of community that facilitates the process of race shifting. In fact, in his study of six "new métis" organizations in eastern Canada, Gaudry argues that they rely entirely on a "relationship to ancestry" in their practice of kinship, as opposed to Indigenous kinship-based relations, which "involve reciprocal relationships with living communities that can demonstrate historical-contemporary continuity and are regularly practiced in a contemporary setting."[22] Once again, blood is all it takes to mobilize novel practices of descent among French-descendant race shifters.

The next section picks up several threads from the first part of the chapter, by focusing specifically on a practice of descent that involves imaginatively re-signifying a seventeenth-century European ancestor as

"Indigenous." Aspirational descent is practised regularly on the forums, as the case studies below illustrate.

INVENTING INDIGENOUS (WOMEN) ANCESTORS: WHEN GENEALOGY, DNA, AND DESIRE COLLIDE

Predictably, the desire to find an Indigenous ancestor in the past, based as it is in *social* and *political* registers, leads to a situation in genealogy forums (and in other social sites) where there is significant debate about whether certain ancestors are Indigenous in the first place. In fact, a number of prominent research projects—such as the Acadian Amerindian Ancestry Project and the Mothers of Acadia mtDNA Project—exist to clarify the racial origins of particular ancestors. The strength of the French-descendant genealogy sector ensures that a wide variety of technological means are expended to (dis)prove a given ancestor's purported Indigenous identity, notably through DNA ancestry testing. Some of these studies are peer-reviewed and appear in academic publications, some are conducted by family genealogists who team up with molecular scientists, and still others are organized through prominent DNA ancestry testing companies in the United States.

Genetic genealogy—what Nelson defines as "the use of DNA analysis for the purpose of inferring ethnic or racial background and aiding with family history research"[23]—on the genealogy forums is used primarily in relation to debates about the origins of a specific woman ancestor in the seventeenth century. Whatever the specific case, molecular technologies are typically mobilized in a manner that shares a commitment to the logics of lineal descent, notably, that the presence of a 350-year-old Indigenous ancestor is the legitimate basis of an Indigenous identity today. After all, as Nash has argued, "genetic genealogy by its very nature emphasizes strictly biological models of genealogical relations."[24] In this context, those who engage with DNA—embedded as it is in scientific discourses of "objectivity" and "accuracy" that authorize its usage—are provided with a great deal of latitude to reconfigure their kinship relations in a manner that reflects their desire. Kramer explains its strength: "Like 'traditional' genealogy, genetic genealogy enables individuals to embed themselves within familial networks and temporal and geographical contexts—creating, rather than revealing, kinship ties and networks through the convergence of bodies, technology, and media."[25] We will see below how Kramer's observation about the *creative* potential of genetic genealogy explains some of the efforts on the online genealogy forums.

Genetic genealogy has been slow to catch on in the main genealogy forums that I visited, since conventional genealogical technologies are both readily available and relatively accurate for French descendants. As its nickname as the "genealogist's paradise" suggests (see Introduction), French-descendant ancestor-seekers normally forego DNA technologies on the forums. I explore some notable exceptions below, many of which connect directly to a search for genes associated with Indigenous peoples. In fact, Kim TallBear's research on "Native American DNA" has demonstrated how family history researchers ultimately use DNA-based ancestry tests to fill gaps in genealogical records, often in search of genes associated with Indigenous peoples. When DNA ancestry testing and/or genetic ancestry were mobilized in the online forums, it was invariably done to mobilize the biological properties of DNA in the service of race shifting. To echo TallBear's concerns, Native American DNA serves as an object with the "power to influence indigenous livelihoods and sovereignties."[26]

A decade ago, anthropologist Deborah Bolnick, joined by thirteen other leading scholars of science, warned the scientific community about the risks involved in genetic ancestry testing—the same type of research undertaken in the genetic genealogy projects explored below. Specifically, they outlined three concerns: "(i) the tests can have a profound impact on individuals and communities, (ii) the assumptions and limitations of these tests make them less informative than many realize, and (iii) commercialization has led to misleading practices that reinforce misconceptions."[27] More recently, Mark Jobling, Rita Rasteiro, and Jon Wetton have reaffirmed those concerns, arguing that "the practice of individual genetic ancestry testing is unreliable and powerfully influenced by cultural and other social forces."[28] Despite the consistent social-scientific critiques of DNA ancestry testing, it continues to be marketed as a means of discovering one's definitive molecular origins and thus is being used to redefine tribal identities in the United States and

First Nation and Métis sovereignty in Canada, posing risks to Indigenous claims to land and life.

We now turn to a series of excerpts from threads on genealogy forums in order to consider how the *creation* of a long-ago ancestor's indigeneity serves the process of race shifting. While this second practice of descent differs from the first and most common form—using an actual Indigenous ancestor from several centuries ago as the basis for an "Indigenous" identity in the twenty-first century—it nonetheless involves a critical amount of discussion on the online genealogy forums under study. Let us turn to three separate cases of seventeenth-century women who have been reconstructed as Indigenous: two from the St. Lawrence settlements (present-day Quebec) and sisters from Acadia (present-day Nova Scotia).

"Until It Is Proven Otherwise, the Métis Consider This Woman to Be Indian": Françoise Grenier, circa 1604

One of the French women most commonly identified as a potential Indigenous ancestor on the genealogy forums is Françoise Grenier (also Garnier), generally believed to have been born in France around 1604 (she died in Quebec City on 1 November 1665). She also appears as an ancestor in my own genealogy—four times through three different children born between 1639 and 1651 in Quebec City. The primary reason that Grenier continues to resurface as a potential Indigenous woman is that historians have been unable to locate either her birth or baptismal certificate in France or her name on a ship manifest from the period. The missing documentary evidence from the early 1600s linking her to France has made her identity open to much speculation. The first time I came across this "controversy," as it is commonly called online, was on the VO forum. In March 2016, Sarcelle posted a request to confirm that Françoise Grenier was in fact Indigenous, though she acknowledged that "opinions are mixed [on her]."[29] Denise, whom you may remember from the previous chapter as a vocal supporter of lineal descent, nonetheless shared the consensus opinion that both Grenier and her husband were French: "Noel Langlois [Grenier's husband] and Françoise Grenier are from France."[30] She then included a link to a well-known genealogical database that lists their birthplace in France.

In an earlier thread on the Ancestry forum in 2011, a poster called Mystery spoke against the common confusion circulating online about ancestors such as Grenier, among others: "All of these names came over directly from France as well as the people they're married to, most of these last names appear in my tree, and I have yet to find native background for any of them. I have left comments for the guy who runs [genealogy website] asking where he got his information from because I've already researched these names, these names are listed on the acadian list. The acadians were NOT indians. The acadians are french people who lived in Nova Scotia who were very devout roman catholic people who farmed for a living."[31] The next day, Martin responded directly to Mystery's claims about Acadians: "As much as Acadians were farmers the majority had intermarried with the native population and were an entirely mixed blood people. Those who would claim otherwise are not old family Acadian."[32] Martin's intervention seemed to sway Mystery; over the course of that evening, they partly walked back their claims about specific "contested" ancestors, reiterating the popular opinion that there are duelling truths about Grenier's origins: "I'm still debating Françoise Grenier, there are some records that say France, some records that say Canada/American Indienne. I have no idea what to believe on that one, I can't find anything that confirms one way or the other."[33]

A debate that took place on the VO forum a few years later, in 2014, further illustrates the tensions that arise when the identity of certain ancestors is debated. An anonymous poster affirmed his "métis" heritage by claiming a number of long-ago Indigenous ancestors, before critiquing many of his acquaintances who have used French women ancestors to obtain a "métis" card:

> Some of them have as an ancestor François Antaya Pelletier who is European and married Dorothée Sauvagesse with whom *there are no descendants*. She died the year after their marriage. Another case that seems even more frequent is that of Noël Langlois and Françoise Grenier, who they consider Aboriginal despite her European name and without any documentation whatsoever.... I question the state of these métis organizations that grant métis status to these people

under such conditions... it's urgent to clean up this mess before we are completely humiliated.[34]

Addressing herself to the anonymous poster, Lory asserted that the "métis" have a different standard of genealogical evidence than theirs: "Did a professional genealogist prove that Françoise [Grenier] was French? No! Until it is proven otherwise, the Métis consider this woman to be Indian. No birth certificate, no proof of her crossing to New France." Before signing off, Lory ended her statement with sarcastic flair: "Where does she come from? The Holy Spirit?"[35] Challenged on her standard of proof by the anonymous poster and a site administrator, Lory simply reiterated her position and later affirmed that Grenier's indigeneity "is a matter of opinion."[36] In this sense, not only did forum posters seem to accept that Grenier's origins were in question, but a type of reverse-onus was placed on researchers and genealogists to *dis*prove Grenier's indigeneity. This in a context where the only reason that Grenier's European origins are questioned in the first place is because of a lack of documentation.

Another example of the use of aspirational descent in the case of Grenier comes from the AOO comprehensive land claims negotiations. In a court hearing held on 17 April 2013 in Pembroke, Ontario, the Algonquins of Greater Golden Lake (an organization created as part of the AOO process) petitioned to include Françoise Grenier as an "Algonquin root ancestor" (as per the AOO's definition) for the purpose of membership in the land claims process. The Algonquins of Pikwàkanagàn First Nation (APFN)—the only federally recognized Algonquin community in Ontario—opposed the inclusion of Grenier, arguing that she was French.[37] The judge tasked with adjudicating the AOO's Master Schedule of Algonquin Ancestors dismissed the application to include Grenier as an Algonquin ancestor, citing a lack of documentary evidence.

There was additional disagreement over Grenier's transformation into an "Indigenous" woman on the forums. After another poster, this time on the GQAF forum, complained that a number of "contested" ancestors are accepted for membership by "métis" organizations in Quebec—including, notably, Françoise Grenier—frequent poster Dominique provided an explanation of the phenomenon: "Many silly hypotheses about the presumed origins of these [contested ancestors] are circulating. Unfortunately, several organizations representing so-called 'Aboriginal' people or self-identified 'métis' people still accept these documents as proof.... We must be wary of the legends about our ancestors that we find on the internet."[38]

Ultimately, a DNA ancestry project (French Heritage DNA) that specializes in French-Canadian ancestry mounted a research project meant in part to identify all of the contested ancestors in French-descendant genealogy. As part of that project, researchers recruited a number of people who can trace their ancestry back through mtDNA to Grenier. Sociologist Troy Duster has outlined the infrastructure used in what he has called the "molecular re-inscription of race" by examining DNA ancestry testing. He explains how we are able to access only a tiny amount of one's ancestral DNA through the two most common types of DNA ancestry tests: Y chromosome DNA testing identifies a male's father's father's ancestry, while mtDNA testing identifies a male's or female's mother's mother's ancestry.[39] In the case of Grenier and other seventeenth-century women ancestors, genetic scientists, DNA ancestry companies, and/or genetic genealogists necessarily employ mtDNA testing, which represents no more than one out of 512 ancestors at a depth of ten generations. Since many of the researchers and/or companies offering mtDNA ancestry analysis do so for intervals of several centuries, they are often providing results based on much less than 1 percent of one's ancestry.

With this in mind, in early 2017 the project released the results: Grenier's mtDNA haplogroup (haplogroup J, subclade J2b1a) that persists among her present-day descendants is associated primarily with western European and Russian descent. Yet even in the absence of DNA associated with Indigenous peoples by scientists and despite the faith that society places in molecular technologies, there continues to be some resistance to the mtDNA results among certain self-identified "métis" organizations, including by the Métis Nation of the Rising Sun, the largest such organization in Quebec (see Chapter 5). Those doubts generally revolve around arguments that DNA ancestry testing is unreliable or that Grenier's otherwise French husband was actually the Indigenous one in the couple. Whatever the precise reason for the resistance, the continued belief in Grenier's (and her children's) Indigenous origins tells us a great deal about the dynamics of aspirational descent.

In contrast to the workings of hypodescent—where one's ancestral connection with the so-called "Old World" marks an individual—my sample from French-descendant genealogy forums generally works hard to disabuse themselves from their European ancestors, turning their back on the Old World in order to reconstruct themselves as Indigenous to northeast America. Turning away from the Atlantic in order to indigenize oneself is another key marker of aspirational descent in the contemporary era. Efforts to move away from European ancestors, based as they are in technologies associated with blood (ancestral genealogy) and genes (DNA ancestry testing), have led many French descendants to remake French women such as Françoise Grenier as "Indigenous," illustrating how contemporary genealogical research mediates a process of strategic self-making.

A French Woman with Algonquin-Siberian Origins? Catherine Pillard, circa 1646

A second example of a previously European woman caught my attention on the forums and in a series of membership documents related to one of the principal "métis" organizations in Quebec. As part of its submission to the Quebec Superior Court in the *Séguin* case, the Communauté métisse autochtone de Maniwaki (CMAM)—the second-largest self-identified "métis" organization in Quebec as of 2017—included about 2,000 genealogical charts representing nearly a third of its membership. I analyzed these charts, compiling a spreadsheet of all the Indigenous root ancestor(s) claimed for the basis of membership. My analysis includes the charts for 1,906 members of the organization who listed 2,344 "Indigenous" root ancestors overall, representing over fifty separate ancestors. Of the fifteen most common "root" ancestors, five are contested in the genealogical community. Overall, about 28 percent of the members count an ancestor who is actually French as their "Indigenous" root ancestor for the purpose of membership. Catherine Pillard (married to Pierre Charron in 1665) appeared as an "Indigenous" root ancestor in about 8.6 percent of the overall member genealogies. Pillard also appeared frequently in the genealogy forums.

I had not been aware of any of the debate over "contested" ancestors prior to visiting, and then transcribing and analyzing, online genealogy forums.

The reconstitution of Pillard as a woman with "Algonquin-Siberian" origins was a surprise. Contrary to the case of Grenier, it is DNA that ultimately "proves" Pillard's Indigenous identity. It was through their participation in the "Amerindian Ancestry out of Mi'kma'ki" research project that genealogists Raymond Lussier, Thomas King-McMahon, and Johan Robitaille first examined mtDNA associated specifically with Pillard.[40] The authors explain that the project was part of an effort to identify the Mi'kmaw ancestors of an unrecognized organization in Nova Scotia claiming to be Mi'kmaq: "The researchers involved in this study are all participants in the 'Amerindian Ancestry Out of Mi'kma'ki' DNA project. The focus of that project is to gather DNA evidence for 'persons of interest' believed to have possible Mi'kmaq Indian ancestry, specifically among historical Bras d'Or Indians of Cape Breton."[41] The organization in question, the Little Bras d'Or Indian Association, is preparing to sue the federal government for recognition,[42] though the Mi'kmaq Rights Initiative—representing the thirteen federally recognized Mi'kmaw communities in Nova Scotia—does not recognize their claim to a Mi'kmaw identity.

There is no explanation, however, of how Pillard—who, according to documents from the period, never set foot outside of the Montreal area—could in fact have been Mi'kmaq (Bras d'Or Lake on Cape Breton Island is nearly 1,500 kilometres east of Montreal, which is itself in the territory of several other Indigenous peoples). Nevertheless, in a research article cited extensively on genealogy forums, the authors explained the basis for Pillard's new identity as an Algonquin-Siberian woman. First published in 2007 in *Le Chaînon*, the newsletter of the Société franco-ontarienne d'histoire et de généalogie in Ottawa, their article was translated and republished online in *Michigan's Habitant Heritage* in 2008. They make clear at the beginning of their article that prior to mtDNA ancestry testing, there was little reason to question Pillard's French origins. A baptismal record existed with her name, dated 30 March 1646, from a parish in La Rochelle, on France's west coast, which also listed her father's full name and her mother's first name. The authors explain the consensus around Pillard's seemingly straightforward French origins prior to mtDNA ancestry testing:

Historically, there has been little reason to bring Catherine's origins into question. There is a baptismal record for Catherine, daughter of Pierre Pillard and Marguerite... dated March in Ste-Marguerite chapel in the parish Notre-Dame-de-Cougnes in La Rochelle, France.... Even with the collective experience in native genealogy and history of the researchers involved in this study, they never considered Catherine Pillard a 'person of interest' in any Native American DNA study before today. The authors knew her origin, her parents, and that a baptismal record had been found in recent years. She was from a period when women are listed on ship records from France to Nouvelle-France. There was no obvious 'red flag.'[43]

Nevertheless, given genetic genealogy's presence at what Nelson calls the "nexus of genetic science, kinship aspirations, and strategic self-making," Pillard would soon appear in conversations about her "Algonquin-Siberian" origins, after about a century and a half as a French woman in Quebec's genealogical circles.[44] After recruiting three present-day descendants of Pillard's (exclusively though their maternal lineages), the researchers identified Pillard's mtDNA as belonging to haplogroup A1, which is most frequently encountered in east Asia, including northeastern Siberia. Essentially, genetic scientists have long associated mtDNA haplogroup A, through its variant A2, with people who are Indigenous to the Americas. The authors explain in their analysis that A1 had newly been associated with Indigenous peoples in and around the Great Lakes. As such, Lussier, King-McMahon, and Robitaille frame their results in the following manner: "Recent DNA evidences [sic] bring the traditional notion of [Pillard's] origins under serious scrutiny. Current DNA evidence now suggests the strong likelihood of her maternal origin in the Americas, specifically in Quebec, and the virtual impossibility of her originating from France. How did this surprising turn of events come about? Advances in DNA testing, its availability to ordinary individuals, as well as remarkable coincidences, led the authors to gather genetic and genealogical evidence about the true origins of Catherine Pillard."[45] The authors do not hesitate to affirm the power that Native American DNA has to intervene in historical and social life, in that a biological substance associated with an unrelated sample of Indigenous peoples' DNA is used to redefine Pillard's identity in the present. A year after the original publication of the research in French, forum posters openly discussed Pillard's new Indigenous identity across a number of forums.

For example, one of the authors of the study is a frequent poster to the Ancestry genealogy forum. In May 2008, in a thread titled "Canadian Metis Organizations," she informed forum members that Pillard was now known as "Catherine Pillard/Pillat/Plat – Native Haplogroup A."[46] Nearly seven years later, in 2015, the thread was still active, and the aspirational nature of Pillard's indigeneity had been replaced by a much more definitive claim. Through the process of strategic self-making, individuals had created an imaginative story cementing Pillard's Indigenous origin. A forum poster going by lrhiebing92 [Bing] expressed the now-common claim about Pillard's indigeneity: "I did recently get some genealogical help and traced my Metis line back to Catherine Pillard Plat (Ouenta, Huron). I have been told that this makes me eligible for enrollment in the Metis Federation of Canada—and I specifically asked if I can apply for membership as a U.S. citizen."[47] Bing expressed the normative logic of Native American DNA, one that circulates relatively freely on this specific genealogy forum. According to that logic, it is no surprise that DNA obtained via a cheek swab from a descendant of a woman who had been otherwise identified as of French descent for more than a century is connected to a DNA mutation found most commonly in relevant scientific samples obtained from people currently living in northern Asia. Further, this ancestral connection is now used by a wide range of race shifters in the United States and Canada to become "Métis" in Quebec and "Abenaki" in New Hampshire (see Table 4). Notably, I count Pillard among my root ancestors three different times through her sons François and Jean Charron (dit Ducharme), born between 1676 and 1684 in towns on the south shore of the St. Lawrence River across from Montreal.

While Bing subtly hinted at Pillard's new identity, Lisa ultimately brought it all home a year later, in March 2016, in a separate thread: "Catherine Pillard/Pillat/Plat was listed as a Fille Du Roi, but her materilineal [sic] DNA was proven to be Native American and now we know her by her birth name Ouenta, daughter of the Great Chief Atsena of the Bear

Clan, Huron Tribe."[48] No longer a humble *fille du roi*—one of the mostly young women and girls from impoverished families in urban France sent to New France by King Louis XIV to bear children—Catherine becomes the daughter of a prominent male Indigenous historical figure, befitting today's race shifters. To be clear, Catherine Pillard was not Catherine Plat nor Catherine Ouenta, and the identity of Chief Atseña's presumed daughter remains unknown.

Despite the widespread circulation and positive reception of Pillard's newfound indigeneity on the forums (and among self-identified Indigenous organizations in Quebec and New England), the Association des Charron et Ducharme—the family association for the descendants of Pierre Charron (dit Ducharme) and Catherine Pillard's twelve children—commissioned its own DNA ancestry testing of Pillard's mtDNA in 2009. The study, published in the association's newsletter and conducted by the highest-profile genetic genealogist in Quebec, confirmed that Pillard's mtDNA signature belonged to haplogroup A, but added a degree of specificity not available in Lussier et al.'s study by assigning it the subgroup A10. After going through the history of that specific genetic mutation in parts of southwestern Asia between the Black and Aral Seas, geneticist Jacques Beaugrand explains that this subgroup has never been associated with populations indigenous to the Americas. Consequently, given his own in-depth molecular analysis and his understanding of the historical movement of people from this region bordering eastern Europe, he concluded that Pillard acquired the A10 mtDNA signature from the migration of people from the Black Sea–Aral Sea corridor into western Europe several millennia ago.[49] In a stinging rebuke of the previous research affirming Pillard's indigeneity, Beaugrand states, "The authors of the article [Lussier, King-McMahon, and Robitaille], had they been more rigorous, would have been able to come up with the same conclusion and avoided unnecessarily fueling the controversy about the origins of Catherine Pillard's mtDNA. Scientific skepticism is an important quality to cultivate, even in genealogy."[50] In this case, a well-known genetic genealogist pushes back against conclusions that not only applied the logic of Native American DNA critiqued by TallBear, but also facilitated race shifting among French descendants.

The Association did not stop with Beaugrand's research, however; it also commissioned a French genealogist to research Pillard's origins in France and a Québécois genealogist to research all documentation referring to Pillard in New France. In both cases, the researchers uncovered material that further corroborated Beaugrand's conclusions, including the documented presence of the Pillard patronym in sixteenth-century parish records near La Rochelle and the existence of dozens of notarized documents with Pillard's name in the archives from New France.[51] In addition, since Beaugrand's publication of his results in 2009, the precise variant of haplogroup A10 that he identified has been observed in individuals in the Italian Alps, as well as other locations farther west. These findings, along with those of the two independent genealogists, led *Michigan's Habitant Heritage*—the publication that featured the English-language translation of the original study—to publish a follow-up article that supported the argument that Pillard acquired mtDNA in France through ancestors who migrated from west Asia. As that author concludes, "In any case, this latest [study] clearly shows a West Siberian origin for a European ancestor, rather than an eastern trek across the Bering Straits for a Native American ancestor. As much as we (her descendants) hoped for Native American roots, the mtDNA still reveals an exotic heritage for Catherine Pillard to capture our imaginations. I, for one, choose to see our many-greats grandmother as a black-haired beauty settling into the Italian Alps with her younger daughters as her eldest daughter and the Huns press on to France."[52] While the author reluctantly abandons a belief in Pillard's Indigenous origins, she nonetheless reimagines a fanciful narrative that places her ancestors at the centre of conflict and adventure on the borderlands of Europe, in a clear example of the type of "creative act of revisionist life writing" that Barnwell argues is at the centre of contemporary genealogical inquiry.[53]

After its careful analysis of all available evidence, the Association des Charron et Ducharme released a statement in October 2017 confirming that it supported the second theory—that Pillard's mtDNA came from southwestern Asia (and not Siberia) due to the genetic and genealogical (documentary) evidence at its disposal. In its statement, the association explains its position:

> The uncertainty about the origin of Catherine Pillard has caused a widespread questioning in our association. We believe that the conclusions we have reached strike an appropriate balance about everything we know concerning Catherine Pillard, whether from a genetics or genealogy perspective.
>
> Does this mean that this position is cast in stone? Not by a long shot. For instance, the discovery of other documents such as a boarding list in La Rochelle or her marriage contract with Pierre Charron could contain valuable information confirming or refuting Catherine's origin, or further development of genetics knowledge could help us in identifying her genetic ancestry more precisely.[54]

As is typical of debates involving genetic genealogy, the association leaves the door open to the eventual discovery of Pillard's Indigenous origins, though for the time being her decade-long run as an "Algonquin-Siberian" woman appears to have officially come to an end.

Despite the availability in French and in English of all the aforementioned research into Pillard's origins, nowhere on the genealogy forums did I encounter any opposition to Lussier et al.'s research. On the contrary, what I did observe on the forums was Pillard's eventual rebirth as the long-lost daughter of a well-known Huron-Wendat chief. These observations also matched my findings from the member genealogies of an "Abenaki" tribe in New Hampshire, in which Pillard's name is changed into a supposed Huron-Wendat name (Plat/Ouenta) to reflect her new patrilineal heritage. Whatever the case regarding Pillard's origins, a remarkable array of research has been conducted to "prove" her racial origins. As it is with Grenier, race shifters appear to select evidence that confirms their beliefs about their "Indigenous" identities, however recent or tenuous these claims may be. In this sense, the practices that I have associated with aspirational descent—a rejection of conventional genealogical research, an openness to mtDNA testing, the fostering of oppositional narratives—all lend themselves to a process of self-making that leads to race shifting among French descendants.

The next case involves two sisters born prior to 1635 in France who settled in Mi'kma'ki in what the French named Acadie (present-day Nova

Scotia). Just like Pillard, the Lejeune sisters have become associated with a prominent male Indigenous chief, lending credibility to their genealogical transformation.

Acadian Sisters in the Service of Aspirational Descent: Catherine and Edmée Lejeune, circa 1630s
Together, the Lejeune sisters appear nearly half a dozen times in a wide range of genealogy forums. Little is known about their early life or their travel across the Atlantic. For a long time, the general lack of documented history meant that both sisters were accepted as Mi'kmaq in genealogical circles. Stephen White, the lead genealogist at the Centre d'études acadiennes at the Université de Moncton, has raised significant questions about this theory, as has the Mothers of Acadia mtDNA research project run by Family Tree DNA, which also verified that the Lejeune sisters' ancestral origins were far outside the Americas.[55] Through that project, genetic scientists associated both sisters' mtDNA with haplogroup U, subclade U6a, which is most concentrated in northwestern Africa (specifically present-day Morocco, Western Sahara, Algeria, and Mauritania), with a much lower frequency in the Iberian Peninsula (Spain and Portugal) and in Iraq, Iran, and the Arabian Peninsula (Saudi Arabia).[56]

Before analyzing material from the forums, though, I would like to point out that in the member genealogies from both the Communauté métisse du Domaine-du-Roy et la Seigneurie de Mingan (CMDRSM) and the CMAM, the Lejeune sisters were listed as the sole "Indigenous" root ancestor for dozens of members. Both organizations are currently involved in protracted legal proceedings (as of winter 2019), attempting to be recognized as Métis under the criteria provided by the *Powley* decision in order to access constitutionally protected Aboriginal rights. A third organization that I analyze, the Métis Nation of the Rising Sun, is also on record as encouraging the use of either of the Lejeune sisters as an Indigenous root ancestor, as we will see in Chapter 5. Of the three different cases of the use of aspirational descent (i.e., Grenier/Garnier, Pillard, and the Lejeune sisters) that I analyze in some depth in this chapter, the Lejeune sisters are the only ones to appear as root ancestors across these three so-called métis organizations.

Returning to the genealogy forums, in a thread on the Généalogie du Québec et de l'Amérique française (GQAF) forum titled "Micmac and/or Maliseet Ancestry" in 2017, I was introduced to the conflict centred around the Lejeune sisters' ancestry. In February, Michel posted the following request: "I'm looking for my Indian ancestors. They say I'm Micmac [sic]. It seems [a genealogist] has published a family genealogy that says we're Maliseet. If a member could please clarify all of this, I'd be very happy."[57] Michel then posted his parents' names, which led frequent poster Yves to provide him with the relevant links from the GQAF's genealogy database. The next day, another frequent poster, Alain, seemed to confirm Michel's Mi'kmaw ancestry: "You certainly do have long-ago Mi'kmaw origins from the beginning of the seventeenth century through your Acadian origins. It's Edmée Lejeune's mother, who's also among my ancestors."[58] Alain went on to provide additional information, including the claim that Frenchman Pierre Lejeune dit Briard married a Mi'kmaw woman in France before 1620. Alain then suggested in passing that these details still needed to be confirmed through the documentary record. A few days later, frequent poster Dominique responded: "DNA tests have proven that Edmée Lejeune and her sister Catherine are both of European origins."[59] She then provided three Web links to the results of these tests and their respective analyses, including a report in *Acadie nouvelle*,[60] a French-language newspaper based in Moncton, New Brunswick, and the full results of the Mothers of Acadia mtDNA research project identifying DNA associated with virtually every Acadian woman in the seventeenth century.

Alain was not deterred by Dominique's introduction of countervailing molecular evidence. On the contrary, he explained that "the confusion comes from the fact that there exists without a doubt two people called Pierre Lejeune dit Briard. Edmée and Catherine's father was born in 1595 and married a Mi'kmaw woman around 1620 in France, while the first weddings in Acadia didn't happen until about 1635. He must've brought his future wife with him to France."[61] To be clear, in order to support his theory about the Lejeune sisters—one that is common among race shifters—Alain hypothesizes that a Mi'kmaw woman married a Frenchman in France, and that the couple later returned to Mi'kma'ki, where the Lejeune sisters were born. In response, Dominique pushed back further against Alain's claims:

"This is pure speculation. There were two Lejeune families that immigrated to Acadia.... The second Lejeune family, who arrived around 1642, is the one to which Edmée and Catherine, and their presumed brother Jean (who married a Mi'kmaw woman) belong.... Since the DNA tests prove that the two sisters (Catherine and Edmée) are of European origins, they cannot be of Indigenous ancestry."[62] Dominique presented the current consensus in the historical and genealogical literature on the Lejeune sisters. In this case, the Lejeune sisters' claim to indigeneity is both *aspirational*, in that their indigeneity appears to be fictive, and *lateral*, in the sense that their indigeneity appears to be connected to the fact that their brother married a Mi'kmaw woman (I return to the practice of lateral descent in the next chapter).

Dominique's dogged efforts to disprove Alain's theory ultimately ended with the mobilization of the "truth" provided through molecular technologies. As we have seen in the two prior sections, whether it stands to prove or disprove the presumed indigeneity of women ancestors in the 1600s, mtDNA is presented as foolproof evidence. Yet, to return to Alondra Nelson's work, genetic genealogy "appeals especially to root-seekers whose prior efforts have failed to yield information sufficient for extensive genealogical reconstruction."[63] Alain illustrated the strategic self-making at the centre of genetic genealogy, in his later recourse to an excerpt from Rameau de Saint-Pierre's book *Une colonie féodale en Amérique, L'Acadie (1604–1881)*, first published in 1889. In the excerpt, Saint-Pierre argues that the Lejeune family was "métis" and lists a marriage between a Pierre Lejeune and a Mi'kmaw woman as evidence. No dates are given in Saint-Pierre's account, nor is there any mention of Edmée and Catherine. "Pierre" might refer to their brother, though his name appears in most records as "Jean." All the same, Alain mobilizes an obscure nineteenth-century text to make his case against the prevalent molecular data. In this sense, his kinship aspirations, rooted as they are in aspirational descent, lead him to confirm his beliefs about his own indigeneity in the face of conflicting DNA evidence. The thread eventually ended, four days after it began, with the original poster, Michel, thanking Dominique for her contribution. This thread introduced me to the world of genetic genealogy among French descendants, since the controversy surrounding the Lejeune sisters' origins casts a wide shadow in Acadian/Cajun genealogical circles.

The next thread on the Lejeune sisters took place on the Rootsweb forum in March 2015, under the title "Questionable Record Lejeune." CJ wrote, "Did somebody make this up? Edmée tested European, right?" and posted a link to a genealogical site (a Rootsweb page) that provided the genealogy of a woman named Marguerite M. Mikmaq.[64] Marguerite is said to have been born in 1585 in present-day New Brunswick, the daughter of Mi'kmaw Grand Chief Membertou (born 1560) and his wife Marie Abénaki (born 1582). According to this online source, Marguerite married Pierre LeJeune Briard II (born 1595) in Vienne in western France and had a child (Pierre Lejeune Briard) there in 1625. The file, updated in 2014 and hosted on a well-regarded genealogical website, repeats some of the same elements of Alain's previous historical narrative. It makes for an intriguing story, especially to race shifters involved in a process of strategic self-making—but, given that the database lists Marguerite's mother (the aforementioned Marie Abénaki) as only three years old at the time of her daughter's birth, among other historical sleights of hand, it poses several incontrovertible problems. The most active forum administrator, Paul, responded right away to CJ's post: "Edmée & Catherine have mtDNA of U6a ['European'].... The explanation [that their mother was Mi'kmaq]—a list of all founding mothers of Acadia that we could not trace back to Europe were assumed to be Amerindian.... This is a false assumption."[65] Paul replied again later the same day, explaining that the genealogist who had entered the data on Rootsweb "is repeating the OLD guestimate that has been disproven by the mtDNA. [The Lejeune sisters'] parents are unknown but we know the two girls were sisters and Jean is probably their brother."[66] He then went on to cite André-Carl Vachon's book on the Lejeune family, which, he claims, debunks previous theories about the origins of the Lejeune family (among others), including those included in Saint-Pierre's work.[67]

Clearly, the fact that the Lejeune sisters' supposed indigeneity has been "disproven" by mtDNA ancestry testing has not stopped individuals and organizations from recognizing them as "Indigenous" root ancestors, at least if we consider the actual frequency of their appearance in membership documents in so-called métis organizations in Quebec (see Table 4). Again, Nelson's conclusion after conducting a similar form of virtual ethnography was that individuals who engaged in online genealogy forums integrated new knowledge about their ancestral past—including DNA-based evidence—in a manner that *confirmed* their established beliefs about ancestry, race, and/or identity. In this case, the fact alone that the Lejeune sisters are at times imagined as Grand Chief Membertou's grandchildren outweighs the strength normally reserved for molecular technologies.

TABLE 4. ASPIRATIONAL DESCENT IN MEMBERSHIP LISTS IN NEW HAMPSHIRE AND QUEBEC

	MANIWAKI MÉTIS QUEBEC SAMPLE = 1,906	SAGUENAY MÉTIS QUEBEC SAMPLE = 27	COWASUCK ABENAKI NEW HAMPSHIRE SAMPLE = 918
Catherine Pillard	8.6% (#5)	0	21.1% (#1)
Catherine Lejeune	1.9%	37.1% (#1)	1%
Edmée Lejeune	2.4%	0	1%

In another thread on the VO forum in 2013, titled "Indian/Métis roots coming from Acadia," a relatively new poster sought to find out more about his Acadian origins. Rods wrote, "Is there a list of Indian or Métis men and women recognized as such and coming from Acadie? My sister and I have done our genealogy and we found four Indian lines coming from Quebec. In my research, I discovered that many of our ancestors are Acadian. Some of them are considered Indian or Métis online, while others are not (according to DNA tests). Any help would be greatly appreciated."[68] Rods received many responses, and the discussion on the thread lasted several months. Before long, Rods responded to a request for a list of the "Indigenous" ancestors that he had compiled with Catherine Lejeune's name, along with two others. Within a couple of days, a frequent poster sent Rods a link to an Acadian genealogy site that mimicked many of the genetic genealogy websites shared by forum posters: contra the available molecular evidence, it favoured a historical narrative that created Acadian-Mi'kmaw kinship relations where none had existed. On it, the Lejeune sisters were definitively identified as "Métis."

Lory, whom you may remember from the previous chapter as a strong proponent of lineal descent, politely encouraged Rods to consider other sources. She writes that "the site that was placed in the thread is very interesting. But again, we should take some and leave some. It all depends on the site's author. As far as DNA goes, I'm very suspicious."[69] A few months later, in April 2014, frequent poster Yves made the final post in the thread: "Lots of Aboriginal lines have their own histories and Catherine Lejeune married to François Lavoie around 1651 is not accepted by the Alliance Autochtone du Québec (AAQ) because there's no legal proof.... The line involving Guillaume Caplan married to an unnamed Indian in Gaspésie is also not recognized by the AAQ. These two lines are quite dangerous, if it's a pastime then fine, but if it's to get an Aboriginal card from the AAQ the bureaucratic answer will be (lack of evidence). Sorry."[70] Yves's post not only pushed back at the use of Catherine Lejeune as an Indigenous root ancestor, but also introduced Caplan ancestry as an example of aspirational descent. The latter is the most common ancestral line claimed as the basis of membership in the largest self-identified métis organization in Quebec (in Gaspésie), to which I return in Chapter 5.

The debate about the identity of the Lejeune sisters shares many similarities with the debates about both Françoise Grenier and Catherine Pillard on the forums and more broadly. In all cases that I encountered on the forums, a 350-year-old family history repeats the heteronormative and patrilineal basis of lineal descent: an intrepid French man whose origins are well documented marries a mysterious "Indigenous" woman whose origins lack precision. Coincidentally, Grenier, Pillard, and Catherine Lejeune are all my direct ancestors, a fact that came to my attention only after I had completed my analysis of their use on the genealogy forums. Combined with three of the Algonquin women from the previous chapter, my own ancestral history includes a number of the main seventeenth-century women ancestors discussed in French-descendant genealogical circles.

When it comes to Grenier and the Lejeune sisters, opposition to their supposed indigeneity, supported by the widely available mtDNA ancestry record, is fairly common on the forums. Nevertheless, some prominent forum administrators and professional genealogists refuse to accept the molecular findings, instead advancing historical narratives that in their arguments substantiate their given ancestor's indigeneity once and for all. It appears that a common narrative strategy in these deliberations is to legitimize an otherwise French woman's indigeneity by connecting her genealogically with a high-profile Indigenous male chief. Such is the case with both the Lejeune sisters and Pillard, who are retroactively imagined as the children of Mi'kmaw Grand Chief Membertou and Huron-Wendat Grand Chief Atseña, respectively. As such, these women's indigeneity is strategically secured by their patrilineal ancestry, which is given gravitas by its chiefly origins. These observations are in keeping with Sturm's research: in the rare instances when an Indigenous man is invoked as a root ancestor among her research participants, he was almost always a well-known warrior or chief.[71]

TABLE 5. LEROUX GENEALOGY, BY FREQUENCY OF MENTION OF SEVENTEENTH-CENTURY WOMEN ANCESTORS

	BIRTH YEAR	BIRTH LOCATION	YEAR OF MARRIAGE	FREQUENCY	GENERATION#
Catherine Pillard	1646	France	1665	3 times	11–12
Catherine Lejeune	1633	France	1665	1 time	12
Françoise Grenier	1604	France	1634	4 times	13–14
Marguerite Pigarouiche	1646	Kichi Sibi	1671	1 time	11
Marie Miteouamegoukwe	1631	Kichi Sibi	1657	1 time	11
Euphrosine-Madeleine Nicolet's mother	1610	Lake Nipissing	N/A	1 time	15

Allow me to address another aspect of the Grenier, Pillard, and Lejeune cases. As we know, mtDNA testing turned up different results for Grenier and Pillard. First, Grenier was deemed haplogroup J, subclade J2b1a—an mtDNA haplogroup associated primarily with western Europe and Russia. Second, Pillard was deemed haplogroup A, and, upon closer inspection, haplogroup A10—an mtDNA haplogroup associated primarily with southwestern Asia between the Aral and Black Seas. In both cases, genealogists, genetic scientists, historians, and forum posters who have faith in DNA-based technologies are able to build a narrative around the specific bio-geographical origins of either of these ancestors. In Grenier's case, her ancestral origins are in France, which overlaps with the specific origins that genetic scientists have attributed to the biological substance associated with her through her descendants today. For many, the molecular evidence supports their understanding of French colonialism. The same is also true for the original molecular evidence in Pillard's case. The fact that her bio-geographical origins were first located in eastern Siberia meant that her story fit the Bering Strait theory of the peopling of the Americas. Through that DNA profile, her "Algonquin" origins were supported by a well-known scientific theory that explains the migration of people from Asia to the Americas about 14,000 years ago. While the association of her mtDNA with eastern Siberia was ultimately rejected by genetic scientists, this theory continues to circulate partly because of the ease with which it fits into existing understandings of the past. In other words, in both cases, the DNA evidence is easily integrated into existing historical narratives.

The Lejeune sisters' mtDNA offers origins that are infinitely more difficult for actors in the French-descendant genealogy sector to explain. Remember that the descendants of both Lejeune sisters were deemed to share haplogroup U, subclade U6a—an mtDNA haplogroup that is associated primarily with the far northwestern corner of Africa (Morocco, Western Sahara, Mauritania, and Algeria) and, to a much lesser extent, the Iberian and Arabian peninsulas. Notably, despite the fact that there is a relatively straightforward explanation for the Lejeunes' association with Africa—after all, a large migration of (North) African peoples into the Iberian Peninsula and across other Mediterranean locales into western Europe occurred much more recently than the Bering Strait timeline— nobody on the forums or in any of the genetic genealogy projects and/or websites openly discusses this possibility. While it may be presumptuous to attribute the relative silence about their origins to an ambient anti-blackness and/or Islamophobia, it is clear that accounting for North African origins presents a stumbling block to some of the same actors who otherwise speculate openly about the bio-geographical origins of a range of ancestors.

To return to my own genealogy, even if Catherine Lejeune had been Mi'kmaq, does that give me an inalienable right to claim an Indigenous identity as "Acadian-métis" or "Acadian-Mi'kmaq" today? Let us return to Pamela Palmater, who has written extensively on Mi'kmaw citizenship codes that oppose the blood-based logics inherited through colonial policy: "Take the example of an Acadian whose parents, grandparents, and great grandparents for four or five generations lived as Acadians, who has always identified with French language and culture, and who one day finds out that he or she has a Mi'kmaq ancestor in their family. Should such a person be considered Mi'kmaq? Assuming that the only connection this Acadian applicant had to the Mi'kmaq Nation was this ancestral connection four or five generations removed, I would say no. Otherwise, I would be basing Mi'kmaq identity solely on blood descent."[72] Indeed, the dedicated efforts to turn the Lejeune sisters into Mi'kmaw women illustrate the perverse nature of bio-racism underwriting the contemporary race-shifting process.

Aspirational descent speaks rather directly to the desire-for-indigeneity that forum posters regularly display on the forums. In this case, French descendants turn to genetic genealogy to confirm the "Indigenous" identity of otherwise French women from the early seventeenth century. I focused on three specific cases (of four French women) that appeared multiple times on the forums. Prior to my analysis of the forums, I was not aware of any of these French women or of the efforts to transform them into "Indigenous" women. In each case, extensive mtDNA ancestry testing by a number of French-descendant research projects ultimately advanced that each of the women was French and not Indigenous. Nonetheless, many forums posters continued to profess a firm belief in the indigeneity of Françoise Grenier, Catherine Pillard, and/or the Lejeune sisters, as do the three largest "métis" organizations in Quebec.

Nelson's argument that individuals turn to genetic genealogy as a way to confirm their pre-existing beliefs about their ancestors is certainly supported by my findings from the genealogy forums. Whether theorized as facilitating a process of strategic self-making, in Nelson's terms, or a process of self-authentication, in Barnwell's terms, the creative use of genetic genealogy by forum posters suggests that molecular findings are most relevant when they support the race-shifting process. When mtDNA results prove unable to support forums posters' avowed desire to become Indigenous, race shifters fall back on speculative histories and affective networks to resituate their kinship aspirations. In this sense, aspirational descent likely demonstrates the obsessive focus on *and* move beyond descent more than the two other practices of descent that I examine in the first part of the book, since one must remain committed to the reconstruction of a seventeenth-century woman's identity in a manner that *literally* bears no relation to their actual lineage as a French descendant. Aspirational descent, as practised on the genealogy forums, is about much more than simply knowing one's ancestral origins. It involves remaking those origins to fit one's desired identity in the present, often in the face of extensive evidence that contradicts one's desire-for-indigeneity. In manifesting their intense desire to become Indigenous, race shifters illustrate the social currency associated with claims to indigeneity and expose the inner workings of the race-shifting process.

Since the practice of aspirational descent engages extensively with a small number of genes associated with a self-identified Indigenous reference sample, Kim TallBear's work on the contemporary circulation of "Native American DNA" also provided a necessary intervention. As TallBear makes plain, Native American DNA has the "power to influence indigenous livelihoods and sovereignties" in a manner that supports the race-shifting process.[73] Most often, French-descendant genetic scientists, genealogists, and/or race shifters employ conventional mtDNA analysis with no apparent regard for how their research may impact upon actual living Indigenous peoples. Instead, their research serves exclusively French descendants.

Chapter Three

Lateral Descent: Remaking Family in the Past

There is no easy consensus on genealogy forums, as participants regularly and openly disagree about the meaning of kinship, family, and identity. What counts as evidence in these debates is highly contentious.

While conducting my virtual ethnography, I observed a third, at times complementary, use of descent on the forums. In *lateral* descent, one relies on an individual ancestor who is *not* a direct ancestor for the purpose of claiming an Indigenous identity today. Normally, there is some form of long-ago familial relation with this specific ancestor; for example, they may be a sibling, great-uncle/aunt, or third cousin to one's direct ancestor. In other cases, the relation appears to revolve simply around the presence of a given patronym. In what follows, I explore a few examples of the use of lateral descent on the forums, including some from my own genealogical reconstruction.

LATERAL DESCENT: WHAT'S IN A NAME?

Everybody Wants to Be a Riel

In a political context in which race shifting has become common, many posters linked the presence of a French-Québécois patronym among the Métis as proof that they might also be Métis. Louis Riel, as the most iconic Métis person in Québécois and Canadian imaginaries, figures prominently on online genealogy forums. As we saw in Chapter 1, he is at times used to support an argument against the Métis Nation's current citizenship code, despite the fact that his fame arises directly from his own commitment to protect the independence and self-determination of the Métis people. Predictably, then, Riel himself is inevitably reclaimed as "Eastern métis" in the forums. In a September 2005 post in the Ancestry forum, Johan sets the stage for Riel's rebirth: "Please know, that in most cases French-Canadian[s] who went West and started the Western Metis already had native/metis ties in Eastern Canada ... some by blood, marriages or even community adoption."[1] Raymond responded favourably to Johan, stating that Riel himself had eastern origins: "Many western metis already had eastern origins before the move. Louis Riel comes to mind as one of note!"[2] As discussed previously, a third poster in this thread went so far as to claim that Riel was born in Quebec, illustrating the efforts that forum posters are willing to undertake in order to support their desire for indigeneity.

To be clear, Riel's paternal grandmother, Marguerite Boucher, was born near the Cree-speaking Métis community of Île-à-la-Crosse in northwestern Saskatchewan to a Dene mother and French father around 1790. Her son, Riel's father, Louis Sr., was born near Île-à-la-Crosse in 1817 and, after Marguerite's death, spent part of his childhood in and around Montreal with his father. Riel himself was born in 1844 in St. Boniface, near Winnipeg in present-day Manitoba, the eldest of eleven Riel children born in the Red River settlement. He had two children; however, both passed away before having children of their own.[3] In other words, Louis Riel has no direct descendants. Nevertheless, it is not surprising that the Riel name is now being used on the forums as part of the practice of *lateral* descent, since Riel continues to be celebrated as a hero in Quebec society (and in parts of French Canada) for taking on the Canadian government multiple times in the nineteenth century. Parks, monuments, schools, streets, and buildings bearing his name abound throughout the province to honour his legacy. Even leaders of so-called Quebec métis organizations have sought to reconstruct their family using Riel's fame as a touchstone. In one such example, anthropologist Anne Pelta describes a ceremony held at the opening of a meeting of about a dozen "Eastern métis" organizations in Sherbrooke, Quebec, in 2009. According to Pelta, the master of ceremonies for the event introduced an individual at the very beginning of the plenary as one of "Louis Riel's descendants," despite the fact that, as just mentioned, no direct descendants exist. That person went on to play a prominent role throughout the weekend proceedings.[4] In a second example, a spokesperson for the Nation Métis Québec introduced himself to the Senate Standing Committee on Aboriginal Peoples 2012 hearings on Métis identity in the following manner: "Please understand that having a Riel here, in Ottawa, is a strange emotional experience. As my mother would say, only one of us was successful in this family, and he was hung. Yes, that's my family."[5] It is clear that Riel's fame continues to be used in a variety of symbolic ways by so-called Quebec métis leaders and organizations.

Linda, posting on the Généalogie du Québec et l'Amérique française (GQAF) forum in August 2015, illustrates the working of lateral descent. In her post, she explained that one of her great-grandmothers, Rosalie Riel, was reclaimed as either Indian or Métis by her father. Linda explicitly brought up Louis in the opening post of the thread: "I've done my own research that connected me to Louis Riel, the defender of the Métis. . . . [C]an you confirm that there are Indians [sic] in my family?"[6] A frequent poster replied within a few hours, confirming Linda's grandfather's date and location of birth and stating that, should Linda be able to confirm that she has Indigenous ancestry, she would automatically be Indigenous. Despite the strong expression of support for lineal descent, a GQAF genealogist confirmed that Rosalie Riel was not directly related to Louis *and* that Rosalie did not appear to have any Indigenous ancestry. Linda expressed disappointment: "Thank you . . . everything that I believed was false, my entire family was wrong, it's not that funny when what I have been told isn't true."[7] Through her disappointment, Linda inadvertently signalled the strength of lateral descent, in which a historical figure—who is nearly always a man of some repute—is imaginatively turned into a family member for the purpose of race shifting, despite a general lack of genealogical precision. In that sense, lateral descent resembles the aspirational form of descent in its clear expression of the desire-for-indigeneity, though in this case, the idea of family is creatively redefined to suit race shifters' kinship aspirations.

In order to verify Rosalie Riel's relationship to Louis Riel and claims about her potential indigeneity, I reconstructed her full genealogy going back to the 1620s using the GQAF database. Rosalie Riel was born in

October 1870 in the Outaouais region of Quebec, about an hour's drive north of Ottawa. I identified 153 root ancestors (i.e., those born in New France post-1620s), all whom were European. This includes 142 French ancestors in the seventeenth century (92.8 percent of the overall total), with sixteen born in Paris, thirteen born in La Rochelle (Poitou-Charente), and eleven born in Rouen (Normandy). As is the norm among French descendants who can trace their ancestry to the early colonial period, I observed several cases of distant consanguinity, with six different French couples repeated twice in her lineage, one of which shows up three separate times. Predictably, Rosalie and I share about a dozen root ancestors, mostly among the earliest French settlers, including common patronyms such as Séguin, Jarry, Beauchamp, Cloutier, Paradis, and Guyon (Dion), the latter of which connects us genealogically to Céline Dion. All of these features of Rosalie's genealogy (and of mine) are in keeping with standard French-descendant genealogy and research in historical demography.

In addition to French ancestors, her genealogy includes the original Riel ancestor—Jean-Baptiste Riel, born in Limerick, Ireland, around 1670—who married Louise Coutu, a French woman born in the colony at Sorel (about fifty kilometres northeast of Montreal), in 1704. Lastly, Rosalie's genealogy turned up ten English ancestors, including the Hinsdale family, which settled in Hartford, Connecticut, along with about 100 other Puritans, in 1637. While Rosalie Riel has only European ancestors for nine generations (from about 1625 to 1850), she nonetheless also has two Puritan ancestors who were adopted by the Mohawk community near Montreal in the early eighteenth century. In fact, both Rosalie and I have among our ancestors one of the most well-known examples of adoption as kin-making in French-Canadian genealogical circles. Notably, the genealogical connection to New England Puritans arises through the French and Mohawk raid at Deerfield, Massachusetts, in February 1704. The raid itself found its way into early American literature, when John Williams, one of over 100 Puritan captives taken north after the raid, wrote *The Redeemed Captive Returning to Zion* after his eventual release and that of four of his children, in 1706.[8] Williams's recounting of his captivity became a narrative central both to teaching about the dangers inherent in Catholicism and to stoking Puritan fears about Native Americans for generations. In fact, historians

Evan Haefeli and Kevin Sweeney claim that *The Redeemed Captive* "has been called a 'masterpiece' of the captivity genre, that quintessentially American literary form emerging from New England colonists' frontier experience."[9] A central reason that Williams's book became so popular was its focus on his daughter Eunice, who ultimately chose to stay among her adoptive kin in Kahnawake after she was given the opportunity to rejoin her Puritan family in adulthood.

Anthropologist Audra Simpson has also written about the place of the Deerfield raid as a staple in the captivity narrative genre, focusing specifically on Eunice's place in that genre. Simpson explains that captivity was quite common in the Northeast at a time when "the wars and sickness that settlement wrought (as well as the wars that they had experienced before) stressed the clan relationships of obligation and reciprocity . . . requiring that others be found to occupy the structural place of affection and obligation required by kinship."[10] She explains that the Deerfield raid likely originated in an effort to console a Mohawk mother in Kahnawake whose daughter had previously been captured by English settlers from New England.[11] In the context of intense internecine warfare in the Northeast fuelled by generations of French and English animosity in western Europe, Williams's captivity narrative became "both an empirical and a mythical moment of awakening within non-Native readership of the horrible possibility of transformation, of a Protestant girl being taken by savages and made into a Catholic Indian, but then, if not to add insult (and disbelief) to this injury, is the social horror of this girl's unwillingness to return to her natal family."[12] For the Puritans consuming her story, Eunice Williams came to "epitomize the spiritual trial posed by the American wilderness, its savage inhabitants, and, perhaps most importantly, the savagery within."[13]

Eunice was seven years old when she was captured, while her Deerfield neighbour Abigail Nims and fellow Puritan child Josiah Rising were four and ten years old, respectively.[14] Like Eunice, both Abigail and Josiah were raised as Mohawks near Montreal, Abigail first at the Mountain Mission in the foothills of Mount-Royal and then at Fort Lorette on the north shore of the island, and Josiah at Fort Lorette. In 1714, Abigail and Josiah both rejected independent efforts made by their relatives to pay ransom and redeem them in New England. Eventually, Marie-Élisabeth Touatogouach

Nims and Josiah-Ignace Shoentakouani Raizenne, as they came to be known, married each other in 1715 at Fort Lorette. In her research on Indigenous kinship-making, Garroutte explains how Iroquois practices at the time involved a period during which family members would introduce a captive to their kinship obligations and assess their success at fulfilling those duties. As Garroutte argues, "The probationary principle fits comfortably with the idea that kinship is not exclusively about ancestral connections but also incorporates an emphasis on behavior that requires time to learn."[15]

Two years after the Raizenne wedding, in 1717, the king of France granted land to the Sulpicians for a mission near the confluence of the Ottawa River and Lac des Deux-Montagnes (St. Lawrence River), about fifty kilometres west of the island of Montreal. French colonial authorities later decided to relocate all Indigenous peoples from the island (including Marie-Élisabeth and Josiah-Ignace) to the new mission in the dead of winter in 1721. Once arrived, the Sulpicians granted the Raizenne couple and their three small children a large estate near the church at the edge of the mission community (in what later became known as the town of Oka), ensuring that they would become prosperous farmers and influential power brokers for years to come. From that point on, the Raizenne family—living in the French-Canadian community at Lac des Deux-Montagnes—appears to have mostly integrated into the broader French-Canadian community. For example, their eldest child, Marie-Anne—Rosalie Riel's direct ancestor—married soldier and businessman Louis Séguin, a major in the French forces, in 1736. Marie-Catherine—my direct ancestor—married Louis's brother Jean-Baptiste Séguin in 1742, following a pattern of Raizenne children marrying prominent French descendants in the region. From this generation onward, all Raizenne descendants married French descendants and spread out into French-Canadian/Québécois settlements north and west of Montreal in the Lanaudière region. Kanien'kehá:ka (Mohawk) community-based historian Éric Pouliot-Thisdale has studied French-descendant families living in proximity to Indigenous communities, particularly at Oka/Lac des Deux-Montagnes, and has concluded that, "historically, as per the archival documents that I have consulted, most [French descendants] living near [Indigenous people] fundamentally had no associated relations with First Nations."¹⁶ Pouliot-Thisdale's observations referred specifically to the Raizenne descendants.

Given their unique place at the nexus of Mohawk and French settler society, several of the Raizenne children played the role of mediator between French Catholic elites and Indigenous society. For instance, three of the eight Raizenne children became key church officials (a priest and two nuns), of which one (Marie) even rose to the rank of Mother Superior of the Notre-Dame Congregation in Montreal, the largest and arguably most important in the colony. As Mother Superior, Marie, known as Sister St-Ignace, had access to the upper echelons of New France's political leaders. All in all, despite their parents' partial upbringing in Mohawk communities around Montreal, the first-generation Raizenne children appear to have been well integrated into the dominant society's cultural norms.

In contrast to the Raizenne adoptees, Eunice Williams (a.k.a. Marguerite Kanenstenhawi Arosen) remained an integral member of the Mohawk community, in this case, in Kahnawake, on the south shore of the St. Lawrence River downstream from Oka/Lac des Deux-Montagnes. In 1713, she married François-Xavier Arosen, a young Mohawk man, and they had three children. Her grandson, Thomas Williams (a.k.a. Thomas Théoragwanegon), became chief of Kahnawake in 1777 and was eventually a signatory of the treaty of 1796 that created the St. Regis Reservation in upper New York State. Unlike the Raizenne descendants, who were key to French-Canadian settlement in regions west of Montreal, many of Marguerite's (previously Eunice) descendants were prominent Mohawk leaders in Kahnawake. In fact, dozens of her descendants continue to live in Kahnawake today.

This brief detour through my own genealogy and that of Rosalie Riel further illustrates the deep ancestral ties among French descendants such as forum poster Linda and I. Unbeknownst to me prior to researching this chapter, it turns out that through the Raizenne connection, Rosalie is my cousin (four generations back) in a similar manner as Louis is Rosalie's (four generations back). In other words, I have a lateral relation with the Riel family. None of these specific ancestral connections are particularly notable, in that distant consanguinity was required for the growth of the relatively tiny French settlements in the colony from the early seventeenth century onwards. What is notable, however, is how these connections are reclaimed today through the practice of lateral descent, a key component of the race-shifting process.

Moving forward, beyond two direct English-but-adopted-Mohawk ancestors—whose child married into a prominent French-descendant military family, establishing a pattern that continued into the twenty-first century—four generations before her birth, there is no evidence that Rosalie Riel had any ancestors other than Europeans in the eight generations after the arrival of her root ancestors in the early seventeenth century. Of course, there is more than biology to kin-making projects, though Linda appears to have depended strictly on biology as the basis for her *lateral* relation to Riel. In the case of Rosalie Riel, she and Louis Riel share one ancestor in common: the original Riel colonist, Jean-Baptiste Riel, born in Ireland around 1670.

As we saw in the two previous chapters, practices related to descent exceed one's *actual* ancestry. As such, the role that Riel plays in French-descendant efforts to become Indigenous finds a parallel in broader efforts to use Riel in Canadian society. For instance, Métis scholar Jennifer Adese explains the ways in which Riel serves to assuage collective Canadian guilt and anxiety about colonialism: "The repurposing of Riel's legacy reflects a more widespread anxiety that is not confined to individual affect. It demonstrates an anxiety that is a defining aspect of contemporary Canadian political, social, and cultural life."[17] In a context in which race shifting among French descendants has taken on a life of its own and the broader repurposing of Riel's legacy is widespread, reclaiming the Riel name as a component of the race-shifting process certainly appears to support Adese's argument about the *collective* anxiety felt by white Canadians struggling to account for our location in ongoing forms of colonial violence. Adam Gaudry advances a complementary reading of the repurposing of Riel in contemporary Canadian society, this time through an analysis of political theory, arguing that "Canadian political theory has internalized Riel by incorporating him (and by extension the entire Métis people), into a foundational mythology describing the founding of Canada as a multicultural métissage [and] this internalization of the Métis has played [a crucial role] in attempts to erase Canada's colonial past, present, and future. Through this process, Riel and the Métis have become a gateway through which political theorists can identify a post-colonial Canada; a project which is, at its core, disingenuous in its erasure of ongoing colonial occupation of Indigenous lands and governments."[18] The representational politics that have led to the widespread circulation of Riel in Canadian society certainly facilitates his reclamation in the race-shifting process. The collective efforts at repurposing Riel as the basis for the existence of a "Quebec métis" community are articulated in a number of sites, not least of which are online genealogy forums.

Having established the basis for what I see as lateral efforts to claim an "Indigenous" identity, the next section examines some other uses of lateral descent from the main genealogy forums, all of which involve efforts to repurpose another Red River Métis family.

The Red River Arcands as "Quebec Métis"

As I suggested above, I was not surprised that carrying the Riel patronym could lead one to claim an Indigenous identity today, especially given his status in Quebec society nearly a century and a half after his execution by the Canadian state. I did, however, find examples of lateral descent in the forums involving other family Métis names, most of which took place on the English-language Ancestry site.

In August 2011 Linda (not the same Linda as earlier) started a thread by introducing two family lines that led her to believe that she may be "Quebec métis," including one (Grenier) that I analyzed at length in the previous chapter: "Hello, I am a novice, so please bear with me. In researching my daughter's tree, I have found Arcands from Quebec, and also Francois [*sic*] Grenier."[19] Linda continues by explaining that she conducted her research with the support of the president of the Maine Franco-American Genealogical Society, before stating her conundrum:

> On November 3, 1718, [Marie-Renée Ursule Chartier De Lotbiniere] married Joseph Arcand in Quebec, who was the great grandson of Antoine Arcan (Arcand) from France. At this point it is pure speculation on my part, fueled by rumors of Native ancestry in the family, as to who Marie-Renee's mother was.... It seems odd that

the mother is unknown, and that she is adopted out of the family. Could her mother have been a Native? ... There are many Arcand Metis in Saskatchewan directly descended from Antoine Arcand. I would like to know if Marie-Renee was a Quebec Metis.[20]

While Linda is not entirely clear in her post about how Marie-Renée Chartier's supposed indigeneity is connected to her Arcand ancestors, it seems that the presence of the Arcand Métis in Saskatchewan is what leads her to speculate openly about both her and Marie-Renée's potential Indigenous ancestry.

Frequent poster Mystery responded to Linda's request two days later by first suggesting that the original Arcand colonist from France may have in fact been Indigenous himself—a rather bold suggestion in keeping with the circulation of aspirational descent on the forums. Mystery eventually offered two other possibilities for the existence of the Arcand Métis: "Actually, there was a book that wrongly noted [that] the original Arcands ... descended from a tribe in Canada. [T]hat may be why they are listed as metis, but I've also found [in my genealogy] pertaining to Marie Angelique Frelon [that] she has an ancestor Marie Sylvestre. ... The [GQAF database] lists some of the Arcands as being the great great grandchildren of Marie Frelon. So that may be part of the reason [the Arcands are identified as Métis] as well."[21] The conversation between Linda and Mystery illustrates some of the speculative leaps that characterize lateral descent. First, a familiar and shared patronym (in this case, Arcand) is associated with indigeneity and/or Indigenous peoples. Linda establishes the connection in mentioning the Arcand Métis based in Saskatchewan, a well-known Métis patronym/family today. Second, both Linda and Mystery raise the spectre of the "Quebec métis," Linda in a direct reference to Marie Sylvestre and Mystery in a reference to her descendants. As I explained in Chapter 1, Marie Sylvestre is the most common Indigenous woman reclaimed as the basis for a "Quebec métis" identity across the forums (and in the membership records that I have analyzed). She has hundreds of thousands of descendants today across Canada and the United States; therefore, it is entirely possible that some of her descendants would have the Arcand patronym.

Third, the supposed Arcand ancestral connection with Sylvestre is presented as the basis for the existence of an Arcand (Quebec) métis family today, where presumably anybody with an Arcand ancestor, with Sylvestre as an ancestor, or with both becomes "Quebec métis." To both Linda and Mystery, one possible explanation for the existence of the Arcand Métis family appears to be that the family were "métis" *before* they ended up in Saskatchewan. These forum posters' apparent lack of knowledge about the origins of the Métis people could be attributable to a general learned ignorance about Indigenous peoples that circulates among white Canadians; that is, they may think that the Métis are an Indigenous people who existed *prior* to European contact and later moved west. The Arcand Métis in Saskatchewan are conflated with the supposed Arcand "métis" in Quebec, which provides a potential answer to Linda's search for Indigenous ancestry (and, perhaps, identity). The belief that the western Métis and the "Eastern métis" are the same people is a useful, if unconscious, strategy that actively undermines Métis self-determination as a *people*, since it contradicts Métis understandings of their own origins.[22] Nevertheless, the actual historical records show a much more complex history, which my genealogical reconstruction of the Arcand Métis illustrates.

The first Arcand to be born in New France, Pierre, was born in 1689 in Grondines, between Trois-Rivières and Quebec City along the St. Lawrence River. Pierre's great-great-grandnephew Joseph was born a few kilometres away from Grondines in Cap-Santé in 1795. Joseph headed west as a voyageur at the very beginning of the nineteenth century, where he first worked for the Montreal-based North West Company (NWC) in the Lower Red River district between Pembina in present-day North Dakota and Saint Paul, Minnesota. It was quite common for French-Canadian men to migrate during this period. Studying the movement of her own Desjarlais Métis ancestors at the time, Heather Devine explains, "Between 1760 and 1830... out-migration of family members became a necessary and accepted part of rural life in Quebec, a response to overpopulation and diminished access to fertile agricultural land."[23] While the nature of the land tenure system was largely responsible for the organization of rural life, and "overpopulation" was a result of this broader system, working-class French Canadians from Quebec nonetheless travelled far and wide in search of work opportunities. In this era, the most common migration route was westward. Starting mid-century, the preferred migration route was south into New

England to work in the burgeoning textile factories. One of my own paternal great-grandparents was born in New England (Lowell, Massachusetts) to parents who joined over 500,000 other French Canadians migrating to industrial cities in the region throughout the nineteenth century.[24]

After the merger of the NWC and the Hudson's Bay Company (HBC) in 1821, Joseph Arcand worked for the HBC until he and Marie Vestro (Jeannot), a first-generation Métis woman, were married in St. Boniface at the Red River Settlement in 1832.[25] From that point on, the couple farmed five acres of land in St. François Xavier parish, a Métis community to the west of the Red River Settlement along the Assiniboine River. Joseph and Marie Arcand had eight children, seven of whom lived to adulthood and married into Métis families at or near the Red River Settlement, becoming prominent members of the second generation of Métis families in the region. They lived during what Métis historian Jesse Thistle calls the "time of Métis prosperity" between 1821 and 1869, "when Métis families continued to travel great distances, exercise freedom of commerce, and practise sovereignty, all while retaining control of their Northwestern maternal homelands."[26]

For example, their third child, Thérèse, married Jean-Baptiste Lafond in St. Boniface in 1852, and their son Jean-Baptiste Tchehasaso Lafond (born 1853) later became chief of the Muskeg Lake band (Muskeg Lake Cree Nation) about sixty kilometres northwest of Batoche, from 1900 to 1914. Three of Thérèse's younger brothers—Joseph, Alexandre, and Jean-Baptiste (born between 1833 and 1840 at the Red River Settlement or in St. François Xavier)—married McKay women from St. Eustache (Josephte, Marguerite, and Nancy Anne, respectively), whose parents (Ignace McKay and Josephte Bercier) were both Métis.[27] Each one of these Arcand brothers worked as a "middleman" for the HBC in the mid-nineteenth century, eventually all becoming "freemen" (free traders) after the Sayer trial of 1849 opened up that possibility to Métis traders. Devine explains that Guillaume Sayer, along with three other Métis traders, were charged with illegally trading furs. At the trial, the jury actually found Sayer guilty but ultimately opted to recommend that he receive no penalty and that the charges be dropped against the three other defendants. The de facto acquittal meant that "the Hudson's Bay Company monopoly was irretrievably compromised and would never be successfully enforced in the region again."[28] The Arcand brothers worked on a riverine trade route that ran along the north–south and east–west axes that went from Lake Superior to the Red River all the way up to the Athabasca region in present-day northern Alberta.[29] By the 1860s, the entire Arcand family was based in the Red River settlement once again.

In March 1869, the Dominion of Canada purchased Rupert's Land from the HBC without consulting any of the Indigenous peoples in the territory, who did not recognize HBC title to the land in the first place. After increasing evidence of white settler encroachment in the region, the Métis formed a provisional government in November 1869 and rose up against Canada under the leadership of Louis Riel. The Dominion government eventually relented and signed the Manitoba Act, which purported to protect Métis land rights. However, through the scrip process, the large majority of Métis in Manitoba were dispossessed of their land over the next decade. Thistle concisely explains the events after 1869: "Canada stalled Metis land claims through a bogged-down labyrinthine scrip process while actively promoting Protestant Ontarian settlement... to tip the balance of power and stop Winnipeg from becoming another French-speaking 'problem' like the one English Canada perceived Quebec to be at the time.... [B]ecause of the stalling and starvation, [the Métis] were obliged to sell their lands at a fraction of their value to predatory speculators who then sold them at premiums to incoming settlers."[30]

In addition to these efforts to dispossess and displace Métis families from the Winnipeg area, Prime Minister John A. Macdonald sent the Red River Expeditionary Force (RREF)—with its 1,000-strong battalion of Protestant Orangemen intent on wreaking havoc on Métis life—to the region. Historian J.M. Bumsted referred to the arrival of the RREF as a "military invasion of Red River" to signify the extreme forms of violence enacted on Métis people of all walks of life in Manitoba at the time.[31] Added to that, the events of the early 1870s severely impacted the health of the Métis (and other Indigenous peoples). Starvation and malnutrition led to an exponential spike in child mortality in Red River.[32] It is no small wonder that the Métis fled by the thousands to territories northwest of Winnipeg, especially near Batoche along the South Saskatchewan River, and also southwest of Winnipeg, into the Cypress Hills and Montana along the Milk and Missouri Rivers.

The first generation of the Arcand Métis born and raised at Red River joined their children and trekked west in the 1870s, to Métis communities near or along the South Saskatchewan River such as Duck Lake and Carlton. François Régis Arcand, Joseph's son and Jean-Baptiste's twin brother, moved to St. Laurent de Grandin by 1875 with his wife, Philomène, and children. There they lived under the St. Laurent government, whose elected leader, Gabriel Dumont, would later become famous as the military leader of the Métis Resistance of 1885. For a short time, the Métis in the region experienced some of their former success as traders, but the scarcity of the buffalo, the onset of white settler encroachment, and the displacement of their First Nation kin onto reserves led to circumstances that resembled those at Red River less than a generation prior.

This time, the Métis, led by Dumont, decided to take up arms, as they believed they had exhausted all other options with the government. They sent a delegation—led by Dumont—and requested that Louis Riel, who was living at St. Peter's Mission in Montana with his wife, Marguerite Monet dit Belhumeur, join the resistance. The Arcand family eventually played an inordinate role in Métis military efforts during the Northwest Resistance in spring 1885. At least eleven Arcand family members were directly involved in the campaign,[33] including six of the first-generation Arcands (Thérèse, Joseph, Alexandre, Jean-Baptiste, François Régis, Marie) as well as several of their children, including twenty-four-year-old Marie-Josephte-Laviolette, Joseph's daughter; Jean-Baptiste Tchehasaso Lafond, Thérèse's oldest son; fifteen-year-old Jean-Baptiste Jr.; and even nine-year-old St-Pierre Arcand, François Régis's oldest son. The latter two boys were trained by their Arcand kin to be munitions envoys and scouts.[34] Further, according to interviews with two Métis elders (Yvonne Richer-Morrissette and Blanche Morrissette) conducted by Jesse Thistle and Carolyn Podruchny in 2013, Arcand Métis women participated in the Resistance by making munitions from melted buttons, kettles, and other kitchenware.[35]

The Métis forces during the Northwest Resistance also included many of their Assiniboine and Cree kin, who fought alongside Riel and Dumont throughout the spring. The Arcand family's commitment to one another and to their Cree/Métis kin manifested the Cree concept of *wahkootowin*, or what Brenda Macdougall has defined as the "expression of a worldview that laid out a system of social obligation and mutual responsibility between related individuals—between members of a family."³⁶

After the defeat at Batoche, the Canadian government enacted severe retribution. Louis Riel was hanged in Regina in November 1885. A short time afterward, eight warriors, six Cree and two Assiniboine—Kah-paypamhchukwao (Wandering Spirit), Itka (Crooked Leg), Waywahnitch (Man Without Blood), Nahpase (Iron Body), Manchoose (Bad Arrow), Pahpah-me-kee-sick (Round the Sky), Kit-ahwah-ke-ni (Miserable Man), and A-pis-chas-koos (Little Bear)—were hanged at Fort Battleford in a spectacle of white settler violence. The largest mass hanging in Canadian history was witnessed by the Indigenous students at the nearby Battleford Industrial School, who authorities marched to the dire scene at the military barracks to bear witness. The Government of Canada also enacted collective forms of punishment, deeming more than twenty First Nation bands to have been treasonous, leading the government to enforce the Indian pass system after the events of Batoche, a policy that further entrenched the confinement of status Indians onto reserves.³⁷ In addition, the government pursued an official policy of dividing the Métis from their First Nations kin through a variety of coercive inducements that led many Métis to withdraw from existing treaty (and, consequently, from living on reserves).³⁸

In this context, the Arcand Métis family scattered throughout Saskatchewan and Montana. In multiple interviews with his Arcand kin who are direct descendants of those who survived the events of 1870 to 1885, Thistle poignantly captured the intergenerational trauma that has been passed down since events at Red River in the 1870s. Thistle explains that much of his Arcand family ended up settling near Prince Albert, north and west of Batoche, where, after another round of unscrupulous settler encroachment, they lived on "road allowances," or parcels of Crown land intended for future road development. Many lived out their lives certain that if the authorities ever caught up to them, they would be hanged, just as Louis Riel and several of their Cree and Assiniboine kin had been following the Northwest Resistance.³⁹ Fast forward more than a century and the Arcand Métis family continues to be a recognizable Métis family in the Prairies, partly due to its active participation and political leadership in Indigenous resistance to Canadian settler violence. What makes the Arcand Métis Indigenous is much more than a genealogical connection with Indigenous women ancestors who lived in the 1600s. Their indigeneity is bound up in their ongoing kinship relations with other Prairie-based Indigenous peoples, their political history of resistance to the Canadian government, and their extreme marginalization in the western provinces.

Returning to the genealogy forums, contrary to both Linda's and Mystery's arguments, Pierre Arcand (the first Arcand born in Quebec, circa 1689) and his eight siblings had absolutely no ancestral connection to Marie Sylvestre, a fact that is easily verifiable on a number of major online databases. The Arcand connection to Sylvestre occurs through one of Pierre's brother's great-grandchildren, who married Marie-Angélique Freslon in 1779. In other words, besides the fact that claiming Sylvestre as the basis for a "Quebec métis" identity today is questionable because of the political use of lineal descent that I outlined in Chapter 1, only those Arcand descendants directly related to Joseph's (the Arcand who left Quebec for Red River) great-great-uncle share the latter's lineage with Sylvestre. As such, any relationship to Sylvestre is a *lateral* one. Clearly, the logics of lateral descent play a role in laying the groundwork for race shifting on the genealogy forums.

As my brief outline of the Arcand Métis lineage illustrates, there exists an entire Arcand line with hundreds, if not thousands, of descendants (many of whom would not carry the Arcand patronym today) who identify themselves—and in turn are identified as—Indigenous today. These Arcand Métis have no relation to any of the so-called "Eastern métis" or "Quebec métis" claiming Arcand origins, beyond a lateral relation three generations *before* the Métis even existed as a people. Linda and Mystery illustrate the inner workings of lateral descent well, wherein the aspirational basis of race shifting combines with the more conventional lineal basis to create long-ago Indigenous ancestors. In order to demonstrate further the workings of lateral descent, I have opted to return to my own genealogy to follow one specific *lateral* line through four generations of Métis life on the northern plains in present-day Manitoba, Saskatchewan, North Dakota, and Montana.

The Politics of Lateral Descent: The Brabant Métis
As I indicated previously, my maternal lineage is through the Brabant patronym. Pierre Brabant (dit Lamothe) was born about 1645 in Aubigny-sur-Nère, a small town (population 5,800 in 2008) in the Centre-Val de Loir region of France, about 100 kilometres south of Paris. He married Anne Goupil, who was born in Sillery (New France), to two French parents, in 1671. Four generations later, their great-great-grandson (and my direct ancestor) Sylvestre Brabant was born in 1794 in Vaudreuil, about forty kilometres west of Montreal. He was the seventh of twelve Brabant children. Sylvestre's older brother Augustin, who was born in 1792, took a route that diverged significantly from those of his other siblings, all of whom remained in the Lanaudière region of Quebec and married fellow French descendants. As you may recall from Chapter 1, my Brabant ancestors settled near the Ontario border in Quebec before finally crossing into Ontario in the middle of the nineteenth century and eventually settling further west, in and around Sudbury, in order to take advantage of the Free Grants and Homestead Act (1868) and the construction of the railway through the region. My maternal grandfather, Phillias, was raised in the Sudbury area at the very end of the nineteenth century and worked most of his life as a lumberjack outside of the city. He died when my mother was a child, and my only image of him is from an old, creased family photo from the early 1960s.

Phillias's great-great-uncle Augustin, unlike his younger brother and my direct ancestor Sylvestre, signed a contract to work in the fur trade and headed west at the end of the first decade of the 1800s. He married twice, both times to Métis women: Marguerite (or Geneviève) L'Hirondelle, near St. Boniface before 1821, and Angélique Lucier, in 1821 in Fort Edmonton. Overall, seven Brabant children were born in Métis communities in the Red River settlement or near Fort Edmonton between 1821 and 1830. For the discussion that follows, I have opted to concentrate on the four children whose mother was Geneviève L'Hirondelle and who were mostly raised in the Métis communities of the Red River Settlement (Geneviève, Charlotte,

Élisabeth, Augustin Jr.). According to Indigenous studies scholar Robert Innes's understanding of Métis ethnogenesis, these children were born between the first and second generation of Métis born at Red River.[40] This first generation of Brabant Métis children each married into prominent Red River Métis families, including the Desjarlais, Sakaban, Gaudry, and Fisher families. They all eventually moved west of Red River, in the Qu'Appelle River Valley at Lebret, Saskatchewan, after the foundation of the Catholic mission there in 1866. It seems that they played key roles in the political, religious, and social lives of the Métis community in Lebret throughout the nineteenth century; their names appear nearly 100 times in church records as witnesses to births, burials, and marriages in less than two decades.[41]

Devine explains some of the economic and social reasons for her own Desjarlais ancestors' decision to move away from the Red River, reasons that no doubt also motivated the Brabant Métis—some of whom were kin with the Desjarlais, most of whom were neighbours. She argues that the "movement of Métis was primarily an economic migration. As the bison populations disappeared, those Red River Métis who had made only an indifferent commitment to agriculture while living in the vicinity of Red River moved westward in pursuit of the waning herds. They settled on the shores of lakes where they could supplement their diet of large game animals with fish and fowl. The Qu'Appelle region was still relatively free of Euro-Canadian settlers, and the Métis could establish their homes on the shores of lakes and rivers."[42] As we saw in the previous section, the aftermath of the signing of the Manitoba Act brought an immense deal of hardship to the Métis who remained around Red River, but before long the Brabant Métis would experience swift changes along the Qu'Appelle River as well.

No doubt anticipating that events at Red River in the first few years after the Manitoba Act signalled a changing political economy in the region, Augustin Jr. was one of thirty-one Métis men living in the greater Lake Qu'Appelle region to submit a petition to the Government of Canada in 1874 requesting that it recognize Métis rights to land, including to hunting and fishing. The petition, archived as the "Petition from Augustin Brabant and Others, Dated Lake Qu'Appelle, 11th September 1874," is addressed to Governor Alexander Morris and began as follows: "Your Excellency,—The Half-Breeds of the Lakes Qu'Appelle and environs offer you to-day their homage, and submit to you the following petitions which they present in their name and in the name of all their brethren scattered over the prairies, and beseech you to give them a favourable hearing, and to remember them in the various arrangements that the Government may make with the Indians."[43] In their recent work examining Métis mobility and politics, historians Brenda Macdougall and Nicole St-Onge specifically highlight the 1874 petition for its expression of a Métis collective consciousness in the face of the emerging power of the Canadian state. According to them, it is one of "fifteen petitions sent to the Canadian and/or American government between 1847 and 1883 [by the Métis], asserting a clear political ideology and determination to be recognized as rights-based communities."[44] In this context, Macdougall and St-Onge read the petitions—and the social relations that they manifest across disparate, yet connected, locations in the northern plains—as representing "kinscapes," or what they define as a "set of relational constellations"[45] at the centre of Métis life. Morris eventually replied to the petition, explaining, "It is the wish of the Government to establish its authority everywhere in these vast territories of the Queen."[46] In the face of Métis (and First Nations) opposition, the Canadian government pushed ahead with its policies of securing the Northwest for private ownership and individual settlement.

Augustin Brabant appears as a signatory in two other petitions from Métis communities in the Qu'Appelle River Valley. The next petition, dated 2 September 1880, is directed to the Marquis of Lorne. In it, the 114 Métis signatories repeat many of their demands from the 1874 petition, most notably "that the Government allow the Half-breeds the right of keeping the lands which they have taken or which they may take along the River Qu'Appelle."[47] Brabant and the rest of the signatories did not receive a response. The second petition was signed at Fort Qu'Appelle, about seven kilometres northwest of Lebret at the head of Mission Lake (Qu'Appelle River), two years later, on 29 August 1882. As already noted, the early 1880s coincide with Canadian government efforts to restrict Indigenous mobility through the creation of reserves in the region, as well as a push to settle European immigrants and white settlers from Ontario and establish the West as an agricultural sphere. This last petition was addressed to Edward Dewdney, the lieutenant-governor of the North-West Territories, and sought Government of Canada redress in the dispossession of Métis lands by the Ontario and Qu'Appelle Land Company. Augustin's sons Alexandre (seventeen years old) and Édouard (twelve years old) were also among the forty-four signatories to this petition. When no immediate response to their grievances was forthcoming from the Government of Canada, Dewdney wrote the Prime Minister's Office a second time, on 6 June 1883. More inaction on the file led the Qu'Appelle River Métis to hire lawyer T.W. Jackson to act on their behalf. On 8 December 1883, Jackson wrote to John Hall, acting secretary of the Department of the Interior, who wrote back on 13 March 1884 confirming that he had received the Métis petition and was unable to visit the Métis due to his overloaded schedule.[48] The Métis never received another response, and within a year most had moved away from their homes, dispossessed by the intense settlement pressure of the OQLC. As we see below, many followed the north–south trade route axis into Montana, where they remain today.

The second generation of Brabant Métis born out west—thirty-two children born mostly in the 1840s and 1850s—demonstrates the type of kinscapes or relational constellations theorized by Macdougall and St-Onge. This generation came of age during the tumultuous events of 1870, following the movement of their Métis kin west. These Brabant Métis were located (primarily in their youth) in and around the Red River settlement in St. Boniface or St. François Xavier along the Assiniboine River; farther south along the Red River at present-day Pembina, North Dakota; in the Qu'Appelle River Valley in present-day Saskatchewan; and farther north along the South Saskatchewan River near Batoche. The available archives (church records, scrip applications, census records) allow us to observe how this generation maintained clear relations with one another and with their Indigenous kin throughout the Lake Winnipeg watershed. Notably, there is at least one marriage between a second-generation Brabant and an Arcand Métis, as well as a Brabant Métis who witnessed an Arcand Métis baptism, both in 1860s St. Boniface.[49] Also, at this point in time the Nêhiyaw Pwat Confederacy/Iron Alliance—a diplomatic agreement (1810s to 1880s) reached between Cree, Saulteaux, Métis, and Assiniboine peoples in the northern plains just prior to Augustin Brabant's arrival in

Red River from Quebec—ensured that the Métis were active participants in regional political events.[50]

The third generation of Brabant Métis (now with a range of common Métis patronyms, especially Fisher, Gaudry, Laliberté, and, of course, Brabant)—162 children born primarily between 1865 and 1885—follow the same pattern as the Arcand Métis, appearing in the archives primarily in the western regions of the Lake Winnipeg watershed.[51] Added to their exile from Red River, they were born at a time when the buffalo herds hardly reached across into Canada, except for a tiny sliver in southern Alberta in the Cypress Hills. The decimation of the buffalo herds was part and parcel of white settler strategies to dispossess and displace Indigenous peoples, including the Métis, who depended on the hunt for their spiritual, economic, and cultural sustenance. As Innes has explained, "Beginning in the 1850s, the buffalo herds began to slip out of southern Manitoba and Saskatchewan, reaching only into southern Alberta and northern Montana, and giving rise to more inter-tribal warfare."[52] The dwindling buffalo herds and the increase in warfare between the Iron Alliance and its opponents, along with the advent of Canadian Confederation in 1867, created a great deal of adversity for the Métis and their allies. This third generation of Brabant Métis entered into the world in this difficult political context. They appear several hundred times as witnesses to a variety of key community events, oftentimes travelling quite a distance to fulfill their social obligations to the broader Métis community.[53] The fact that virtually all of the Brabant Métis in this generation married Métis spouses further confirms Macdougall's observations about the lack of outsider men past the first generation.[54]

During this period, several Brabant descendants (with patronyms such as Sansregret-Henderson, Fisher-Constant/Gariepy, Desmarais-Azure, Desmarais-St-Germain) turn up southwest of the Qu'Appelle Valley across the U.S. border in present-day Montana. Just over a decade before the movement of this generation south, Montana had twice deported Métis, first in the spring of 1875 and again in the summer of 1879, when General Nelson Miles forcefully sent the Métis across the border.[55] Therefore, Montana, much as Métis territories northeast, did not welcome Métis territorial claims sympathetically. Following bison herds south into North Dakota or Montana and trading products arising from the hunt had been a common Métis practice for generations, as Macdougall and St-Onge demonstrate.[56] In fact, hundreds of Métis living along the Milk River about sixty kilometres south of the Cypress Hills (in present-day Saskatchewan) were born and raised in what became the United States. On 6 August 1880, Louis Riel sent a petition to the same General Miles, signed by sixty-three Métis men requesting the creation of a reservation for the Métis, along with other social and political rights. The document, signed by some Brabant Métis descendants with the Gariépy and Azure patronyms, made the following request:

> We ask the government to set apart a portion of land as a special reservation for the halfbreeds, as, scattered amongst other settlers, it becomes a very difficult matter for us to make a living and owing to our present limited means and want of experience in economy, we cannot compete with the majority of our fellow countrymen.
>
> Our want of legal knowledge has also been a stumbling block in our way, as often defrauded by tricky men, we have again been as individuals put to expense in the law courts uselessly, and this alone has rendered us often unable to remain more than four or five years at a time in our place without becoming completely impoverished.[57]

It took nearly four decades after the petition for a reservation to be created, and in the meantime, all of the Brabant Métis families in question are recorded in towns or settlements that either are on an Indian reservation (Blackfeet Reservation), are within ten kilometres of an Indian reservation (Fort Belknap Reservation), or would become part of an Indian reservation (Rocky Boy's Reservation).[58]

The fourth and final generation that I consider here mostly straddles the last decade of the nineteenth century and the first two decades of the twentieth century and represents an additional 149 descendants of the original Brabant-L'Hirondelle union (circa 1820 or so). This generation was born well after the Canadian state's post-Confederation Indian policy began to take full effect, including through the confinement of First Nations people onto reserves. Despite repeated attempts by the Iron Alliance, individual First Nation bands, and Métis leaders to have the government recognize

Métis land claims through treaties, the government refused, opting instead to implement a Métis scrip system.[59] In this context, government policy tore at the fabric of Métis kinship relations, as most Métis ended up landless outside the parameters of the numbered treaties and the Indian Act.

This generation of Brabant Métis born in Métis communities on the northern plains followed many of the same economic, social, and cultural patterns on display among previous generations, though the Canada-U.S. border notably enforced new forms of identification among the Métis as the nineteenth century ended. Once again, I take Macdougall and St-Onge's guidance: "To see the Métis as historical actors, we need to erase the border and understand the contexts of treaty making, economic colonialism, and the military occupation of the northern Plains by emergent nation-states."[60] Besides the literal occupation of Indigenous lands by an influx of white settlers after the Métis Resistance at Batoche in 1885, the materiality of the border had a lasting impact on the kinscapes that had been maintained by Métis peoples for up to five generations. Despite the deployment of new border surveillance, the Métis nonetheless maintained certain aspects of their *wahkootowin*.

Those Brabant Métis descendants who stayed across the border in the United States were most often either enrolled as "Indians" or enfranchised as white citizens.[61] For instance, the Sansregret family, who lived on the Blackfeet Reservation and in communities south of the reservation, ultimately became enrolled citizens of the Rocky Boy's Reservation when it was created in 1916. A town in Rocky Boy's is, furthermore, named for the Azure family, who are direct descendants of the original Brabant Métis family in Red River and were enrolled early in the reservation's history. In another example, the Desmarais family enrolled as members of the Little Shell Tribe of Chippewa Indians of Montana, which, after fraudulent dealings on the part of the U.S. government in the 1880s, is still waiting for federal recognition.[62] Little Shell members were originally located in and around Turtle Mountain and Pembina in North Dakota but moved west after government officials showed no interest in negotiating a treaty in good faith.[63] Besides those who became enrolled Indians, the majority of Brabant Métis in Montana who were enfranchised appear to have upheld the principles of *wahkootowin* through intermarriage, though the technologies enforced through the Canada-U.S. border and at the boundary of the Indian Reservation continued to present a disruption to Métis mobility and independence. Despite these at times violent disruptions, the Brabant Métis continued to travel across the international border to fulfill their responsibilities under *wahkootowin*, like the thousands of Métis people living in the United States today.

Before this brief interlude through Métis territories across the northern plains, I began with a discussion of Augustin Brabant (born 1792), my direct ancestor Sylvestre's older brother, who, after signing a work contract, found himself at the centre of the fur trade at the Red River Settlement. Here he married a first-generation Métis woman, Marguerite (or Geneviève) L'Hirondelle, and settled in the Red River Settlement. Before I conducted my genealogy in 2017, I had never heard of either Sylvestre or Augustin Brabant: it was only by doing research for the present study that I uncovered any of the Brabant line past my maternal grandfather at all. From there I discovered, by accident, that Augustin signed a contract as a *voyageur*, which is what led me to his time in and around Red River. Of course, it is precisely this type of tenuous connection—my great-great-great-great-great-grandfather Sylvestre's brother Augustin had Métis children—that has led people on the forums to claim a distant, *lateral* relation to people like Louis Riel or Joseph Arcand, a "fact" that is then mobilized to self-identify as Indigenous today. As Nash has explained, relatedness defined only as genealogical links "exclude[s] the flexible, elastic, and practiced nature of familial relatedness and kinship."[64] It also, as Doerfler, Palmater, and Barker have argued previously, undermines Indigenous political sovereignty through the continued insistence on the racialization of Indigenous polities.

In contrast to Joseph's trajectory out west, Sylvestre Brabant's branch of the family tree was well integrated into the fabric of French-Canadian society. He was married in 1815 to a French-Canadian woman in Rigaud, about sixty kilometres west of Montreal, and the couple became some of the first French-Canadian settlers in L'Orignal (Ontario), forty kilometres upstream (west) on the Ottawa River, sometime mid-century. All of Sylvestre and Rose-de-Lima Legault's four children were married in L'Orignal between 1843 and 1858 and worked as farmers and labourers in the growing settlement. The two eldest children received a dispensation from church authorities, because they both married second cousins, who also happened to be siblings (Sylvestre's niece's children). My direct ancestor, Adolphe Brabant (born 1831 in Rigaud), married Delphine Labonté, whose French-Canadian family originated downstream in Laval, north of Montreal. They had one child, Théodule-Ferdinand-Xavier, around 1860. My maternal grandfather, Phillias, was born in the 1890s across the Ottawa River from L'Orignal in Grenville, Quebec, where his parents, Théodule and Élovie Quesnel, were married in 1889. They were farmers who, along with their two children, followed the railway west and settled in Hanmer (Ontario), just outside of Sudbury, joining an increasing number of French-Canadian settlers to the region who were promised land by the Government of Ontario. Both Phillias and his one sibling, sister Bernadette, were married in Hanmer in the 1920s.

This brief exposé of four generations of Brabant history illustrates the specific ways in which the lives of Sylvestre Brabant and his French-Canadian settler descendants diverged significantly from those of Augustin and his Métis descendants. The first generation of Brabant Métis were born in the immediate aftermath of the Pemmican Wars and the Battle of Seven Oaks—when most historians consider the Métis to have first articulated a clear vision of themselves as a distinct people in and around the Red River Valley.[65] The second generation were raised as buffalo hunters, farmers, and traders who were key nodes in the greater network of Métis settlements and sites in the Lake Winnipeg watershed. They were present during the Métis Resistance of 1870 and continued to press settler governments for Métis land rights as an Indigenous people. The third generation maintained their social obligations throughout the watershed. Facing intense white settler pressure in the region, this generation left traces in a number of petitions, letters, and other documents pressing the nascent Government of Canada to live up to its promises to Indigenous peoples. As those appeals led nowhere and settler violence against the Métis and other Indigenous peoples in the northern plains intensified, some of the Brabant Métis and their kin participated in the Métis Resistance of 1885. The devastating aftermath of that conflict, combined with the militarization of settler states and the violence of white settlers in the region, led many to seek refuge farther afield. Faced with a settler colonial logic that refused to recognize Métis demands for land

and treaties, many Métis struggled to maintain their kinship relations—some entered treaty as Indians in the United States and Canada, others opted for scrip in Canada, while others also maintained *wahkootowin* in the northern plains without any formal recognition as Indigenous people.

It is clear that any effort to indigenize the thousands of Brabant family members who have no connection to the Brabant Métis—except a generations-old *lateral* one—would resemble the efforts to indigenize all non-Métis Arcand and Riel individuals on the forums today. Kinship as practice stands in stark opposition to the multiple uses of descent on the forums. As Nash explains, "Thinking of relatedness as a practice in which those who count as close family . . . depend on the ongoing practice of kinship, through which a range of family forms are continuously enacted, stands in contrast to a strictly genealogical account of who is related to whom in the past and in the present."[66] One element of the practice of *wahkootowin* that became evident in reading about the Brabant Métis was their continued effort to maintain good relations with their First Nations kin, which is manifested not only in four generations of intermarriage with Cree and Saulteaux people, but also in their sustained presence as witnesses to key events in the lives of other non-Métis Indigenous peoples.

Rob Innes's research illustrates how, despite several generations of living under the effects of the Indian Act, the impacts of residential schools, and the intergenerational trauma produced by the Canadian colonial regime, Métis citizens of Cowessess First Nation—between the Red River Settlement and the settlements near Qu'Appelle in the Qu'Appelle River valley—managed to maintain and even nurture their kinship relations with Plains Cree, Assiniboine, and Saulteaux kin into the twenty-first century. Innes argues that multicultural bands such as Cowessess were common in the region and were held together by Cree-influenced Elder Brother stories that conveyed "traditional law to the people and thus functioned as a legal institution."[67] According to Innes, this legal institution governs people's interactions, particularly as it pertains to kinship patterns, ensuring that *wahkootowin* is at the centre of community life.

In contrast, at no time in the forums did anybody inquiring about a long-ago ancestor or claiming some form of genealogical relatedness with an Indigenous person ever discuss *existing* Indigenous kin. To race shifters, then, genealogical practice is a way to "commune with the dead," to borrow a phrase from Adam Gaudry.[68] Returning to my own family history, it is difficult to tell the extent to which my maternal grandfather (Phillias Brabant) was aware of his Indigenous ancestors in the 1600s. It is possible that he would be aware of his ancestral connection to the Raizenne couple, given that they represent a rather famous example of war captives from New England who were adopted by the Mohawk. The stories that circulated in my mother's familial social milieu about having Indigenous ancestry, though apparently not directly expressed by my grandfather, could be reasonably explained by the well-known nature of Raizenne family history, whether due to their capture at the Deerfield raid or to the eventual influence of many of their children within the Catholic Church.

Phillias and his parents, grandparents, great-grandparents, and great-great-grandparents did not live in (or near) Oka (where the first generation of Raizenne children were raised), nor did they settle in towns in proximity to Indigenous people. Instead, as did tens of thousands of French Canadians at the time, they set off west into Ontario following the signing of the Robinson-Huron Treaty (1850) and the Free Grants and Homestead Act (1868). A notable aspect of the family stories circulating among my Brabant kin is that there was no discussion of any ongoing, sustained relationship with an Indigenous person, let alone any Indigenous kin, nor did any of my Brabant kin practise such relations. To me, that is the most crucial indicator that my Brabant family has absolutely no claim to an Indigenous identity today, except of course, through the practices of descent that I have previously outlined, all of which facilitate the contemporary race-shifting process.

Lateral descent involves mobilizing a long-ago ancestor as the sole basis of one's Indigenous identity, in addition to inventing indigeneity in the past. The practice of *lateral* descent varies, though, in that it entails moving into an "Indigenous" identity on the strength of sharing a family name (patronym) or relationship with an actual Indigenous person. Métis leader Louis Riel—who was executed by the Canadian government in 1885 and remains a much-revered hero among French descendants—is the most common individual reclaimed as the basis for a broad Eastern/Quebec "métis" identity on the forums. At times, Riel, who has no direct descendants, is reclaimed as a direct ancestor to race shifters claiming an "Indigenous" identity, and at other times, he is (wrongly) said to be born in Quebec. Whatever claims are being made on behalf of the Riel name, we are again presented with evidence of the *creative* use of descent to invent indigeneity where it did not exist beforehand.

Through reconstructing the genealogy of one contemporary Riel descendant, I explained how her relationship to Louis Riel is a lateral one, meaning that one must move back to Louis's great-great-grandfather's brother to find a genealogical connection. In fact, through this study I discovered that I count one of Louis Riel's fourth cousins as an ancestor, which is unsurprising given the extent of distant consanguinity in New France. The Riel patronym was not the only Métis name to turn up on the forums, as my discussion of the Arcand Métis demonstrates. In order to contrast the historical experiences of the Arcand Métis and the so-called Quebec métis, I reconstructed the genealogy of four generations of Arcand in the northern plains, starting with the original Arcand man who travelled to the Red River settlement from rural Quebec at the dawn of the nineteenth century. It turns out that the Arcand Métis were key political actors in Métis resistance to the Canadian government and remain a prominent Métis family to this day. Conversely, by and large the Quebec Arcand have no apparent kinship (or other) relationships with living Indigenous peoples; claims to indigeneity rely on a lateral relationship with the original Arcand settlers in the seventeenth century.

In order to illustrate the workings of lateral descent in more detail, I turned to my own genealogy once again. In this case, I reconstructed the genealogy of a Brabant man who travelled to the Red River Settlement at the beginning of the nineteenth century and whose children were among the second generation of Métis children. By juxtaposing four generations of Brabant Métis life on the northern plains with four generations of Quebec Brabant life in western Quebec and east-central Ontario, I illustrate the specificity of Métis existence, particularly through ongoing kinship relations with Prairie-based Indigenous peoples. Many Brabant Métis descendants now reside on reservations in northern Montana and North Dakota (Rocky's Boy and Turtle Mountain Chippewa), which is a far cry from my own Brabant kin, who have no known relationships with living Indigenous peoples.

Some readers might reasonably be wondering how the race-shifting process among French descendants impacts Indigenous peoples. My concern to this point has been to document the mechanics of descent—to expose its inner workings—as a way to explain the precise details of how specific ancestors are being reclaimed, transformed, and reimagined to fit white settler desires. The next part of the book, divided into two chapters, each exploring a specific self-identified Indigenous organization in Quebec, gets at a question that has thus far gone mostly unanswered: How does race shifting impact upon Indigenous self-determination and sovereignty today?

Part Two

RACE SHIFTING AS ANTI-INDIGENOUS POLITICS

Chapter Four

After *Powley*: Anti-Indigenous Activism and Becoming "Métis" in Two Regions of Quebec

Early colonial relations between French settlers and the Innu on the north shore of the St. Lawrence continue to be at the heart of the myth of peaceful coexistence present in Quebec society (and in French Canada). It is along these rugged shores, particularly at Tadoussac near the mouth of the Saguenay River, that Champlain and his associates met the Innu, whom they called "Montagnais" (People of the mountains), on their fateful journey in 1603. Sociologists Pierrot Ross-Tremblay and Nawel Hamidi explain that Innu oral history tells a radically different version of events in the early seventeenth century than the dominant story that promotes the chimera of métissage (see Introduction). The Innu version of events "tends to assert that relations quickly deteriorated after [the alliance in 1603] and that, the more the French population increased, the more relations deteriorated with the Innu. Thus, arithmetic made it less and less necessary for Eurocanadians to respect their word and the alliances of friendship and cohabitation that had been reached. Four hundred years later the oral tradition carries this memory.... The behaviour of newcomers would therefore gradually change from explorers to masters of place and law. Destitution and deceit led to the repression of the Innu."[1] Ross-Tremblay and Hamidi's work contributes to exposing the chimera of métissage as a contemporary narrative that furthers the usurpation of Innu sovereignty and self-determination. That different elements of Quebec society invest so much nationalist energy in believing in the myth of peaceful coexistence is certainly one of the engines propelling race shifting forward.

With its origins in Chicoutimi, at the head of the Saguenay River, the Communauté métisse du Domaine-du-Roy et de la Seigneurie de Mingan (CMDRSM)—created on 4 January 2005—became the first Quebec-based organization to attempt to meet the *Powley* test, in a case it submitted to the Quebec Superior Court in March 2006. The organization's incorporation, and the subsequent creation of the regional "métis" community, was directly tied to white, French-Québécois opposition to the negotiation of a comprehensive land claim in the area between the federal and provincial governments and an organization representing a few of the Innu communities in the region. The opposition came together in the four years immediately prior to the *Powley* decision (from 2000 to 2003), after which time much of the leadership of the anti-Indigenous, white rights movement shifted into a nascent "métis" identity, as I outline throughout this chapter. The CMDRSM's origins in anti-Innu activism are well known in the area.

As a way to expose the specific political machinations of race shifting in these regions, I explain how it emerges as a strategic way to protect and consolidate white settler access to territory and resources. Once again, Circe Sturm's research allows us to consider the role that "extended social contact with other race shifters" plays in encouraging individuals to become "Indigenous" ("métis," in this case). Race shifters, Sturm explains, "required external prompting from someone who could relate to their situation and almost sense their [Indigenous] potential. The social context is crucial: when and how racial shifters learn of their [Indigenous] ancestry matters less than the social process by which it was given greater meaning."[2] The analysis in this chapter provides an in-depth consideration of the social processes that led thousands of otherwise white French descendants to identify as Indigenous in a relatively short period of time and in two delimited geographies. In order to do so, I begin with a brief historical and political overview of the origins of the CMDRSM, before continuing with my analysis of some of its organizational documents.

LA COMMUNAUTÉ MÉTISSE DU DOMAINE-DU-ROY ET DE LA SEIGNEURIE DE MINGAN: THE *POWLEY* DECISION, LAND CLAIM NEGOTIATIONS, AND OPPOSITION TO THE INNU

Since an August 2017 visit to the Saguenay–Lac-Saint-Jean and Côte-Nord regions of Quebec, I have assembled a large archive of thousands of documents related to the principal "métis" organization in these two regions. These documents are almost all related to the *Corneau* case, which dates back to 2006. The case originally involved one defendant, Ghislain Corneau, whom the provincial government ordered in 1999 to take down a hunting camp illegally built on public lands. In March 2006, the CMDRSM submitted his defence against the charges, affirming Corneau's "Aboriginal" rights to hunt, fish, and gather as a "Métis" person (over twenty members of the CMDRSM also eventually joined in the case as plaintiffs). The Quebec Superior Court rejected their claim in 2015, judging that the plaintiffs did not meet the *Powley* test. The case was heard on appeal in May 2017, the first *Powley* case to make it to the appeal stage in Quebec. The Quebec Court of Appeal upheld the lower court decision in July 2018.

Since the *Corneau* case was first submitted to the Quebec Superior Court, Quebec courts have released judgements in nine other cases brought forward by organizations or individuals seeking recognition as Métis under the *Powley* test (*Bolduc* and *Noël* in 2016; *Paul* in 2017; and *Delarosbil*, *Gagnon*, *Vallée*, and *Tremblay* in 2018; and *Marchand* and *Lehoux* in 2019). Courts in Quebec have also ruled against twenty-three other individuals who were members of the CMDRSM in cases joined to the *Corneau* case (*Simard*, *Duchesne*, *A. Lalancette*, *C. Lalancette*, *Perron*, *Lavoie*, *Minier*, *Jean*, *Riverin*, *Gagné*, *Pelletier*, *Corneau (Miville)*, *Corneau (Stéphane)*, *Gobeil*, and *Gagnon* in 2015; *Tremblay*, *Savard*, *Bouchard*, and *Desbiens* in 2016; *Pelletier* in 2017; and *De Launière*, *Gagnon*, and *Tremblay* in 2018) and two other individuals in the preliminary stages of their cases (*Séguin* in 2016; and *Parent* in 2019).

Besides these thirty-five cases in Quebec, at least twelve similar cases have been heard in New Brunswick (*Castonguay* and *Chiasson* in 2002; *Castonguay et al.* and *Faucher* 2003; *Daigle* in 2004; *Chiasson* in 2004;

Castonguay and Faucher in 2006; *Hopper* in 2008; *Brideau and Breau* in 2008; *Vautour* in 2017; *Caissie* and *Castonguay* in 2012) and two in Nova Scotia (*Babin* in 2013 and *Hatfield* in 2015). Notably, none of the forty-nine "Eastern métis" (or "Quebec métis" or "Acadian-métis") court cases heard in these three provinces has managed to pass the *Powley* test.

Even so, in early 2019 there were at least five other *Powley* cases of similar provenance on the dockets in Quebec—and several others waiting in the wings.[3] Because *Corneau* was the first *Powley* case to reach the Quebec Court of Appeal, thousands of documents have been filed in the case. All of the documents that I analyze herein are publicly available, having been submitted as part of the court case. As far as I can tell, some of these documents have twice before been used in scholarly analyses outside of the legal process, but both times in an only limited fashion.[4] I have decided against analyzing the actual court decisions, primarily because I do not think that Canadian jurisprudence is a fair or just gauge on Indigenous identity or Indigenous rights. As Chris Andersen has argued, court decisions are not "objective sources of validation ... somehow free of the racialized/colonial logics that shaped previous official documentation, historical analysis, or even ethnohistory."[5] Instead, I analyze here a series of thirty-one interviews led by anthropologist Denis Gagnon, via a research assistant, with CMDRSM leaders and members that was presented as part of the group's expert testimony in the *Corneau* case. The CMDRSM hired Gagnon—the then Canada Research Chair in Métis Identity—to coordinate research into their existence as a Métis people under the *Powley* criteria. As such, the interviewer was widely recognized as a friendly associate and was welcomed to the organization's annual general meeting in 2007, when he was introduced to the membership. The interview participants include ten of the sixteen original CMDRSM board members, as well as eight additional board members of four "clans" associated with it. Overall, these interviews covered just under twenty-three hours in the summer and fall of 2007.

In order to add context to the analysis, I made extensive use of the interview guide, which was included alongside the interviews. Given the organization's interest in providing evidence for the existence of a historic Métis community, the interviewer stuck closely to the interview guide. At no time in over 400 pages of transcribed interviews did the interviewer critique or otherwise push back at any of the claims brought forward by participants. The interviews focused primarily on self-identification; the distinctions between either local white people and the "métis" or the Innu and the "métis"; and the specific dimensions of regional "métis" identity. For the most part, participants seemed to treat the interview as an opportunity to record their opinions about a range of material related to the emergence of the CMDRSM.

Finally, in addition to the interviews, I have analyzed the twenty-seven ancestral genealogies provided to the court as part of the CMDRSM submission in the *Corneau* case. I have access to the genealogies of all the plaintiffs going back on average twelve generations, or to the arrival of the first French settlers in what they called New France. While a handful of plaintiffs count an ancestor six or seven generations back as the basis of their indigeneity, the large majority rely on one ancestor more than ten generations back (normally in the 1600s) as the only basis for their (recent) claims to indigeneity. The average generational depth for the root ancestors identified by the twenty-seven plaintiffs is 8.6 generations (or to the mid-1700s). Anne Pelta's doctoral research on the CMDRSM bears out lineal descent as the sole basis for belonging to the organization: "The capacity to demonstrate genealogical ties with an Aboriginal ancestor authorizes an individual's inclusion as a member of the CMDRSM.... Blood constitutes the basis for the feeling of solidarity among CMDRSM members."[6] There is some overlap between the interviews and genealogies, as three of the interview participants are included in the archive of genealogies. As a whole, the genealogical profiles allow me to demonstrate further how the use of both lineal and aspirational descent is at work in recent claims to indigeneity in the region—claims that emerge initially to oppose existing Indigenous peoples politically.

Two events were crucial to the race-shifting process in these regions, and to the eventual creation of the CMDRSM. First, public opposition to the land claim negotiations between settler governments and several Innu communities, between 2000 and 2004, provided the context for some of the early social contact among a range of race shifters. Through joining anti-land claim and/or white rights organizations and mobilizing together as opponents of the land claim, several eventual race shifters created lasting social bonds. Second, the *Powley* decision (2003) opened up an avenue for their claim to an Indigenous identity as "Métis," with the express aim of putting an end to the land claim negotiations and accessing Aboriginal rights under section 35 of the Constitution Act, 1982. I begin the analysis with a consideration of the impact of the Supreme Court of Canada's 2003 decision in the two regions.

"Powley Told Us, 'Defend Your Rights'":
The Powley *Decision and the Politics of Race Shifting*

The *Powley* decision played an unmistakable role in the appearance of "Eastern métis" organizations in Quebec and in other provinces in eastern Canada. A quick look at the Statistics Canada data confirms a marked increase in the number of individuals identifying as Métis after *Powley* (the decision was made public in September 2003). For example, after two censuses of flat growth (1996 and 2001), the number of individuals identifying as Métis in Quebec nearly doubled between 2001 and 2006, from 15,850 to 27,985.[7] In his study of the racialization of the Métis in the Canadian census, Andersen foreshadowed the role that state categorization would play in undermining Métis *peoplehood*, noting that "the construction of this population estimate clearly requires a certain level of discursive violence which shears 'Métis' of any national or even historical political roots and supplements these with a simple emphasis on mixed ancestry."[8] The fact that Statistics Canada has so far refused to add to the census a Métis category that clearly distinguishes those identifying with the Métis *people* ensures that the category continues to be used by race shifters eager to self-indigenize.

The largest regional increase in Métis self-identification in Quebec, according to the 2006 census, was found in two census divisions in the Saguenay–Lac-Saint-Jean region (Le Fjord-de-Saguenay and Lac-Saint-Jean-Est), which saw its self-identified Métis population more than double between 2001 and 2006.[9] Another key statistic from the 2006 census involves the overrepresentation of men among those who self-identify as Métis during this period. For instance, in the three primary census agglomerations in the Saguenay–Lac-Saint-Jean region (Saguenay, Alma, and Dolbeau-Mistassini), about 15 percent more men than women identified as Métis in the 2006 census.¹⁰ In contrast, 1 percent more women than men identified as Métis across Canada in 2006. Further, the statistics from the 2016 census continue to bear out the gender discrepancy. For instance, in the same three census agglomerations, 18.7 percent more men than women identify as Métis, even though the population of these regions comprises about 2.1 percent more women.¹¹ The significant gender gap in self-identification, in addition to the discrepancy between regional and national figures, is explained by the regional movement's origins in struggles over hunting and fishing rights and the specific platform it created for dominant displays of masculinity.

Many interview participants confirm that the creation of the CMDRSM in 2005 was directly linked to the possibilities provided by the *Powley* decision.¹² Race shifting, then, must also be read in conjunction with larger social and political trends, including legal ones, that occur outside the actual region in question. For example, a founding board member participant (#4) explained *Powley* in these terms: "*Powley* opened doors, and it closed others. Of course, it provided recognition for the East, now, *Powley* helps us here. *Powley* told us, 'defend your rights, demand them, ok, recognize yourselves as Métis, those who are Métis, defend your rights, demand them!' And that's what we're doing."¹³ A second board member, this time the founding vice-president (and president-chief in 2019), expanded on some of the ideas above: "We quickly understood that [*Powley*] was the way to have your Aboriginal identity recognized, get with it, let's go, things are going by the Métis route, there's no other way to play it, don't try to play another hand, you lose from the outset, that's why we decided to create the [CMDRSM]." These two board members—neither of whom had ever identified as Indigenous prior to *Powley*—expressed the common sentiment that *Powley* provided a legal context favourable to race shifting, which emboldened regional actors to create the CMDRSM in order to lobby for distinct Aboriginal rights to hunting and fishing in a region where such political efforts on behalf of a distinct "métis" people had hitherto not existed.

Another of the founding board members and the "chief" of one of the "métis clans" associated with the CMDRSM was adamant that *Powley* was a turning point in the region: "*Powley* was like lightning in a blue sky, it was, those people, we have to, us Métis should put up a monument to them, it was really *Powley* that started everything. What the 'Ontario Métis Nation' [*sic*] just won is huge, they won [rights] for all of Ontario ... and Quebec is next. It'll happen fast now, we'll also experience the same lightning [here]." Before his sudden transformation into a "métis" leader after *Powley*, this board member was the founder, president, and spokesman for a white rights organization called l'Association pour le droit des blancs (Association for White Rights), which was created in 2002 to oppose land claim negotiations with the Innu. A newspaper article in January of the same year described him as "the first defender of white rights" in the regions.[14] I analyze the organization's role in local politics in the next section.

Interview participants, particularly those involved in organizational governance in a formal capacity, commonly referred to the *Powley* decision as *the* key event that triggered "métis" political mobilization in the region. The founding vice-president also picked up on this narrative thread: "They woke us up in 2003 with *Powley* when they told us: 'Well, self-identify as métis', you know, they didn't say, 'self-identify as Indians or off-reserve Aboriginal or this or that.' They said, 'if you're Aboriginal, you're one of these three categories.' We didn't have much of a choice, they forced our hand, and said, 'identify yourselves.' So, today if you're Aboriginal and you feel Aboriginal, that's my case, well I'm necessarily métis." On an individual note, both of these board members, just like the previous two, also affirm that previous to *Powley*, they had never identified as Indigenous. In this sense, *Powley* not only led to the creation of a political organization but facilitated individual jumps from ancestry to identity.

Participant #11 confirmed the common understanding of the importance of *Powley* in the organization's genesis, explaining how it provided members with the impetus to make use of their Indigenous ancestry: "So, we looked at what happened in the Powley decision, which was in Ontario I think, we were saying that Métis have the same rights as Indians [*sic*], so we went to see what rights we could have because like I explained, we knew we had Indian ancestry but we weren't using it." This participant speaks to the tension present in the interviews between ancestry and identity and also between the individual and community. As we know, *Powley* set out a number of criteria for individuals to be recognized as Métis in order to access Aboriginal rights granted by section 35 of the Constitution Act,

1982. With only a few exceptions, interview participants explained that prior to events in the early 2000s, they simply did not identify as "métis." In fact, the majority of interview participants were not even aware of their Indigenous ancestry prior to undertaking genealogical research on the matter for the purpose of joining the CMDRSM as members. Again, *Powley* provides the legal environment for the mobilization of a long-ago ancestor by French descendants in these regions of Quebec. Whether aware of their ancestry or not prior to the SCC's *Powley* decision, interview participants "used" their ancestry, as the last participant explained, to claim a "métis" identity that mirrored the *Powley* test.

On this note, it is instructive to consider how participants identified themselves socially prior to *Powley* in order to clarify the dynamics of race shifting in the post-*Powley* environment. Evoking my analysis of online genealogy forums in previous chapters, when the founding president was asked about the ancestral basis for his "métis" identity, he explained that "my mother would say that there was Indian [blood] in our family." He later went on to say that one of his ancestors was a "pure" Innu, before explaining that he had *at least* thirty Indigenous root ancestors. Yet, my analysis of his genealogical chart, submitted by the CMDRSM as part of its claim in the *Corneau* case, indicates otherwise. As a matter of fact, the president's chart identifies only one Indigenous root ancestor, not thirty, as he claimed. That single root ancestor is none other than Marie Sylvestre, an Indigenous woman born around 1624, who is used extensively as the sole root ancestor by race shifters claiming a "Métis" identity in Quebec and Ontario, an "Abenaki" identity in New Hampshire, Vermont, and Quebec, and an "Algonquin" identity in Ontario. According to my calculations, Sylvestre has at least 800,000 direct descendants in Canada and the United States, making her the most common root ancestor in the organizational records that I have analyzed (see Table 1). Furthermore, the woman whom he names in the interview as being 100 percent Innu is actually a tenth-generation descendant of Sylvestre, her only Indigenous root ancestor, who was Abenaki, not Innu. The president's initial statement relies on the conventional use of lineal descent ("Indian blood in the family"), but then appears to use a form of aspirational descent to further legitimate his claim: an ancestor (from all accounts, a French-Québécois woman) becomes a "pure-blood" Innu woman in his statement. In addition, one Indigenous ancestor in the 1600s (Marie Sylvestre) becomes thirty root ancestors from the same period.

The president's apparent inability to pinpoint accurately the basis for his Indigenous identity was not unique among interview participants. Participant #12, a regular member, made similarly creative claims about his ancestry, at least based on the genealogy submitted to the court by the CMDRSM. For instance, he answers a question about how long he has known about his indigeneity in the following manner: "I always, I always thought that I was Métis.... [M]y parents always said that my Mom was an Indian, she had, actually, my [Indigenous] origins come from my Mom.... Once in a while they'd tell me about other guys in the family, that they were real Indians, that they lived like Indians.... I've never tried to gain [Indian] status, but that'd probably be easy." The participant's genealogy points to a single Indigenous root ancestor (Françoise Ouechipichinokwe) married to Frenchman Nicolas Pelletier in 1677, 330 years before the interview. In spite of his air of confidence, the participant's genealogy indicates that he is *at least* eight generations away from Indian status under the Indian Act (or about 250 years), a fact that he imaginatively glossed over in this interview. In this case, the participant appears to *indigenize* his mother, as she retroactively becomes Indigenous on the strength of an Indigenous ancestor born in the mid-to-late 1600s. Having secured his mother as Indigenous, the participant is able to claim a "métis" identity, in following the normative blood-based equation used by participants (Indian parent + white parent = métis child), an equation that openly opposes Métis peoplehood as defined in previous chapters.

Along these same lines, participant #2, the defendant in the court case, provided a partial explanation of his origins that seems to support his current claims to an Aboriginal identity as "métis": "My father would say, 'we have Indian ancestry.' . . . [I]t took me three years to find my Indians [*sauvages*], so it was long, it was a long time. . . . I said, 'I have to find the Indian [blood] and then I'll go get my cards.'" As the Quebec Superior Court decision in the case makes clear, despite knowing about his limited Indigenous ancestry from childhood, the defendant only started to identify as Indigenous after he was charged with a hunting-related offence in

1999. He then joined an Alliance autochtone du Québec (AAQ) local, for which he claimed to be a non-status Indian on the strength of an Innu ancestor born in nearby Charlevoix around 1785. It was only after the AAQ refused to defend him in court that Corneau began to identify as "métis" and joined the CMDRSM, which agreed to finance his legal defence. At six generations back, this Innu woman represented the earliest root ancestor among the twenty-seven genealogies presented as part of the CMDRSM's submission to the court.

Notwithstanding his Indigenous ancestry dating back to one Indigenous woman born over two centuries ago, participant #2 discusses—openly, and throughout his interview—how *Powley* led him to identify as "métis." As one of only two interviewees (out of thirty-one) who identified as Indigenous in some manner prior to *Powley*, his turn to a "métis" identity post-*Powley* is particularly notable. In the three cases of interview participants for whom I have ancestral genealogies to corroborate their ancestry and/or identity claims, each one credits the *Powley* decision for their definitive move to a "métis" identity.

Still other participants discussed their ancestry without explicitly referring to the *Powley* decision. In all cases, genealogical research was the primary means through which they sought to confirm their supposed indigeneity. For instance, in answering the question about how long she had known about her indigeneity, participant #6 explained the central role that genealogy played in her identification of Indigenous ancestor(s) and ultimately of becoming "Indigenous": "Well, no, we never talked about it [growing up], and there was no term associated with this state, to say, 'well, I'm of métis ancestry.' We knew we had [Indian] blood, but to what extent or degree... I'd say that it has been a year-and-a-half, maybe two years since we've known more on a genealogical level." Participant #16, another founding board member, confirmed participant #6's statement about the recent vintage of "métis" claims in the area: "We use the word Métis more and more I'd say. But it's a word we've used for, what, 2 or 3 years, because before it was Indian [*sauvage*], there was no distinction, there were no métis and Aboriginal, we never identified as Aboriginal... we never said that we were Métis, it wasn't a word that existed in the Saguenay vocabulary, in any case I never heard it, they would say that people had Indian [blood] in them."

Participant #29, a political adviser for the largest clan associated with the CMDRSM, also argued that prior to *Powley*, nobody in the region self-identified as "métis": "We didn't even know the term Métis [before *Powley*], well, we knew it, but only in terms of the mixing of blood, we didn't know it through culture." The clear consensus among interview participants was that the term "métis" was never used in the region prior to *Powley*.

Remarkably, almost all interview participants further justified their recent Indigenous identity claims by arguing that the "métis" represented the large majority of the regional (or, at times, provincial) population. The numbers ranged: participant #11 stated that a minimum of 50 to 60 percent of the regional population was "métis," while the president stated that he "sincerely thinks that there are 300,000 Métis [in the region]," which was equivalent to about 85 percent of the regional population at the time. About half of the respondents used a figure closer to 80 percent to quantify the regional "métis" population, placing it well over 250,000 people, even though at the time of the interviews the CMDRSM represented no more than 4,000 people. To put this figure into context, in the 2006 Canadian census, 108,425 people in Quebec identified as Aboriginal (i.e., First Nation, Métis, or Inuit). If 80 percent of the population of the two regions at the time (total population about 350,000) claimed to be "Métis" (Aboriginal), the overall Aboriginal population of Quebec would have been nearly tripled.[15] In that scenario, First Nation and Inuit people would have represented only about 20 percent of the Aboriginal population of Quebec, down from about 75 percent at the time. Notably, none of the participants who estimated hundreds of thousands of regional "métis" people explained why only a small fraction of them—anywhere from 1 to 2 percent—ultimately joined the CMDRSM.

Several other interviewees provided sweeping rhetorical statements about *all* of the regional population being "métis." For instance, participant #10, a regular member, was adamant that all local people were Indigenous: "Whether you like it or not, everybody in Saguenay-Lac-St-Jean is Métis one way or the other. If somebody says that they're not Métis and he has a very dark skin tone, and you know, he lives near a lake or something like that, there's something going on." While participant #10 focused on skin tone and living in the woods as the basis for one's indigeneity, participant #27, a vice-president of one's of the CMDRSM's clans, focused on one's citizenship status: "Well, in Quebec there are about 4,110,000 [French descendants], but in the overall population only those who still have their immigration certificates in their pockets are not Métis, that's about it. So, the movement for [Métis] recognition has huge potential." Unlocking this potential required a great deal of social activism and mobilization in the region. While *Powley* was the main reason provided by participants for re-signifying ancestry as identity, key CMDRSM board members nonetheless played a crucial role in the race-shifting process. The interviews confirm that race shifters in the region "required external prompting from someone who could relate to their situation and almost sense their [Indigenous] potential."[16]

In fact, six separate participants identified the same founding board member as having introduced them to the *Powley* decision and encouraged them to explore their Indigenous ancestry in order to claim an Indigenous identity to oppose Innu land claims. That same board member—who, according to his own interview, was an active member of one of the anti-land claim organizations that I discuss in the next section—chaired the CMDRSM's membership committee at the time of the interviews. He became a household name in francophone Quebec when a video of him testifying at a provincial government commission on secularism in 2014 went viral.[17] In the video, both he and his wife (a fellow founding member of the CMDRSM) testify about the threats posed by Muslims to Quebec society. She started their joint presentation off by sharing in cringe-worthy detail their visit to a mosque in Morocco: "There were men on all fours on the ground, I mean, what are they doing? And the guide said, 'They're praying.' C'mon, I said, praying on the ground on all fours ... I couldn't believe it. I got back on the bus, and said, 'What the hell?' Praying on all fours on a rug." Her mocking tone reflected her disgust with what she had witnessed.

He picked up where his wife left off at the hearing by briefly complaining about the presence of the call to prayer on a visit to Istanbul, before raising the familiar spectre of anti-blackness: "About twenty years ago I would walk around alone on the streets of Montreal and I was safe ... but not anymore, because street gangs have taken over." The couple's contribution to the commission was widely derided in the media, but when he was interviewed by a sympathetic *La Presse* over two months later he did not back down, even using his "métis" identity as cover for his anti-immigrant position: "I'm Métis and have been fighting for almost twenty years to get my rights recognized. I don't understand that an immigrant who just landed here has more rights than me. It doesn't make sense."[18] In fact, by his own admission in his 2007 interview, the first time that he identified as "métis" or Aboriginal was in his 2006 tax filing, less than eight years before his interview with *La Presse*.

This board member's by-now-infamous entry into the public domain points to some of the more disturbing intersections of white settler colonial, anti-black, and Islamophobic discourses at play in the region. The specific way that he mobilizes his supposed Indigenous identity—while also exaggerating its scope—to argue against an imagined immigrant threat to his "rights," illustrates how claims to a "métis" identity in the region are used for much more than opposition to the Innu. As chair of the membership committee, he led the CMDRSM's recruitment efforts in the first few years of its existence, when the organization went from an initial seven members in January 2005 to 3,354 members by 20 October 2007. At the 2007 annual assembly, he reported that only 15 percent of these members had submitted proof of their Indigenous ancestry, which means that 85 percent of members had simply signed a sworn statement affirming their "métis" identity. This continues to be a common practice among the post-*Powley* organizations in Quebec.

For example, one regular member (participant #19) explained, "I made my solemn declaration [that is required of members without documented evidence of Indigenous ancestry] not very long ago, I still don't have my card. So, it was [chair of membership committee] who spoke to me about this group, and I was interested in finding out more. The [CMDRSM] did the research about my family to find out if I have Aboriginal blood." The same member who testified at the government commission about the mosque in Morocco also explained the joint efforts of herself and her husband to recruit new members: "[He] phones people and speaks with them as soon as he sees one [potential member]. He speaks with them, me too, I do the same thing. When I was at my friend's place, I said, 'so, are you going to join or what?' She still doesn't know, yet they, she's younger than me, but still, her parents lived in the woods." In both cases, a potential member joined the organization due to the prompting of CMDRSM officials prior to undertaking any genealogical research and/or providing verification of their ancestry.

Another board member of the largest clan associated with the CMDRSM (participant #29) explained his success at recruiting members in a small town about sixty kilometres southwest of Sept-Îles earlier in 2007: "I arrived there with a lot of knowledge, I had been on the board for two years. I got there and spoke about the 'métis,' I told them what it was all about, and in three days, sixty new members had signed up, bang!" Without a doubt, a stubborn belief that everybody with any Indigenous ancestry—whether through lineal, aspirational, or even lateral descent—was in fact "métis" centrally organized the social processes at work in the CMDRSM's recruitment efforts. The same board member who claimed to have recruited sixty new members in three days explained his prowess in the following manner: "Everybody who comes from the Côte-Nord before 1949 are clearly Aboriginal, 'bing bang,' hey, there are many, all of the towns, all of the towns are 100% métis, wall-to-wall, it's not a big deal, and often in the same town, they're Indian Métis. Yes, it has been, it's a fact." Again, Circe Sturm's work among self-identified Cherokee in the United States provides us with an apt parallel: "Whether established race shifters try to convert family members, friends, or strangers, they approach the world as if it is filled with potential Cherokee."[19] So it was with leaders of the "métis" movement in the Saguenay–Lac-Saint-Jean and Côte-Nord regions of Quebec during this period, where virtually everybody was imagined as the bearer of constitutionally protected Aboriginal rights as a "métis" people.

Claims that a majority of the regional or provincial population were in fact "métis" mobilized the logic of lineal descent, based as it is in strictly blood- (and at times, gene-) based understandings of indigeneity. The majority of participants focused intently on the biological basis of their presumed indigeneity, repeating statements that were common on the genealogy forums: "[insert family member] has Indian blood," "[insert family member] always said we had Indian blood," or "we have Indian ancestry." Focusing on long-ago racial mixing is a useful strategy, since it elevates one's claims to this nascent form of indigeneity and undermines Métis peoplehood based in the northern plains. All the same, the intense focus on blood also challenges the participants' own legal claims about the presence of a historical "métis" community in the two regions, since the *Powley* test clearly states that Indigenous ancestry is itself not enough to meet its criteria. Besides, over 90 percent of the Indigenous ancestors identified in their genealogical sample had no territorial relationship with the regions in question, almost all were non-Innu, and none had any kinship ties with any other, according to the organization's own submission. Moreover, a significant majority of members rely on a single ancestor married in the 1600s as the sole basis for their current claims to indigeneity, including the most common "Indigenous" root ancestor in the CMDRSM genealogies—a French woman, Catherine Lejeune—in a clear manifestation of the practice of aspirational descent.

Notwithstanding the manner in which CMDRSM members undermine their own legal efforts, the Supreme Court of Canada's *Powley* decision paved the way for the self-indigenization of French descendants in the Saguenay–Lac-Saint-Jean and Côte-Nord regions of Quebec. Starting in 2004, thousands of French descendants in the region began their rather quick transformation into "Indigenous" people. As individuals in the region began to identify with the juridical definition of Métis identity provided by the SCC, the *Powley* decision was the single most important dimension pushing people in the region from ancestry to identity, in the terms that Sturm has developed. Notably, none of the thirty-one interviewees— including the CMDRSM's founding president and vice-president (current "chief"), eight other founding board members, four clan "chiefs," and the three co-founders of its women's committee—identified as Métis prior to 2004. Just the same, by the time of the interviews in 2007, all had joined an organization whose two main pillars were support for white rights and opposition to the Innu.

Yet, it was events prior to the *Powley* decision, between 2000 and 2004, that ultimately laid the groundwork for the social process that gave greater meaning to French descendants' claims that a tiny amount of Indigenous ancestral substance made them Indigenous. The next section turns to how regional claims to indigeneity were directly linked to French-descendant opposition to Indigenous peoples' political claims in the region. I consider how "extended social contact with other race shifters," as Sturm has posited, created the context in which otherwise white French descendants were prepared to take the plunge and claim to be "Indigenous" in the immediate aftermath of the *Powley* decision.[20]

"The Métis Community Is the Only Way to Counter the Innu": The Spectre of Whiteness

Following a series of SCC decisions recognizing Aboriginal land title (notably, the *Calder* decision in 1973)—in the aftermath of changes to the Indian Act in 1951 that loosened restrictions on the hiring of legal counsel—Indigenous peoples across Canada sought increasingly to negotiate land claims with the federal government. Also following *Calder*, the Government of Canada changed its negotiation strategy and established the Indian Claims Commission to address the numerous comprehensive land claims on its docket. Shortly thereafter, the Innu and Atikamekw nations came together to create the Conseil Attikamek-Montagnais in order to submit a comprehensive land claim to the Indian Claims Commission in 1979.[21] Negotiations began in 1984, when Innu journalist Bernard Cleary was named chief negotiator. Eventually, the Attikamek dropped out of the negotiations to pursue their own political strategy in 1994, and several Innu communities protested the negotiations by dropping out of the Innu organizations involved in the land claim. By 2000, or the beginning of the period under study here, four Innu communities (Mashteuiatsh, Pessamit, Essipit, and Nutashkuan) created the organization Mamuitun and remained in negotiation with the federal and provincial governments. A framework agreement was released publicly in early 2000, eventually leading to the mobilization of a significant anti–land claim/white rights movement in the two regions in question led primarily by men protesting the potential expansion of Innu harvesting rights. The movement expanded significantly after the release of the agreement-in-principle in May 2002. The framework agreement was called "Approche commune" (Common approach) by the parties, though that term later became associated with the entire land claim negotiation more generally, which is how I use the term throughout this chapter.[22]

Mobilization against the land claim negotiations prior to the *Powley* decision was significant and provided the type of social contact necessary for the creation of the CMDRSM. As the discussion above suggests, opposition to what became known as the Approche commune was (and continues to be) widespread among the Innu as well, for reasons that are quite separate from the French-descendant opposition.[23] I do not intend to enter into the dynamics of that opposition here, since my focus is specifically on the workings of race shifting at the time. Nonetheless, Pierrot Ross-Tremblay and Nawel Hamidi provide a cogent outline of grassroots Innu opposition to the Approche commune: "Given past events and our experience in the negotiations with the Innu, it seems more and more reasonable to doubt both the Crown's ability to honour its promises and the validity of First Peoples' consent to the extinguishment of their own sovereignty founded in an ancient and complex juridical culture. . . . In fact, what is too often relegated to oblivion and appears imperative to mention are the colonial and ethnocentric foundations that permeate all of the Crown's relations with the First Peoples of Canada, including in the territorial negotiations with the Innu in Quebec."[24]

In the interviews, one could observe significant ambivalence in participant claims about (their) whiteness in particular. It was not uncommon for CMDRSM members to equivocate between their former identity as "white" Québécois and their new identity as "Aboriginal métis," through either asserting that their sympathy was with white people or slipping into a discussion of their relative whiteness. As Sturm explains, "Though [race shifters] would prefer to keep the specter of whiteness under wraps, it still manages to emerge in their narratives in a variety of ways."[25] One of the principal ways that whiteness explicitly emerged in the narratives of interview participants was through an extended discussion of their past political collaboration with local white rights organizations. For instance, in the first interview, conducted with the founding president of the CMDRSM, we find out that many individuals who would come to self-identify as "métis" were actively involved in such activist organizations in the two regions:

> The general (white) population agrees with [our approach] and it is not difficult to see why, because the Métis community is the

only way to counter the Innu, who want to control the entire territory. Okay, so, [white people] tried with other organizations, for example, [Fondation] Équité territoriale, which brought together Québécois and some Métis as well, and then, well, they failed because to effectively counter a treaty, you have to be a part of it. To be a part of it, you have to be, you're either the government or you're Aboriginal. [White people] then see that our approach is to stop the treaty process so they're quite happy with that, they then support the organization. We'll be half-allies with white people.

Anne Pelta's own interviews with members of the CMDRSM in 2009 and 2010 corroborate the president's statement. For instance, a board member explained to her how

> Slowly it began to get tense, things became tense in the city and [authorities] were scared that it would turn into a civil disturbance because there were some injuries... they were scared, they were very scared. But then they put the cover back on the pot, so they stopped the [negotiations], they decided to stop [the negotiations] to re-study it all, they formed committees in the [two] regions but they were all garbage committees that led nowhere. While [the negotiations] were stopped, me and [Pierre] said, 'shit, let's stop the train, we have to get on now.' Do you get it? We have to get on the train, how can we get on the train legally, without being thrown off? So, that's when we started to do research on the Métis and those things.[26]

The violence that this board member seems to describe—but fails to name explicitly—mostly involved physical attacks perpetrated against Innu-identified individuals in towns across the two regions.

Clearly, in order to understand race shifting in these specific regions of Quebec, one must fully consider the political context that led to it. The fact that many previously white Québécois individuals shifted to a "métis" identity after *Powley* is only one part of the story. For the most part, the few scholars who have studied the emergence of the CMDRSM have avoided explicitly discussing the overlap between the leaders of the anti-Innu/white rights mobilization and its eventual founders, despite the abundance of public documents plainly illustrating these connections. Even so, philosopher Dominique Leydet has described the "hostile reactions" that the framework agreement brought about among French-Québécois people in the region: "Their mobilization resulted in the formation of activist organizations, in at times virulent public statements and debates in local and provincial media, as well as in protests by some elected officials."[27] Anti-Innu sentiment in the region was by no means a new phenomenon, as I explore further in the next section, but its renewed intensity during this period was noteworthy.[28]

The interviews illustrate that in the period leading up to the creation of the CMDRSM in January 2005, many eventual race shifters were in extended contact with one another through organizing with (fellow) white French-Québécois people against Innu land claims. This section considers one of the legacies of the CMDRSM to be the consolidation of white opposition to comprehensive land claims negotiations in the region.[29] The eventual emergence of whiteness in participant narratives is anticipated by Sturm's work: "Race continues to haunt their narratives of indigenous reclamation in a variety of ways. Both implicitly and explicitly, race-shifters define their [indigeneity] in terms of whiteness, and they do so to an extent that makes movement between the two [whiteness and indigeneity] possible."[30] The CMDRSM president's previous statement in support of the white population betrays his own involvement in one of the main anti–land claim/anti-Innu organizations at the time as a white Québécois person. The interviews are telling in that they expose the extent to which former leaders of the anti–land claim/white rights movement in the region became leaders of the nascent "métis" rights movement. In reviewing the interviews, it becomes clear that the strategy to oppose Innu land rights through becoming "Indigenous"—espoused previously by the founding president—had been embraced by the organization's membership.

To return to the mobilization of anti-Indigenous hostility in the regions at the time, the organization Fondation équité territoriale was one of three principal anti–land claim organizations that formed in the aftermath of the release of the framework agreement in 2000. In his statement above, the CMDRSM's president used the shared opposition to the Innu by local white and "métis" people as evidence of their wider social bond. In their new identity as an "Aboriginal" people, these "métis" were able to intervene rather directly in the land claim negotiations—a form of opposition not available to the white community. In his narration of events, the Innu are all-powerful, bringing the majority-white population to its knees. Of course, as is common in mobilizations against Indigenous land claims and rights in the rest of Canada, the scope of opponents' claims about Indigenous rights is inevitably exaggerated.

Anthropologist Paul Charest, who worked alongside Innu negotiators for more than a decade and grew up in the region, has been razor sharp in his criticism of the three anti–land claim/white rights organizations that emerged between 2002 and 2004. He lays much of the blame for the increase in social tension, including a discernible rise in physical attacks against Innu youth in local cities, squarely at the feet of these organizations as well as several local media outlets that fanned the flames of discontent. Charest goes so far as to say that the three organizations were likely spreading "deliberate misinformation meant to bring as many people as possible against the [negotiations]."[31] Earlier in his study, he made an apt historical comparison: "We weren't far from a localized collective paranoia, stemming from heated rhetoric that claimed the Indians wanted to seize the territory and expel the Québécois with the complicity of the Quebec government. A feeling of anxiety, even of collective fear took over a part of the population. One could even imagine being back in the early days of [New France], what with the great fear of the 'savage Iroquois.'"[32] In a study of regional media coverage a decade later, Charest identifies only one media article in 2005 that openly questioned the existence of the new regional "métis" community: "Only one discordant note in the concert of approval: Innu Senator [and former Mashteuiatsch chief] Aurélien Gill questioned the existence of the métis, which led to a spanking [in the media] by CMDRSM leaders."[33] As I explore further in this section, interview participants— including some who were leaders and/or founders of local anti–land claim/ white rights organizations—openly promoted several key rhetorical devices used in regional opposition to the Innu, including in media coverage.

A second founding board member (participant #11) specifically discussed his involvement in Fondation équité territoriale as directly linked to the anger in the region at what he explained as "white people giving the land to the Indians." In particular, he outlined the degree of opposition in the region in stark terms: "When we spoke about that, about the Approche commune at the start, everybody was pissed, and we were scared and we wanted to kill everything that had to do with Indians." From there, he links the creation of the CMDRSM, and his own coming out as métis, to government betrayal: "Those people who betrayed us, who sold us out, I will never have anything to do with people like that again, that's why I call them white people now. I don't consider myself white anymore, because those people betrayed us." Earlier in the interview, the slippage between his previous identity as white Québécois and his newly embraced identity as "métis" was clear: "I consider myself less white than I did before [the Approche commune], because they betrayed us, in my opinion, they're Judas. . . . [T]hose people are supposed to be there to represent us, to defend our rights." Research participants outlined the dynamics of race shifting in clear, unambiguous terms: they traded their previous white, Québécois identity in for a more strategic identity in order to oppose territorial negotiations, because in their estimation, settler governments were no longer representing their interests fairly.

The discourse of betrayal was particularly strong in the region in the years following the 2000 announcement. In 2001, participant #5, a founding board member, was one of six local white French-Québécois men to self-publish an edited collection meant to oppose the negotiations on behalf of the French Québécois. At no point in the book—entitled *Le pays trahi* (A betrayed country)—do any of the authors discuss the existence of a regional "métis" community. In fact, the book self-consciously aims to mobilize the white, French-descendant population against existing Indigenous peoples in the region. The following is an excerpt from the introduction:

> In fact . . . this treaty [Approche commune] is the death knell of *our French-Canadian community* and it marks the starting point of a historic rupture between our two peoples—and of Quebec! It ends up robbing us of our citizenship, of the possibility of making decisions for our collective future, of having a say in our development and natural resources, of planning for better days for our children. . . . I can mull this over in every which way, but I'm unable to accord to

some of us—even if they *were* our Aboriginal brothers and sisters—
the privilege to build their prosperity ($$$) by dispossessing me
of my future.³⁴

Again, the book does not raise the spectre of "métis" rights; in fact, no
local publication before 2005 discussed the existence of a distinct métis
population in the region.³⁵ Regardless, betrayal—in this case, by elected
officials and government bureaucrats in a faraway urban centre—centred
the grievances of a vocal minority of residents who openly opposed Indigenous land rights and self-determination, even in the case of the narrow
parameters developed in the negotiations. The environment of hostility
created by white rights organizers, including at least two of the editors
of *Le pays trahi* who would come to identify as "métis" within a couple
of years, led to the creation of a government commission in the region in
order to review the land claim negotiations.³⁶

In his interview, the founding vice-president also reflected on the social
bonds created between French-Québécois activists and so-called métis
people in their shared mobilization against land claim negotiations: "The
public is supportive as well because the Approche commune created a lot
of worry, there's a lot of worry in the [white] population about the treaty
negotiations... when they see that we oppose its ratification and that we're
organized.... I'm convinced that it, that in their eyes we're doing the right
thing, so that's why they see us in a positive light." For his part, participant
#5, one of the editors of *Le pays trahi*, explicitly connected his embrace
of a "métis" identity with his opposition to the land claim negotiations:
"The Approche commune was definitely the alarm bell, wow, just wait a
minute. Yes, I felt that they were outright denying a part of my past." This
member continued in his explanation of the trigger that led him to mobilize
a "métis" identity for the first time: "You're Québécois, shut your fuckin'
mouth, and speak Chinese if you like, but we don't care. For us, it was like
that. Wait a second there, they were taking the territory, but that's too bad,
we're connected to this land, and now you want to take it away to do God
knows what with it. We're just as linked to the territory here as the Innu
in the area." Interviewees repeatedly linked their eventual identification as
"métis" to their opposition to land claims negotiations.

As another example, participant #9, co-founder of the CMDRSM's women's committee, focused intently on the negotiations in her race-shifting narrative. After admitting that nobody in her family had ever discussed their supposed Indigenous ancestry in her youth, she explained the central role of the land negotiations in her new identification: "Well, since the Aboriginal people, anyways, since the Approche commune, that was the trigger, the feeling that something was being taken from us, that, that, that, that's it, it like angered me, and it was then, yes, that I woke up." Even when the interviewer tried to bring her back on track by focusing on other potential reasons for her self-identification, she insisted, "Sure, sure, but that wasn't the trigger. It was really the Approche commune. . . . [W]hen they started talking about it, then I started to read about it and it really angered me because, anyways, I have river lots with my partner and they were included in the, in the claims, and I said from the beginning, I told myself, 'I'm going to go get my card because I don't want to lose my home.'" We see here the common trope that the Innu were on the cusp of expropriating land and property in the region, leading to certain calamity. Yet, as has been consistently communicated to the regional population since at least the mid-1980s, land claim negotiations have never opened up the possibility of expropriating private property, despite the repeated claims to the contrary by interview participants.[37]

Finally, another founding board member and the lead defendant in the court case (participant #2)—who continues to be the most prominent member of the CMDRSM in the regions—openly discussed the role that the so-called métis community played in local racial politics: "For sure, white people are pleased with us, this is evident because we're going to protect them, and also, we'll be able to chat, um, we won't play both sides. . . . [T]hey're protected." This board member minced no words: the local "métis" population will protect white settler interests over land and resources from the perceived threat(s) posed by the Innu. A wide range of statements expressed by participants confirm that the CMDRSM was founded by active leaders of white rights and anti–land claim organizations in the region, many of whom were concerned with access to the land for hunting purposes.

"Where Did My Rights Go?": Hunting and Fishing in Dispute
As part of their submission to the Quebec Superior Court in the *Corneau* case, the CMDRSM included genealogies for twenty-seven members, primarily hunters, including a few leaders of the organization (i.e., founding board members). These genealogies included thirty-five root ancestors reported to be Indigenous, including the infamous Catherine Lejeune (born 1633), one of the two sisters from early Acadia whose name came up repeatedly on the genealogy forums (see Chapter 2). Lejeune presumably ends up among the ancestors of so many CMDRSM members because several Acadians fled to these two regions to avoid deportation from present-day Nova Scotia in the 1750s, including Marguerite Savoie, Lejeune's great-great-granddaughter and my direct ancestor. Marguerite, her mother, and three siblings trekked across parts of present-day New Brunswick to Prince Edward Island in 1755 after her Acadian father was deported to Georgia by British authorities. They eventually made it by boat to Quebec, but not before two of Marguerite's siblings had died en route. This is but one example of the Acadian migration west into Quebec in the 1750s and 1760s—a phenomenon that has led historical demographers to estimate that Acadian ancestry accounts for, on average, 1 percent of French-Québécois ancestry.

Besides the incredible fact that Lejeune alone represented nearly 40 percent of the CMDRSM root ancestors overall *and that her actual indigeneity has been disproven*, about 65 percent of the root ancestors were born in the 1600s. It appears that lineal and aspirational descent are not just artifacts of the genealogy forums; both forms of re-signifying indigeneity are mobilized in organizational spaces in order to access constitutionally secured Aboriginal rights. Moreover, in considering the founding president's statements about being the "half-allies" of white Québécois people in the region, it seems relevant to repeat that he himself apparently claims a lineal connection to Marie Sylvestre as the sole basis for his move to indigeneity. In the transcript of his interview, he details his actions in the white rights movement prior to shifting to an Indigenous identity with apparent pride. We can see here how descent, in both its lineal and aspirational forms, provides the scaffolding that supports the construction of new "Indigenous" individuals and organizations in the region.

While several of the CMDRSM's founding board members were active members of the Fondation équité territoriale and/or had published anti-land claim tracts before shifting into a new "Indigenous" identity, others were involved in perhaps the most anti-Innu organization in the region at the time: the Association for White Rights (AWR), based in Sept-Îles, nearly 600 kilometres northeast of Chicoutimi.[38] The association was founded in 2002, in the lead-up to the announcement of the agreement-in-principle. Its founder, who eventually became a key founding board member of the CMDRSM, recruited at least 2,000 regional members to the AWR in less than a year.[39] As such, he became a notable representative of regional opposition to the land claim in media reports throughout 2002 and 2003.

André Forbes became especially well known for promoting the idea that the Innu were wresting control of the entire territory from white settlers, contributing to the heated rhetoric about which Charest expressed consternation at the time. After only a few months of concerted action, under his command the AWR amassed over 4,500 signatures for a petition calling for an end of the "secession" of the Côte-Nord region from Quebec.[40] After the signing of the agreement-in-principle in May 2002, Forbes penned an editorial for the daily newspaper *Le Soleil*, in which he argued that the land claim negotiations represented "hateful politics that bring social tension that leads to the situation in Israel."[41] Arianne Loranger-Saindon, whose master's thesis in anthropology outlines the anti-Innu opposition to the land claim negotiations, illustrates that it was common at the time for local residents, including many who were members of white rights/anti–land claim organizations, to compare the situation of the regional white, French-descendant population to that experienced by Palestinians under Israeli occupation or by the Black majority under apartheid in South Africa.[42] Despite this apparent support for the plight of Palestinians under Israeli occupation, the AWR's president nonetheless coined the term "Red Taliban" to refer pejoratively to Indigenous peoples in the region, mobilizing a toxic mix of anti-Indigenous and Islamophobic symbolism.[43] All the same, in his position as the president and spokesperson of the association, he was provided with consistent coverage in several newspapers, where he continued his campaign to mobilize white residents against land claim negotiations that, in his estimation, would transform over a quarter of

Quebec's territory into Innu "property."⁴⁴ Needless to say, he became infamous for stoking anti-Indigenous fires through mobilizing racist imagery, to the point where Charest has called Forbes "the principal leader of the cabal against the agreement-in-principle."⁴⁵

Shortly after his intense turn as the founder and spokesperson of a major white rights organization, he became a founding board member of the CMDRSM, as well as president of one its five "clans," in 2005. He was an outspoken CMDRSM board member for several years before political disagreements led him and other "métis" from the Côte-Nord to create their own organization in 2012. Even though his conduct caught up to him in 2011, when the Liberal Party of Canada dropped him as its candidate in the federal riding of Manicouagan for his racist (particularly anti-Indigenous) statements,⁴⁶ he remains (as of January 2019) a board member of the Association Métis Côte-Nord, which ultimately signed "treaties" with two national organizations advocating for the "Eastern métis": the Métis Federation of Canada (in 2014) and the Council of the First Métis People of Canada (in 2017). He actually became one of the latter organization's three "ambassadors" in 2017, further cementing his reputation as a leader of the "Eastern métis" movement nationally. The transformation of a figure publicly renowned for his particularly incendiary leadership of an anti-Indigenous movement into an "Indigenous" leader in the region might seem to be an extreme example of race shifting. But as I indicated above, interview participants not only slipped back and forth between their previous white identities and their new "Indigenous" ones, as Sturm's work anticipates, but specifically discussed their involvement in white rights/anti–land claim organizing as building the type of social bonds necessary for their political work as "métis." This last dimension of the study—direct and verifiable evidence that white rights activists became prominent race shifters—contrasts with Sturm's findings and with those of other scholars who have been studying self-indigenization movements in the United States and Canada. To bring this point home, anthropologist Mathieu Cook—who conducted the most in-depth study of the anti–land claim movement in the regions—reports that he was unable to find any archival trace for the existence of either the Fondation équité territoriale or the AWR in the regions after the creation of the CMDRSM in January 2005.⁴⁷ As such, Cook's research, and my own, strongly suggests that much of the membership of the two organizations, including that of the most virulently racist white rights organization, followed their leaders and transferred into the CMDRSM.

Throughout the interviews, participants consistently described how their alliance with local white activists had been built on ambient anti-Innu sentiment in the regions, to which future (and current) CMDRSM leaders made significant contributions. At no time in over twenty-three hours of interview time did any of the participants mention how they opposed or resisted anti-Indigenous racism in the region. Instead, they take advantage of and contribute to this form of racism, as in the case of participant #16, a founding board member of the CMDRSM:

> We benefit from [the fact] that public opinion is on our side, people detest Aboriginals because of the Oka Crisis, blocking roads before that, every time that we heard about Indians [sic] they were alcoholics, they were, they were folks who don't pay taxes, they live backwards on their Reserves, so, there's an unfavourable prejudice, there's an unfavourable public opinion of Indians [sic], but us, public opinion is on our side. People clearly make the distinction, there's a wall between the two, there's a universe [between the Innu and the 'métis']... [W]hat they know about us is that we publicly said that, 'we have as many rights as the, we're métis, we're a bit Indian and a bit white, and that's it.' We explained that clearly in public, we never went and did something like a road blockade, so public opinion is very favourable towards us. [White] people see that we are trying to establish equilibrium in the treaty negotiations, this suits white people and, well, we're just like them, you know, they see [sic] us on the radio, they see us in the newspapers, they know us, we shouldn't forget that there was a lot of resistance to the Approche commune around here, there was an uprising against it.... [P]eople were very scared, people with [hunt] camps, are scared that they'll lose their camps, that the Indians will hunt on their lands.

Not only does participant #16 reflect on the tight social bonds between white activists and the so-called métis in the region, but the spectre of whiteness once again emerges, as when he states rather boldly that the "métis" are just like white French-descendant people. The slippage is unsurprising, since the same participant had already explained that prior to *Powley*, or three years before, he had never identified as Indigenous.

His statement also points us to a crucial piece in the puzzle of local race-shifter resistance to the land claim: much of it is tied directly to concerns about access to the territory for hunting and fishing. That hunting and fishing became the flashpoint for white settler resistance to the land claim makes sense given the long history of efforts to prohibit Innu access to land in the region. From 1864 onwards, the Innu were restricted from salmon fishing on the ribbons of rivers that flow into the lower section of the St. Lawrence in their own ancestral territory. Essentially, private clubs had exclusive rights to the rivers and would actively exclude Innu from the fishery. Cook has explained how, with the eventual changes to the Indian Act in 1951, provincial authorities were tasked with policing Innu hunting and fishing, which led to a number of new conflicts. In the 1970s, the Innu, along with the Mi'kmaq across the St. Lawrence, began to mobilize along the rivers of the region to access the salmon fishery, which led to a protracted battle with the local French-descendant population.[48] In an interview in the academic journal *Recherches amérindiennes du Québec*, a lead commissioner at the Quebec Human Rights Commission during the 1970s explained the emergence of what became known as the "salmon war(s)" in Innu territory:

> People decided that it was time to openly defy the law. That's when the conflict erupted—there were even gunshots. At Romaine, a security guard at a private fishing club was sentenced for shooting at Indigenous people. On the Moisie River, two Indigenous people who had been night fishing were found dead in the days that followed. The circumstances were murky, and the Innu immediately suspected an incident with the game wardens. . . . In Natashquan, Antoine Malec, the chief of the community, was night fishing with a friend when the fishing club's manager rammed them at full speed. His own boat was nearly cut in half and he almost lost his life. And these were key moments. In Natashquan, people said, "Enough, that's enough!" and that's when the fight for the recognition of their rights to the river[s] started. In Mingan . . . the chief Philippe Piétacho made a symbolic gesture by placing a fishing net in the river. And that was

in front of everybody. That's when the riot squad arrived. It's what we call the "salmon war."[49]

As the land claim negotiations began in the midst of the so-called salmon wars at the very end of the 1970s, Innu land claims were particularly contentious among local white people. Bernard Cleary, the chief negotiator through part of the 1980s, has written about the tense political climate that existed near the beginning of the land claim negotiations. He quickly realized that opposition to Innu ancestral and territorial rights in the region ran deep and organized a series of public events aimed at raising awareness about the negotiations. In a book that he published on the topic, he outlined several parallel efforts made by other Innu people in the mid-1980s, including a trek across the region to "meet white people once again to explain to them the issues related to the territorial negotiations . . . to try and gain support in the non-Native community."[50] While some of those efforts led to new forms of political solidarity in the region, Cleary, with his experience as chief negotiator in the first five years of land claim negotiations, nonetheless concluded that "several people or groups, especially hunters and sport fishermen . . . are intent on creating myths about this [land claim] negotiation so that the Innu and Atikamekw [who were involved in the negotiations at the time] fail to achieve their social goals."[51] Anthropologist Brieg Capitaine's more recent study of anti-Innu racism on the Côte-Nord confirms some of Cleary's observations from the 1980s. Capitaine interviewed white French-descendant fishermen and government bureaucrats involved in regulating the commercial fishery just a year before the Corneau interviews. In his analysis, he points out that research participants firmly believed that the Innu did not belong in the commercial fishery. According to Capitaine, two principal tropes circulated among his interview participants that supported their position against Innu access to the fishery: that Innu people are inherently lazy, and that the Innu lack a fishing history and tradition.[52] Both tropes support the claim that the commercial fishery in the region is best reserved for white fishermen. It is unsurprising, given the history of opposition to Innu harvesting rights in these two regions, that much of the opposition to the land claim negotiations continued to be organized by hunters and fishermen.

Participant #13, who became a member of the CMDRSM at the urging of one of the recruiters described previously, expressed the common concern with access to land in response to a question about why he had started identifying as "métis":

> A large part of it was the land claim that was coming, we didn't want to lose our rights too. It seems to me that we have just as many rights as [the Innu] to the forest, to our lots, those are our resources. The electricity [produced in the region] also belongs to us, I mean, those are our resources. Why would they give them to only a part of the population that represents, I don't know, no more than 2% of the population. I'm not upset with them, for example, I think they're a people, a [distinct] people, but we're also a people, I want to continue my activities, I want the, the children after us to continue as well.

Overall, interview participants openly discussed the strategic value of identifying as "métis," in terms of both how it positioned them favourably vis-à-vis the white French-descendant population and how it offered them an avenue to obtain expanded hunting and fishing rights. Participant #12, a regular member, explained, "Governments must absolutely take us seriously, it's official, if they don't it's going to explode, you can feel the tension. I'm not a, I mean I'm not violent, but like I said earlier, my rights, if I have any, they're valuable, I want to have them. I always made a living, I always worked and paid taxes, and if today they recognize us, well they're going to have to, or at least don't bug me, if I decide to go out in the woods tomorrow morning, don't come bug me." Besides the fact that he raised the spectre of violence should the so-called métis go unrecognized—a strategy that the president of the AWR used regularly in the media—it is also notable that this interviewee relied on the presence of an Indigenous woman born around 1650 as the sole basis for his own claim to an Indigenous identity. He wrapped up his statement as follows: "There are three or four peoples [*peuples*] here, white people have to live here too, you know." Again, his statement alerts us to the fact that the "métis" movement—whose origins can be traced to the emergence of the region's white rights/anti–land claim movement—has repurposed descent to intervene politically in Indigenous land claims and territorial rights to the advantage of the white French-descendant population.

The Innu Are Métis Too: The Emergence of the "Disappearance Thesis"
The final theme in this section revolves around individual conceptions of local Innu (Indigenous) people, whom many of the participants are (imaginatively) reclaiming as kin and as the basis for their own Indigenous identity. Reading through the interviews, it was difficult to see much of a difference between the type of everyday racist tropes that circulate widely in Canada about Indigenous peoples and those expressed by CMDRSM members and leaders. Participant comments ran the gamut of white settler perspectives on Indigenous peoples, from the ugly and abusive to the ignorant and cold.

One of the most troubling aspects of the interviews is how participants completely ignore historical or contemporary colonial violence as experienced by Indigenous peoples. There is no mention of the extensive civilizing efforts of missionaries in the region, or the legacies of residential schools (there were three in the regions) or the Sixties Scoop that came out of those efforts, nor is there any consideration of the insidious forces that continue to regulate Indigenous life. Instead, participants cast the Innu in a negative light for *choosing* to be "Indians" (under the Indian Act). For example, when asked what differentiates the so-called métis from the Innu, participant #6, co-founder of the CMDRSM's women's committee, stated,

> I think that it's the, the, the choice that their ancestors made to fall under government guardianship... when reserves were created, I think that their way of life or of survival was highly influenced by those decisions, the choices that ancestors on both sides made then, either to let oneself fall under federal jurisdiction or on the other side, they said, 'well, I'm going to get by as a free person'... we had more independence in that manner, in terms of choice, and I also think at the level of cultural transmission, whether it's language or a way of life because, they [Indians] don't know freedom.

The focus on an innate need for independence was a recurring trope in participant claims about *the* distinguishing characteristic of the so-called métis—despite the fact that local French-descendant freedom/independence itself relied on the strict regulation of Innu lifeways, as in the forced relocation of the Innu onto reserves or the complete ban of Innu commercial fishing well into the twentieth century. Nonetheless, in contrast to the so-called métis, the Innu were faulted for their dependence on government or, more generally, on the "system." We can also observe in the previous statement a rather awkward effort to suggest that the métis—keep in mind that this board member had only started identifying as "Indigenous" a year prior to the interview—were more adept at cultural transmission, such as language, than the Innu. On that note, it is worth mentioning that over 10,000 people reported speaking the Innu language in the 2016 census.[53] The very fact that the Innu language is spoken at all is due entirely to the incredible efforts of Innu people to transmit the language through nearly 500 years of contact with European invader-settlers. This board member's Eurocentric, colonial attitude toward Indigenous cultural survival was common among the interviewees, downplaying Indigenous resilience in favour of a form of nationalism that promoted French-descendant efforts to speak French in the face of the dominance of the English language.

In another example, the founding president explained the "métis" need for independence in terms that appeared to compare Indigenous people living on reserves to zoo animals. In the first part of his statement, he imagines reserves as zoos surrounded by fences to keep their charges from escaping: "We're not used to living fenced off in a zoo, where as soon as you hop the fence, well look . . . it's over." While Indigenous people, like the Innu, are used to living caged on a reserve, in his estimation, when they escape they are unable to live a normal life: "Those who are inside are fine, but those who are outside are all being watched, so that's not right, it's not right, it's the wrong way to be." The CMDRSM leader, however, says nothing about the coercive legal basis for the confinement of Indians on reserves. In the common understanding promoted by participants, the entire bureaucratic apparatus regulating the lives of "Indians" acts as evidence of an innate lack of Innu independence. Participant #12 further manifests a normative lack of understanding of federal Indian policy: "The Indians want to be autonomous, that's normal. They've never been autonomous, governments have stuffed their faces with money in order to control them, they weren't even able to control themselves, so they had a warden on the reserves." In order to construct the Innu as a threat to the local white and "métis" population, participants readily doubled down on common ideas about Indigenous peoples as innately dependent and uncivilized, supporting their narrative that the so-called métis are a reasonable party better suited to white society's civilizational norms.

Participant #7, a CMDRSM board member and another co-founder of its women's committee, who compared reserves to "ghettos" and complained that today's Innu were not as "traditional" as the "métis," also took the idea that the "métis" had a natural instinct for freedom—a trait lacking in the Innu—a bit further: "There's a desire for freedom [*liberté*], a desire for independence that we have as Métis that is different than in the reserves. Indians [*sic*] accept the system, you know, they chose to become dependent, they let themselves become dependent of the government on the reserves. They're dependent, and that's what the Métis didn't want to do, we went against the system, we stayed outside the system. . . . They're really dependent in every way, and that's the difference between the reserve and the Métis." The specific discourse outlining the independence-dependence dialectic was quite productive for interview participants, in that it allowed them to solidify "métis" claims to the region at the same time as it undermined Innu claims. By framing "being an Indian" as a *choice* made at the time of the creation of reserves, primarily in the nineteenth century, participants were able to avoid casting a light on both past and current violence that sustains the Indian Act regime (and their ancestors' role in its creation and maintenance). As such, at no time did participants question the legitimacy of the "reserve" as a space of confinement or the role that it played in constituting their very freedom; instead, it marked the boundary of their authentic "Indigenous" selves. The equation—independence + freedom = métis—was repeated over and over again in the interviews, inasmuch as it served to undermine Indigenous self-determination.

As another example, participant #5, who was one of the editors of *Le pays trahi*—the book published as a way to mobilize the local French-Québécois population against the Approche commune—argued that all Innu are in fact "métis":

> What do we tell [the governments]? Even the Innu with whom you are getting ready to sign a treaty, they're also Métis for the most part. Not only are they Métis, but we're also Métis, but we're Métis with our own culture. You recognized them as Indians because you put them [*parqué*] on reserves, and you weren't able to put the others on reserves... and that's typical of the Métis, we don't need a 'band number,' thank you very much, I don't give a shit, that's very typical of the Métis, we don't need that, if we needed it, our ancestors would've gone to live on the reserves.... [O]ur ancestors were right at home here.

Central to the interview narratives of participants is the belief that the Innu, and, presumably, status Indians, acquiesced to British colonial control, a fate that the "métis" smartly chose to evade. The aggressive manner in which participants dismissed colonial violence *and* Indigenous agency ensured that the so-called métis stood out as the most authentic "Indigenous people" in the two regions. The self-serving nature of this argument is evident. Besides casting the Innu as less Indigenous, participants openly shared a narrative that perpetuates colonial violence through erasing the existence of the Innu as a distinct Indigenous people in the region. These insidious efforts are an example of what Sturm calls "symbolic inversion," in that the regional "métis" are now claiming that they are *better* Indigenous people than the Innu, and ultimately, that the Innu no longer exist, in keeping with the origins of the CMDRSM.[54]

The previous statement by participant #5 points to another idea commonly expressed by participants that takes up a key premise of Russel-Aurore Bouchard's work going back two decades. Back in 1995, Bouchard, a regional historian, self-published a book titled *Le Dernier des Montagnais* (The last of the Innu) that popularized what scholars generally refer to as the disappearance thesis (*thèse disparitionniste*).[55] While Bouchard's book received a cascade of negative reviews, including by Innu commentators,[56] a sympathetic Radio-Canada television report on its flagship national news program *Téléjournal* in March 1996 nonetheless legitimized her arguments. Cook explains how the disappearance thesis spread in the region following its mainstream treatment on Radio-Canada, foreshadowing how Bouchard's ideas would be used against the Innu only a few short years later: "The coverage [on *Téléjournal*] was an important moment in the spread of [Bouchard's] thesis [...] the coverage was based on the popular impression that [the Innu] are not true Indians [*sic*] after all. So, if they're not real Indians, why give them ancestral rights?"[57]

In his overview of Bouchard's work, historian Louis-Pascal Rousseau has argued that the disappearance thesis is foundational to Bouchard's later research on the regional "métis" population, work that the CMDRSM relies on extensively in its claims to an Aboriginal identity, even though at no point in *Le Dernier des Montagnais* does she argue that a Métis people distinct from the Innu exist in the region.[58] Essentially, according to Rousseau, Bouchard's theory presents the following order of events: (1) at the beginning of the seventeenth century, there were about 4,000 Innu individuals; (2) by 1671, there were only a few hundred Innu people; (3) to avoid their disappearance, Innu survivors mixed with the "interethnic diaspora" created by individuals of other Indigenous groups, which led to the creation of the "new Innu"; (4) by the beginning of the eighteenth century, about 750 "new Innu" occupied a much smaller range of their previous territory; and (5) to avoid disappearing, the "new Innu" intermarried with white individuals in order to form a "new race of Innu."[59] Bouchard's single-minded focus on purity as the basis for authenticity foretells the supposed demise of the Innu as a distinct political community. Near the end of the book, Bouchard anticipates the central role that her work would play in the opposition to Innu land claims: "A particularly troubling observation that might serve to sharpen the cynicism among Canadians confronted with the latest land claim devised by contemporary Aboriginal leaders, census takers in 1845 already established that the Aboriginal population of Lower Canada was but a Métis 'nation,' as it was hardly possible to find a single pure-blooded Indian."[60]

Bouchard's writing had long served exclusively to promote the interests of the white, French-Canadian population in the Saguenay–Lac-Saint-Jean region. As such, she was one of the most fervent opponents of the land claim negotiations between 2000 and 2004.[61] Her writing began to shift in 2003, when in a brief presented to the government commission tasked with mediating the conflict in the regions—written after the release of the agreement-in-principle but before the *Powley* decision—she included three regional "ethnicities" in her work for the first time: French Canadians, the Innu, and a new category of "Aboriginal French Canadians" (*autochtones canadien-français*). She argued that the latter and French Canadians were the same people, but that the new category of people should nonetheless be considered Aboriginal.[62] But it was only after the *Powley* decision—when Bouchard herself started to identify as "métis"—that she self-published a series of books on the "métis" history of the region. The first three books were published with the support of a $25,000 grant from the City of Saguenay, whose then mayor Jean Tremblay was a visible opponent of the land claim negotiations. As an example, on 31 March 2004—the day that the agreement-in-principle was signed by all three parties—the city flew its flags at half-staff in mourning.

So important was Bouchard's contribution to the CMDRSM that its president praised her at the opening of each of its first two annual general meetings. In November 2005, Tremblay opened the plenary by acknowledging Bouchard's intellectual contributions to the organization. At its second annual general meeting, at the Hotel Le Montagnais's convention hall in central Chicoutimi in October 2006, Tremblay recognized Bouchard's work in a more approving manner: "The chief highlights the titanic work done by Russel Bouchard, our link to the past [*lien de mémoire*], who in sixteen months has written three works that will contribute greatly to establishing the necessary proof for the existence of the historic community, for that community's continuity to today, and for its distinctive métis culture."[63] Tremblay ended on a combative note: "Russel, weapons in hand (her pen and her words) made it a duty to defend the [CMDRSM] in the media against anybody who attacked our credibility and legitimacy. The chief encourages you to buy her books. It's a duty for all Métis to know our history and to share it with our children."[64] It appears that the CMDRSM continues to hold Bouchard's work in high regard: when I visited the organization's headquarters in downtown Chicoutimi (Ville de Saguenay) in August 2017, the administrator pointed me to a bookshelf full of Bouchard's books. She cheerfully encouraged me to buy Bouchard's books as a way to find out the truth about the regional "métis" community.

Another prominent researcher on the origins of the CMDRSM is genealogist Alexandre Alleman. He self-published a short book, *Nomenclature des Métis du Domaine du Roy et la Seigneurie de Mingan*, as a way to support the genealogical work of the CMDRSM.[65] The City of Saguenay subsidized the purchase of the book to the tune of $12,000, as a show of support for the "métis" movement in the region. Alleman's genealogical work started from Bouchard's premise that the Innu no longer existed as a distinct Indigenous people. Accordingly, Alleman argues throughout his book that as of the eighteenth century, there was only one single Indigenous nation present in the territory—none other than the "métis people." Rousseau explains how Alleman transforms his genealogical data to fit his political argument: "Overall, the content of Alleman's repertoire is a list of weddings involving Innu families (considered an integral part of the "métis people" by the genealogist) from [the Innu communities of] Mashteuiatsh and Betsiamites [Pessamit]."[66] In fact, Rousseau points out that about 80 percent of the people in Alleman's "métis" database are in fact Innu (likely with status), while the remaining 20 percent are Innu who married outside either of the two largest reserves. In other words, Alleman transforms present-day Innu people into "métis" people on the basis of blood-based biologics, in following Bouchard's historical narrative. Both Bouchard and Alleman made crucial contributions in the lead-up to the CMDRSM's creation in January 2005.

Given the CMDRSM's efforts to promote Bouchard as the official historian for the organization and the actual embeddedness of her ideas in the local "métis" movement, it follows that the interviewer and participants discussed her work and/or ideas on a number of occasions.

For instance, participant #26 explained his vision of the Innu: "Look, in my opinion, they're as Métis as us, as we are, because there was a time on the Côte-Nord that there were no more Indians [*sic*], they all died from disease. The only ones who survived were the mixed-race people [*gens métissés*].... At the root, we all come from the same gang. It's not complicated, it comes from France. You know, it's, it comes from Europe." Somewhat counterintuitively, the Innu, and by association, the regional "métis," become French descendants, in following Bouchard's biological argument. Clearly, under this bold vision any claims to a distinct Indigenous political community—either by the Innu or by the so-called métis—are at best questionable. After a long statement defending himself against potential charges of racism, participant #27, the vice-president of the largest clan and a member of the CMDRSM's legal committee, repeated the idea that European biological substance saved the Innu: "The Indians would all be dead if there hadn't been any métissage." Not content with this simple biological equation, he subsequently argued that the Innu lacked a cultural and historical consciousness: "It's incredible that, even today, you go to bookstores near Quebec City with antique books, and [Innu people] went by and bought all of the books. They're Indians [sic], it's funny, but it's because they're searching for a history, I think that's what's going on." Besides the fact that this participant does not share how he might have acquired such detailed information about the customer base for several bookstores that are more than 300 kilometres southeast of his residence, it is worth noting that it is the CMDRSM that has been involved in a number of incredible efforts to rewrite regional history to suit its political objectives. Nonetheless, the large majority of interview participants adopted a range of interrelated ideas—that the Innu disappeared in the 1700s, that all Indigenous peoples today are in fact "métis," that the Innu have no historical knowledge about their existence and/or are unable to transmit distinct cultural practices—meant to undermine Innu peoplehood.

Participant #10, a regular member, confidently boasted, "I'm sure that the Indians [sic] all know that we're Métis, sure, sure, of course, it's evident. Maybe not the English, but the French, they know that we're Métis, for sure. Still, I think that there aren't any pure Indians anymore, because the English killed them all in wars and there were epidemics. That's what I think and if there are pure Indians, they should get tested. I would like to see that because there are some that are more Indian than us, that's for sure." What stands out from participant understandings of their so-called métis identity is that they rely on notions of purity that deny Innu identity as a distinct Indigenous *people*. Finally, participant #4, a CMDRSM board member, confirmed to the interviewer that he agreed with Bouchard's arguments, before explaining that "there aren't any more pure Indians [sic], there aren't any more, all of the pure

Indians [*sic*] have died.... I believe [Bouchard's claim] that the Montagnais [Innu] were wiped from the map. I also believe that." As further evidence of the extent of the circulation of Bouchard's ideas in the region, Charest—who was born and grew up in Saguenay–Lac-Saint-Jean—explains that it remains common for people to ask him whether or not today's Innu are related to the same people that the French encountered in the seventeenth century: "The idea that there are no more 'real Indians' in Quebec has been implanted in a segment of the general public that asks no better than to believe it. Thus, sometimes I am asked whether it's true that the Innu of today are the descendants of those encountered by the supposed discoverers of New France."[67] Consequently, to understand the anti-Innu discourse of interview participants, one must return to Bouchard's early work in developing the "disappearance thesis." Of course, in a context in which an active white rights movement developed in the region—and Bouchard was herself one of the key architects of that movement prior to becoming "Indigenous"—denying the existence of the Innu remains a potent political strategy.

Finally, one last dimension of participant claims regarding the Innu is notable for its *absence* from the interviews. After I had carefully waded through hundreds of pages of transcribed interviews, one unmistakable dimension came into view: the participants had no relations, kin-based or otherwise, with Innu in the region. While participants struggled to explain the *cultural* dimensions of their "métis" identities—and when it was discussed, by far the most common response to that question involved a combination of hunting, fishing, and being out in the woods in one's cabin—it became clear that their presumed culture was not based in knowledge of or relations with actual Indigenous peoples. Instead, to participants, being Indigenous was above all about a long-ago blood relation, pure and simple. Yet, as we have seen previously, while blood is often used as a metaphor for family, and the two concepts certainly intersect, there are important distinctions in Indigenous ontologies.

In this chapter, I have explained the genesis of the CMDRSM as the first organization in Quebec to seek legal recognition as a distinct Métis people under the *Powley* test, mainly through an analysis of member interviews from the period. First, in the aftermath of the *Powley* decision, CMDRSM leaders strategically consolidated their anti–land claim, anti-Indigenous, and pro–white rights politics into a new imagining of indigeneity in the region. Participants themselves are quite forthcoming about the belated entry of the "métis" into the regional political fray—a few leaders even suggest that it was the most strategic political avenue available to them as opponents of Innu rights in the region. Nonetheless, through triangulation with available member genealogies we find that both lineal and aspirational descent are crucial to race shifting in the region. Either a long-ago Indigenous ancestor or a long-ago European ancestor who is refashioned as Indigenous serves as the sole basis for an Indigenous identity in the majority of member genealogies.

Second, we find that several leaders and members of the CMDRSM are in fact former leaders of the anti–land claim/anti-Indigenous movement and/or the white rights movement. Many of the eventual founders of the CMDRSM worked closely together building a coalition of French-descendant groups that opposed the Innu on the ground, including in anti–land claim, white rights, hunting rights, and landowner associations. This type of extensive social contact among eventual founders of the CMDRSM laid the groundwork for the race-shifting process in the two regions after *Powley*. Two figures in particular were renowned for promoting violent anti-Innu imagery prior to shifting into a new Indigenous identity after *Powley*, though several CMDRSM members have continued to promote anti-Indigenous and, especially, anti-black/Islamophobic ideologies in the intervening years.

Third, despite bold claims about their own indigeneity, CMDRSM members circulated typical anti-Indigenous sentiment during their interviews. The first common trope involved representing the Innu as less civilized than the so-called métis. Taken together with a belief that the Innu *chose* to live on reserves under the Indian Act and that the "métis" chose to remain free, the self-serving nature of their statements is most apparent. Another popular theme expressed by CMDRSM members involved the argument that the Innu disappeared as a distinct Indigenous people sometime in the early eighteenth century, paving the way for the ascension of the "métis" as the only truly authentic Indigenous people in Innu territory today. In these interviews, race shifters demonstrate how adept they are at situating their claims as on par with—and at times, as superior to—those of the Innu.

My examination of the CMDRSM exposes how creative uses of descent facilitate a race-shifting process that has as its origins an openly white-supremacist movement against Indigenous peoples (and racialized people). The details of the CMDRSM's origins take us far away from the ongoing and at times painstaking efforts that individuals who have been disconnected from their Indigenous kin—through the Indian Act, residential schools, the Sixties Scoop, or today's child welfare and criminal justice policies—undertake to reconnect with their Indigenous kin. What we see in the case of the CMDRSM are efforts to deny the existence of Indigenous peoples as political entities with distinct land-based and kinship-based relations that tie them to a specific territory. The impacts of such an intentional denial, particularly among a group of people who now claim to be Indigenous, are potentially far reaching.

Chapter Five

The Largest Self-Identified "Métis" Organization in Quebec: The Métis Nation of the Rising Sun

In 2006, nine local hunters in the Gaspé Peninsula who were opposed to a Mi'kmaw territorial agreement founded the Communauté métisse de la Gaspésie. The group later merged with several smaller organizations to become the Communauté métisse de la Gaspésie, des Îles-de-la-Madeleine et du Bas-St-Laurent, and is now known primarily as the Métis Nation of the Rising Sun (MNRS), the self-identified métis organization with the largest membership in Quebec (and the second-largest in Canada). It was at its special general membership meeting on 10 September 2016 that the organization adopted its current name.[1] As of 2017, it claims to represent between 16,000 and 20,000 registered members—more than triple the number of members of the next-largest organization in Quebec.[2] I have examined the MNRS's self-representation in some previous work, especially as it pertains to its opposition to Métis self-determination and its use of Native American DNA.[3] What follows is an effort at explaining its origins in the organized opposition to Mi'kmaw land claims in the region.

Similar to the CMDRSM (the third-largest "métis" organization in Quebec by membership in 2019), the MNRS is in court seeking recognition of its members' Aboriginal rights. It had four active court cases on the dockets in 2018: the *Marchand* case, which the MNRS lost in Quebec Superior Court in January 2019; the *Vallée* case, which it lost in Quebec

Superior Court in April 2018; the *Delarosbil* case, which it lost in Quebec Superior Court in December 2018; and the *Parent* case, in which the Quebec Court of Appeal ruled against the MNRS in its request for financial support in March 2019. All four cases involve the arrest of a member of the MNRS for illegally harvesting fish or game or for building a permanent hunting structure on public land, followed by a subsequent attempt to meet the *Powley* test in their defence. The documents that I have assembled come from the *Parent* case, named for Éric Parent, a member of the MNRS who was arrested for overfishing flounder in 2010. As part of the preliminary inquiry, the current president of the organization and the defendant—both founding members of the MNRS—provided testimony to the Crown prosecutor about a range of issues related to the MNRS, including its membership, its origins, and its legal claims to an Aboriginal identity. Both MNRS members were questioned for about five hours (with frequent recesses) by the prosecutor, in the presence of two lawyers working on behalf of the MNRS. The testimony took place on two consecutive days in the middle of October 2016.

In addition to these two transcripts, I have assembled and analyzed a number of public documents and statements produced by the MNRS and/or its leadership in the ten years since its creation in 2006. Among these are meeting minutes and other documents from its website, public statements by the organization's founding president, a few media reports from the time of its creation, and statements by Mi'kmaw stakeholders regarding the ascension of the MNRS in the region. Together, this documentation provides a crucial resource for understanding the rise of one of the most politically significant self-identified métis organization in Canada, at a time when its legal claims to Aboriginal rights are proceeding through the courts.

THE MÉTIS NATION OF THE RISING SUN: THE "MÉTIS" MOVEMENT IN GASPÉSIE

The Gaspé Peninsula is home to the largest (by proportion) self-identified métis population in Quebec. At over 30,000 square kilometres, the peninsula is equal to over 50 percent of the total area of Nova Scotia, or about 20 percent of the total area of New England. According to the 2016 census, the three Mi'kmaw communities in the region had over 5,000 citizens combined, including more than 3,000 living on two reserves—Listuguj and Gesgapegiag—out of a total regional population of just under 130,000.[4] The peninsula includes the administrative region of Gaspésie–Îles-de-la-Madeleine (six census divisions) and the census divisions of Matane and La Matapédia. Overall, about 6,700 people in the eight census divisions on the peninsula identified as Métis in the 2016 census, which represents about 5.2 percent of the region's population.[5] As a comparison, about 3.6 percent of the population (or 12,960 people) of the two regions in the previous chapter self-identified as Métis in 2016.[6]

The number of people self-identifying as Métis between 2011 and 2016 continued to rise precipitously in Gaspésie. For example, four of the top six provincial rates of increase per census subdivision between 2011 and 2016 were in the Gaspésie region.[7] The rates of Métis self-identification in Gaspésie continue to far outstrip those in other regions of Quebec. What's more, within these four specific census subdivisions, 17.1 percent more men self-identified as Métis, a clear parallel with the regions studied in the previous chapter.[8] The MNRS's origins as a hunting association opposed to a Mi'kmaw territorial agreement at least partially explains its sustained appeal to men a decade after its creation. Again, race shifting in Quebec appears to be tied to a process of the consolidation and maintenance of dominant forms of white masculinity.

The two transcripts from the preliminary testimony in the *Parent* case provide a great deal of clarity about the history and politics of this so-called métis organization in Gaspésie. As with the CMDRSM, the MNRS was founded in the immediate aftermath of the Supreme Court of Canada's *Powley* decision. The MNRS was incorporated in June 2006, about eighteen months after the creation of the CMDRSM. Similar to the CMDRSM's genesis, several of the MNRS's founding members were actively involved in a social movement opposed to Indigenous territorial rights prior to publicly declaring their "métis" identity. I have divided the analysis of the MNRS documentation into three sections. First, I examine the organization's origins as a hunting association aimed at putting a stop to a territorial agreement between the Gesgapegiag Mi'kmaw community and the provincial government. Second, I examine the precise ancestral claims made in the two transcripts from the preliminary inquiry and by the MNRS in its member documentation, in order to outline the practices of descent at work in the race-shifting process in the region. Third, I explore how the MNRS mobilized the logic of Native American DNA starting in 2015 in order to make a number of bold territorial claims that oppose Mi'kmaw territorial rights.

"We Stopped the Indians' Project": From Hunting Association to "Métis Nation"

Similar to what transpired in the Saguenay–Lac-Saint-Jean and Côte-Nord regions, the origins of the MNRS are tied directly to regional opposition to Indigenous territorial rights. Back in 1999, the Government of Quebec signed an agreement with the Mi'kmaw community of Gesgapegiag, on the south shore of the Gaspé Peninsula. The agreement centred on the development and creation of a Mi'kmaq-controlled hunting, fishing, and camping *pourvoirie* near the centre of Gaspésie—about sixty kilometres north of Gesgapegiag—that would also include an interpretative centre and hiking and horseback riding trails. A *pourvoirie* is an outfitter that manages a strictly delimited geographical space that is normally leased from the province. The operators turn a profit by charging a fee for access to the territory and for providing services such as accommodation, guiding, meals, and other amenities associated with their mainly hunting and fishing clientele. According to the latest statistics of the provincial association for outfitters—Les pourvoiries du Québec—619 outfitters operated in Quebec in 2008, collectively hosting 471,734 clients.[9] Overall, outfitters provided 3,459 jobs in rural regions in 2008, which explains part of their attractiveness.

Much of the territory in question had been a wildlife reserve until 1991, when it reverted to "unorganized" public land. There are over a dozen privately owned outfitting territories in Gaspésie, and many others in Quebec managed by Indigenous communities, including one operated by the Mi'kmaq. Throughout the negotiation process to establish the *pourvoirie*, the Gesgapegiag negotiators insisted that the project was central to their economic development portfolio, as it would employ about twenty community members.

As the project picked up steam, it began to find opposition among hunting and fishing organizations in the region. Much of that opposition was organized by people who, after the *Powley* decision, would begin to identify as "métis" and claim Aboriginal rights. The actual origins of the MNRS in this local opposition to Mi'kmaw territorial rights became clear only through reading the extensive testimony provided by two of the organization's founding members (one of whom is the long-time president, now "grand chief"). Both men spoke openly about the organization's origins as an association advocating for non-Aboriginal hunting and fishing rights. Although the narratives expressing opposition to Mi'kmaw territorial rights in the region did not speak about the protection of "white rights" in the same stark terms as did CMDRSM's founders, all founding MNRS members nonetheless first met and bonded over their mobilization against Indigenous rights. Anthropologist Fabien Tremblay—who conducted interviews with members of the MNRS's membership in 2007 as part of a project led by anthropologist Denis Gagnon—attests to the organization's genesis in active opposition to negotiations involving Indigenous territorial rights: "It was in a context of tension and opposition to an eventual agreement between the Government of Quebec and the Mi'kmaw community of Gesgapegiag that the Communauté métisse de la Gaspésie (CMG) was founded in 2006. At the start, the CMG only brought together a few dozen Métis people, who for the most part were hunters who fiercely opposed the agreement being negotiated."[10]

In his preliminary testimony in the *Parent* case, retired police officer, long-time MNRS president, and now "grand chief" Benoît Lavoie discussed the organization's origins in some detail. He explained that the MNRS got its unassuming start in a large tent erected on a former wildlife reserve in the Chic-Choc Mountains, just south of Gaspésie National Park. It was there that Raymond Cyr joined his cousin and future founding "chief" Marc Leblanc's hunting party during the moose season in October 2004. Cyr and Leblanc, who had been hunting in the area since 1992, were joined by Lavoie and Éric Parent, who each hunted in adjacent territory, as well as a few other hunters. They all had a habit of meeting in a communal tent every evening during the week-long moose season to discuss the day's hunting. During one of their nightly get-togethers in 2004, the conversation turned to the territorial agreement between the Gesgapegiag Mi'kmaw community and the provincial government, which included the specific territory where the men hunted. As a way to intervene in the negotiations, Cyr suggested that members of the hunting party claim an Aboriginal identity, outlining that all of them likely had long-ago Indigenous ancestry.

Cyr's plan was met with some skepticism at the time, as Lavoie recalled saying: "We've never had rights, only Indians have had rights, us, we don't have any." According to Lavoie, Cyr boldly responded with the following four fateful words: "Read the *Powley* decision." Hunting side by side, season after season, this same group of hunters had nurtured social bonds that would prove useful in the battle ahead. When he was questioned about the role that the *Powley* decision had played in the organization's genesis, Lavoie answered that it was only after Cyr told him to read the *Powley* decision in 2004 that he was able to see a way forward to protect his hunting rights:

> From that point on, it, [Cyr] told me how to spell it, and I went on the internet and I searched for "Powley." Then I read through the entire decision. Afterwards, around this time we were... we had started the Hunting and Fishing Association because the Gesgapegiag Indians [*sic*] wanted to set up an outfitting territory in Baldwin County.... So, they were taking our hunting territories away and ... so, in the research that I conducted, an Aboriginal nation cannot infringe upon the hunting rights of another Aboriginal nation. And we, well we had been hunting there since... 1992, and we hunted next to them, they were our hunting territories.

Similar to the founding president of the CMDRSM in the previous chapter, the current MNRS "grand chief" recounts his discovery—through the *Powley* decision—of a political strategy to oppose Indigenous rights in the region: to become an "Indigenous nation" claiming its own Aboriginal rights.

Another parallel with the CMDRSM is that MNRS founders literally came to know one another in their organized opposition to Indigenous territorial claims. In the case of the MNRS, four of its key founders—all of whom hunted in parts of the proposed outfitting territory—first formed a hunting and fishing association to advocate for their rights as white French descendants. Later in his testimony, Lavoie explained the basis for what would become the "métis" movement in the region:

> We met again in 2005 and we decided... I had begun my genealogical research, we decided to start... to reclaim our rights. Because in *Powley*, they said... the Supreme Court judges said that if we didn't reclaim our rights, we'd lose them forever.... We got incorporated and started the movement. That's how it happened, and that's why Éric Parent is among our founders because he came to these same meetings.... We were all complete strangers, whether it was Éric Parent or [founding president] Marc Leblanc or me. Éric Parent hunted on one side, I was in the middle, and then Marc Leblanc was on the other side.

His recounting of events from more than a decade previous confirms the crucial aspect that social contact played in propelling race shifters forward in their eventual coming out. In this case, a small group of moose hunters organized themselves to oppose a proposed Mi'kmaw-controlled, land-based project.

Finally, near the end of his testimony, Lavoie reiterated the role that *Powley* played in pushing some hunters in the region to identify as Métis, before explaining that "other [court] judgments that we read said that an aboriginal nation cannot take away the rights of another nation, so we said, 'They won't be able to remove us from here even if they proceed with their outfitting project, we'll retain our hunting rights.'" Post–*Powley* decision, local white hunters organized to intervene politically in regional decisions involving access to land. Consolidating their access to hunting territory was crucial to their political movement.

A day after Lavoie's statement, the defendant in the case, Éric Parent, corroborated his testimony, explaining how the plan to claim Aboriginal rights was hatched while out hunting in the fall. The following excerpt includes a back-and-forth exchange between Parent, one of his lawyers (DL1), and the prosecutor (P), during the former's court testimony:

P: Now I'm going to ask you questions that are linked to the organization. You're one of the founders?

PARENT: Yes, I'm the ninth founding member, we were nine when we started.

P: OK, and how did it happen? How did it all start?

PARENT: We met in the woods while hunting... because Marc Leblanc was the president of the métis community—

P: OK.

PARENT: And then there was Raymond Cyr, there was Benoît [Lavoie].

P: [Current president] Benoît Lavoie.

PARENT: We would meet in the woods and we'd talk about all of this: "Hey, I have Indian ancestry on this side" and all of that. "My great grandmother is from Restigouche." Then, Raymond was listening to all of this [and he'd say], "Yes, but there's more to it than this."

P: Approximately what year did this take place?

PARENT: About 2006. 2007. 2009.

P: OK.

PARENT: Around then.

P: When did you create the organization?

DL1: In 2006.

PARENT: We probably created the organization a bit before that.

DL1: OK.

PARENT: It could have been 2005, because... we would talk in the woods when we were hunting, when we'd see each other. Because I hunt there, Benoît is there, and so are the others.

P: Yes, you're close.

PARENT: We're all in the same hunting sector. The entire gang is concentrated in the same sector.

P: I'm going to ask you a question. The reason that you know Benoît Lavoie, for example, is not because he's your neighbour in town?

PARENT: I met Benoît in the woods while hunting.

P: You met him while hunting, right?

PARENT: And I hunted for deer with [MNRS founding president] Marc Leblanc back in 1983, 1984, 1985, 1986 on the Anger River here in Gaspésie.

Parent then began a harrowing deer hunting tale from the 1980s involving him and Leblanc navigating a swelled river while driving in chest waders, as the water flooded into the driver's side through the vehicle's floor. His second defence lawyer—who had hunted in the same area around the same time—recounted his own version of a similar experience. Parent finished the anecdote with a story from his childhood, when he was instructed to sit on a deer that had just been shot by a family member for a photo, only to have the deer stand up and throw him to the ground. In that sense, the courtroom itself, much as the hunting grounds described by Parent, became a site for the construction and maintenance of dominant forms of masculinity. Parent built on Lavoie's previous statements, illustrating how race shifters required social support from fellow race shifters to redefine their identities. Hunting, as a social practice involving extensive male bonding, provided the type of social contact needed in this case. After the long tangent, the discussion returned to the scene in the woods in fall 2005.

P: So, you all met while hunting, and you said, "Listen . . ."

PARENT: Then, we—

P: You spoke about your ancestors.

PARENT: Then, we started saying that we're Métis and all of that and that it's too bad, but we're going to lose our hunting spots because [Gesgapegiag] was on this project to take away the [former] Baldwin [wildlife] reserve from . . . where we all hunted.

In his testimony, Parent was quite clear that the case of local hunters becoming "Indigenous" was directly tied to losing access to a specific hunting territory. However, in actuality, the outfitting project would exclude the hunters only inasmuch as they would lose *free* access to hunt in that specific territory. They would continue to be able to hunt on public lands elsewhere without cost.

We pick up the discussion between the Crown prosecutor (P) and the defendant where it left off above:

P: So, it was the Mi'kmaq who wanted to do this?

PARENT: Yes, they wanted it. For all of the Gaspésiens who already hunted in that area, it was a real kick in the ass, and get lost.

P: OK

PARENT: So, then we were talking about it, and Raymond Cyr said: "Well, yes, we could start our own métis organization [*communauté*], we all have Indian [*sic*] blood and all of that."

P: uhum, uhum

PARENT: So, we started an organization. And then, we opposed the [Gesgapegiag] reserve project, and it worked, it was put on ice, and—

P: Hold on, I want to know more about this story. What happened exactly? What did you . . . because that's quite an exploit, to succeed in stopping—

PARENT: We stopped the Indians' outfitting [*pourvoirie*] project.

P: How did . . . how did you manage to do that?

One of the defendant's lawyers interjected at this point. A brief back-and-forth between the participant's primary lawyer and the Crown prosecutor ensued, before the latter continued his line of questioning: "No, but I'd like to hear more about what happened with the Mi'kmaw project. Now that's—"; the Crown prosecutor was cut off again, and before long, the MNRS's two lawyers, including its long-time lawyer (DL2)—one of its honorary members—volunteered to answer the Crown prosecutor's inquiry on behalf of their client:

> DL1: Yes, well the answer is that [the project] was shelved because these folks opposed it—
>
> DL2: There's a part that I know about, if you like I could share.
>
> DL1: Yes, sure—
>
> DL2: There was a secret hand behind all of this... but they never played it, they couldn't, but there was a hand that included [another] hunting territory.... It was paid for by the government. They had instructions to negotiate, but they weren't. They were only negotiating with the Indians [*sic*]. From that point on, there was... I guess we could call it a revolt, not a physical revolt, but there was a public outcry. This outcry principally involved hunters, since they say that 80-odd percent of the region is Métis, there are lots of Métis people.
>
> P: OK, essentially... yes, I get it.
>
> DL2: And then, we sent letters.
>
> P: OK.
>
> DL2: We sent letters to the federal government, I could produce them for you if you like, advising them that they were dealing with Métis territories... to not... to be careful not to confer rights to [these] territories and that we should be called to the negotiating table before any territorial rights were conferred... and so the effect was to stop the entire thing. All of it, they realized that there would be a physical revolt or there would be—

At this point in counsel's explanation, the defendant's other lawyer interjected and a twenty-minute recess ensued.

The testimony by the two founders reveals a great deal about the MNRS's origins in a struggle over asserting hunting rights for French descendants. Time spent out on the land by a small group of hunters led to the creation of a hunting and fishing association to lobby governments and encourage local residents to oppose the Mi'kmaw territorial project. After one of the hunters became aware of the *Powley* decision, he spread the word to his hunting brethren and together they decided to move from ambiguous knowledge about their Indigenous *ancestry* to an affirmation of an Indigenous *identity* through claims to being "métis." In fact, much like several key members of the CMDRSM from the last chapter, a few of the original members acted as key promoters for the idea of the existence of a "métis" identity in the region, as well as agents of recruitment for the organization.

In his ethnographic study a year after the creation of the MNRS, Tremblay explains the central role that social contact played in the spread of race shifting in the region: "First contact with other members and 'leaders' of the [MNRS] was crucial in the process of identification among the Métis that we interviewed in the region: it revealed the existence of a Gaspésian Métis identity and, especially, it interpellated Gaspésians into claiming their rights as Métis."[11] Tremblay goes on to explain that the majority of his respondents were first approached by existing MNRS members soliciting their membership in the organization before they actually undertook genealogical research into any possible Indigenous ancestry.[12] In this sense, Sturm's observations that race shifters normally "required external prompting from someone who could relate to their situation and almost sense their [Indigenous] potential" certainly appears to be indicative of the type of social process that emerged in the region.[13] What's more, the fact that Quebec is home to the smallest proportion of Indigenous peoples of any Canadian province (2.2 percent in 2016) accords further with Sturm's observation that race shifters "tend to avoid states with a large Native American population."[14] In the case of Quebec, race shifters can reliably depend on general confusion about Indigenous lifeways, including those associated with citizenship and kinship.

The discussion above in court shows that the idea of a conspiracy, involving the Mi'kmaq and government officials, continued to circulate even a decade later, when the second defence lawyer (and honorary MNRS member) discussed it in open court proceedings. This, even though the provincial government in 2007 dispatched a facilitator to the region—to meet with different stakeholders—who eventually recommended shrinking the amount of territory in the agreement by more than 60 percent.[15] Later, in 2008, the government dropped the proposed entry fee for a second time under pressure from the MNRS, the hunting lobby, local municipalities, and opposition politicians. Nonetheless, protests fuelled by misinformation persisted in the region, and the idea of a government- and Mi'kmaq-led conspiracy continues to hold influence today.

As part of his own ethnographic study on the "Eastern métis," anthropologist Emmanuel Michaux interviewed Denis Jean, a local historian long associated with the MNRS, in February 2010. Four years after the creation of the MNRS, and with the Mi'kmaq's outfitter project shelved, the historian promoted a normative white settler perspective that inevitably cast the so-called métis as victims of government and Mi'kmaw aggression, in terms similar to what we saw in the previous chapter. According to Jean, "The Government of Quebec wanted to give a large portion of Gaspésie to the Mi'kmaq to create an outfitting territory. And they would've had to expel, I think . . . 300 Métis hunting families or groups from the territory. So, people thought that this was an injustice. Up until then, the Métis had lived within the system, even though it was unfair and they lived in poverty. But, when things go too far, you have to react, and that's what woke up the Gaspésie Métis. . . . We call it the Baldwin Affair."[16]

Besides the fact that the total proportion of the Gaspé Peninsula under negotiation had originally been around 1.7 percent at most, the overall number of so-called métis hunters who would have had to find another hunting territory was no more than fifteen. I came to this estimate by taking the number of individual hunters in the existing territory reported by the media (estimates ranged between 150 to 500; I chose 300) and multiplying it by the proportion of people identifying as "métis" in the region according to the 2016 census. Of course, in the early to mid-2000s, none of the hunters appear to have identified as "métis" at all, so even identifying fifteen "métis" hunters is an overestimation. Jean's claim of 300 métis *families* or *groups* is an exaggeration of even the high range expressed by the MNRS (500 *individuals*) and assumes that all of the hunters in the territory at the time were "métis." Jean—a prominent member of the MNRS—readily circulated the type of anti-Indigenous narrative that was common in the region at the time, exaggerating the impacts of the project on the so-called métis while spreading rumours about a nefarious plot to subvert local white settler mobility. In another example of the type of academic research that has supported the MNRS, Tremblay, who has been relatively careful in his wholesale recirculation of organizational rhetoric, nonetheless promoted a number of questionable claims. For instance, he argues that negotiations between the provincial government and the Mi'kmaq "constituted a threat to the Métis because they may put into question their access to hunting and fishing territories used by some of their families for generations."[17] As Lavoie explained in his testimony, they had been hunting in the territory that was originally being negotiated for no more than fifteen years by the time of the founding of the MNRS in 2006. In these cases, 1.7 percent of the territory becomes a "large proportion of Gaspésie," fifteen hunters (at most) becomes "300 families or groups," and fifteen years becomes "generations."

Many similarities can also be found in the early statements of the CMDRSM leadership and some of those expressed by the MNRS leadership. For example, the MNRS's founding chief, Marc Leblanc, was active in the media in the immediate aftermath of the organization's creation in 2006, responding in particular to Mi'kmaw claims about how the nature of racism in the region had limited their historical access to land. Leblanc featured prominently in a regional newspaper article on 30 July 2006 that opened with the following sentence: "The Gaspésie Métis Community represents the most important strategy to prevent the community of Gesgapegiag from creating an outfitting territory."[18] The article goes on to explain that the MNRS had about ten members at the time, before quoting Leblanc: "By following the right approach, there might be a way to obtain an injunction against this project (Aboriginal outfitters). We're going to tell the federal government that we have Métis people in Gaspésie and that our territory is currently being stolen. We'll ask the Government of Canada to give us time and the financial means to survey the number of Métis, write the history of the Gaspésie Métis community, and stop the outfitters project."[19] We can see here a striking parallel with the statements of the CMDRSM's founding president—both leaders make it plain that their organization (and "community") was created to put a stop to Indigenous territorial claims. The MNRS was so emboldened by its reading of the *Powley* decision that even with only nine members, it asserted territorial rights that circumvented Mi'kmaw claims.

The overwhelming majority of media reports and online traces (on online hunting and fishing and/or Aboriginal-themed forums) about the "Baldwin Affair" available a decade later represent the dominant white support for the "métis" position against the agreement favourably. In the following statement, titled "Setting the Record Straight"—posted and then circulated on a number of online hunting and fishing forums and on the Nation autochtone du Québec (NAQ) forum that you may remember from Chapters 1 and 2—Leblanc responds to Mi'kmaw concerns about the MNRS's legitimacy as it pertains to Aboriginal rights:

> Now, when it comes to this paragraph, "Several Indigenous communities, including the Mi'kmaq of Gaspésie, don't agree with Métis claims." We're not claiming this territory, it already belongs to us, and has for a very very long time, since we've practiced hunting, fishing, and gathering in a traditional manner for 100 years. We've had camps here for moose hunting for more than seventy years. . . . This is what we call "tradition"!!! And now, when another Aboriginal people asks for this territory in order to create a private outfitter through the ancestral tradition of a reserve-based Aboriginal band, I'm flabbergasted!!! Among people who say that they are civilized, Indigenous law doesn't exist!!![20]

Leblanc, himself a prominent hunting and fishing guide in the region, played a role similar to that of several leaders of the anti-Innu movement, outlined in the last chapter. The MNRS president did not stop with the denial of Mi'kmaw territorial rights, the denunciation of Mi'kmaw ancestral tradition, or the repudiation of Indigenous law. Instead, he went on the attack against the project later in 2006 on a number of online forums:

> As far as [chief of Gesgapegiag Mi'gmaq] goes, he who's offended by our suspicious Métis community, I have this to say: "If 1604 hadn't happened, he wouldn't be of this world, since he himself is Métis." And from the pedestal of his status and the millions [of dollars] that come from the federal government largely through income and sales tax taken from off-reserve Aboriginal people, he should look in a

mirror to see who he really is.... Neither the [MNRS] nor any of its members have been racist towards his community. That's false, he's playing the victim (and politics).[21]

Clearly, Leblanc fanned the flames of discord in the region.

The intense level of disregard for Mi'kmaw life expressed by opponents did not dissuade some Mi'kmaw leaders from jumping into the fray. The chief of Gesgapegiag at the time, John Martin, explained in a regional news report that the project would, in part, aim to decrease moose hunting pressure by managing the number of hunters in the specific territory. In 2005, 102 moose had been killed in the territory of the proposed project— seven by Mi'kmaw hunters, and the remaining ninety-five by non-Mi'kmaw hunters.[22] In addition, the Mi'kmaw spokesperson for the territorial project responded to much of the opposition online in a post on the NAQ forum: "[Many people] claim that 500 hunters use the territory, but according to the numbers we received [from the government], about 150 currently use the territory. Where did these '500 hunters' practice their 'favourite sport' before 1995, when it was a wildlife reserve that banned hunting?" Besides a general concern with the validity of the data circulating online, and in the media, she pointed to the crucial relationships that the Mi'kmaq have with this *specific* territory:

> Quebec is a huge province where Québécois hunters can find other hunting spots while being in their culture (Quebec culture). But Gaspésie is the traditional territory of the Mi'gmaq, we can't do our traditional hunt in the Laurentians (for example) because our culture is based here on our traditional territory. It's here that we've lived for millennia, it's here that we speak our language. Québécois people can travel throughout Quebec, speak their language, and work in an environment that favours their culture, but we don't have the same opportunities. We must stay here, develop here, and work here if we want to preserve our Mi'gmaq history and culture.[23]

The Mi'kmaq, as in this example, spoke out strongly about the importance of developing their relationships with the land in the region even though they faced intense white settler opposition to their project. Finally, the same spokesperson explained how attempts to sever Mi'kmaw relationships with the land and water of Gespe'gewa'gi (Gaspésie) can be directly traced to the appearance of Euro-descendants in the region: "You're afraid of being 'expropriated' and 'displaced' but First Nations have faced this for at least 200 years. Our land was expropriated and we were displaced and contained on Indian reserves. Nobody 'consulted' us and it wasn't our choice. Now, we simply want a sliver of the territory to establish an economic base for our community. . . . Our project is not to 'the detriment of white people,' as many have said. If you look at things from our perspective, you'd see that resource development currently takes place to the detriment of the Mi'kmaq."[24]

Despite the repeated participation of Mi'kmaw leaders in regional deliberation, the MNRS continued its aggressive public campaign against the Mi'kmaq (and other Indigenous peoples) in subsequent years. In October 2007, sixteen months after the organization's creation, it presented a brief to a provincial government commission (the Commission on Accommodation Practices Related to Cultural Differences, or the Bouchard-Taylor Commission) that made several audacious historical claims: "We present this document to you as the only direct descendants of Quebec's First Peoples whose members were not all killed by microbial shock. We stand as witnesses to the errors of Official History, which teach us that there are Métis and Indians while there is only one Indigenous Nation in Quebec."[25] In this case, the "Quebec métis" construct themselves as withstanding biological elimination due to their European lineage, which offered them immunity to disease. Their presentation at the high-profile commission confirmed that the "disappearance thesis," which had first made its controversial entrance onto the public stage across the St. Lawrence River in Innu territory, had now become a cornerstone of the "métis" movement.

The MNRS's statement continued along the same lines as many of the interview participants in the previous chapter by further setting out its logic for being the only authentic Indigenous people in Quebec: "Your creation of reserves, which began in 1831–32, forced only the most miserable among us to live there. . . . [We] refused to die on 'your' reserves. We assert before you and the Québécois descendants that we accepted on our soil that we are not on 'federal' land, but on Québécois 'provincial land.'. . .

We assert that our ancestors refused the reserves and that we remained free due to [our] inhuman efforts. Diseases that came from Europe ... killed the [Indigenous] half of ourselves. Only the descendants mixed with Europeans survived these plagues."[26] The biological racism animating their brief promoted an image of the colonial past as a simple matter of "survival of the fittest." In this case, besides their innately superior European lineage, the "Quebec métis" survived due to their choice to remain free of the Indian Act regime, unlike the "miserable" Indigenous peoples who opted for life on a reserve and, presumably, for the range of remarkably violent policies enacted under it (including, but not limited to, more than a century of child abduction and residential schools).

In fact, for the "Quebec métis," resisting life on reserves—where the majority of Indigenous peoples in Quebec either live or have kinship relations—is a badge of honour that defines their existence as an "Indigenous" people today. Status Indians are constructed as "sell-outs" for having "chosen" to live on reserves and for adopting Indian Act provisions, while the "Quebec métis" are lionized for their resistance to (British) government encroachment and their commitment to freedom. Through it all, the MNRS astonishingly erases the ongoing existence of over 100,000 Inuit, Cree, Innu, Mi'kmaw, Maliseet, Anishinaabeg (Algonquin), Mohawk, Huron-Wendat, Abenaki, and Atikamekw people across more than 1.5 million square kilometres. Eventually, the MNRS's political strategy overrode the government's previous support for the Mi'kmaw project. Once again, a regionally based, new "métis" organization pushed a negotiated agreement to the back burner and fostered anti-Indigenous sentiment and conduct on behalf of the white population.

Lineal and Aspirational Descent in Gaspésie
One of the elements that manifested itself over and over in the preliminary testimony of the MNRS leaders that was not present in the interviews cited in the previous chapter was a detailed discussion of root ancestors. In particular, the "grand chief," the defendant, and/or their lawyers spoke about specific long-ago ancestors on several occasions. In this sense, we are offered a glimpse into how long-ago ancestry is the backbone of the narrative of "métis" identity in the region. Most references to ancestors focused

on Acadian ancestry, which can be explained by Acadian migration to the peninsula after the ethnic cleansing of the Acadians that took place farther east, in present-day Nova Scotia, in the mid-eighteenth century. A local college history instructor, Jean-Marie Thibault, started promoting the idea that 85 to 90 percent of the Gaspésie population was "métis" on the basis of its Acadian ancestry in a July 2006 news report—a month after the creation of the MNRS.[27]

The news report included a statement by Thibault—"I'm Métis myself, as my great-grandmother was a pure Indian"—before paraphrasing his version of the peninsula's history: "The historian explained that at the time of the Acadian Deportation, the young Acadian men who migrated to Gaspésie were between 20 and 25 years old. 'White' women were quite rare after this migratory movement [in the latter half of the eighteenth century], so 'Indian' women were there and took family names that are well known in the region." Thibault went on to opine that more than 75 percent of all communities in Quebec were "métis"—including all First Nation communities—and that the Government of Quebec was unlikely to recognize the Aboriginal rights of métis people in the province "because too many would claim this status."[28] Due in part to the historian's opinion, the figure of 90 percent continues to circulate in the region a decade later; the MNRS even includes the figure on its registration form for new members, no doubt to aid in its recruitment efforts. As in the case discussed in the previous chapter, the MNRS promotes the idea that almost all French-descendant settlers in the region are Indigenous, sensing "their [Indigenous] potential," in Sturm's terms, all the while normalizing its opposition to the Mi'kmaq in the process.

Returning to the testimony from the preliminary inquiry in the *Parent* case, the MNRS's primary lawyer mobilized both lineal and aspirational descent linked to seventeenth-century Acadia in his explanation of the basis for a significant portion of its membership:

It's a man named Membertou who is the [root] ancestor of many members of our community. . . . [H]e was in touch with Poutrincourt and etc., around Port-Royal, and etc., etc. So, I'll give the mandate to [our researcher] to respect the *Powley* criteria through

demonstrating that the historic community started with one of the
Membertou ancestors. We'll put together a clear and precise text
on this character's history.... In some cases, there was another one,
Modakawendo [sic], Acadia Park in Maine knows this person quite
well, but we'll have to hire experts to read the literature in order to
redo the history for Quebec.

In his explanation of the ancestral history of the so-called métis community, the MNRS's lead counsel traces the ancestry of many of its members back to Membertou, the Mi'kmaw grand chief who is frequently evoked as the maternal grandfather of the Lejeune sisters (Catherine and Edmée), as noted in Chapter 2. Of course, this history is purely speculative and involves believing—among other significant leaps of faith—that Membertou's wife was a child when her own child was born, as I pointed out previously. Besides, genetic scientists involved in the Mothers of Acadia mtDNA project have repeatedly identified the Lejeune sisters' mtDNA as belonging to a haplogroup and subclade whose highest frequency is found in northwestern Africa—a part of their story that has contributed to their contested status as an "Indigenous" ancestor today. In its own reliance on the Lejeune sisters' indigeneity, the MNRS displays a remarkable faith in aspirational descent.

MNRS counsel did not stop with Membertou and the Lejeune sisters, though; he also mentioned another ancestor specifically associated with Acadian history. Marie-Mathilde Madokawando married French officer Jean-Vincent d'Abbadie de Saint-Castin in the 1670s, likely in Penobscot territory in present-day Maine. As such, in his only statement on the historical ancestry of the MNRS membership, the lawyer focused intently on (at least) two women born in the 1600s. In the first case, an intricately concocted historical narrative provides Mi'kmaw ancestry for two sisters who are otherwise European in the historical records. *Aspirational* descent is at work in the case of the Lejeune sisters, inasmuch as two European women are remade into Mi'kmaw women despite DNA evidence to the contrary. As Alondra Nelson has suggested, kinship aspirations justify one's beliefs about their social identity in the face of conflicting DNA evidence.[29] *Lineal* descent is also key here, since ancestral lineage with Membertou (and Madokawando), a lineage more than three centuries old, appears to be at the basis of MNRS claims to indigeneity. In this case, a simple blood connection with one ancestor among over 4,000 (at generation 13) is all it takes, in an extreme example of blood logics. That these arguments work principally to facilitate the MNRS's efforts to oppose actual Indigenous peoples ensures that lineal and aspirational descent will continue to be used in the service of race shifters in the region.

In another example of aspirational descent in its membership policies—an aspect of the MNRS's specific politics that was corroborated on the genealogy forums was its lax registration practices—the organization embraces other root ancestors whose indigeneity is commonly contested in Quebec genealogy circles. The "grand chief" illustrated this dynamic, when he defiantly explained that Françoise Grenier is openly accepted as a root "Indigenous" ancestor for the purpose of membership:

LAVOIE: Well, I could tell you that many [of our members] have Françoise Garnier Grenier [in their genealogy]—

P: OK, who's?—

LAVOIE: Who's Noche Kouhana's [sp] daughter, married to Noël Langlois in 1634.

P: No, no, I mean, why are you telling me this?

LAVOIE: It's because she's very contested by a lot of people—

P: OK.

LAVOIE: —who say that that she's not métis, but we have documents from the period that say that there were no European women on the territory—

P: OK.

LAVOIE: —in those years. That means that we're going to recognize her [as an Indigenous ancestor]. So, [MNRS member's name] has her [as a root ancestor], but many others do as well.

The chief concedes that Grenier is "contested by a lot of people," but that the MNRS nonetheless continues to recognize her as Indigenous. Yet, Lavoie's statement about there being no European women on the territory that Grenier inhabited in 1634 is plainly false. I have identified more than half a dozen other European (French) women in my own genealogy who were located in the St. Lawrence Valley by 1634—in addition to Grenier, who appears four different times in my genealogy. The "grand chief," and by association, the MNRS, seems to be of the same opinion as some of the forum posters whom I cited in previous chapters: in the absence of any evidence to the contrary, Grenier can be safely assumed to be Indigenous. Remarkably, the "grand chief" went significantly further here than did anybody on the genealogy forums when he gave Grenier's mother a name; this is the only time—including within the considerable online debate about Grenier on genealogy forums and blogs—that I found any mention of her mother's potential name. You may remember Grenier as one of the women I discussed in Chapter 2 in relation to my development of the concept of aspirational descent. Genetic scientists, through buccal swab tests of her descendants, have associated her with haplogroup J (subclade J2b1a), which is most frequently found in western Europe and Russia. Again, we see how, among race shifters, kinship aspirations are at the forefront of a strategic self-making process.

Another set of siblings who are contested Indigenous root ancestors are the four Caplan sisters, who are most commonly at the basis of Gaspésie "métis" claims. In his testimony, Lavoie singles out the Caplan line, as he calls it, as one of the MNRS's "solid genealogical lines." When questioned about how he became one of the organization's nine original members, Parent explained his own ancestral history, which leads to Catherine Caplan (born 1701), in the following manner:

P: Ok, Hélène Huard [root ancestor] is a member of which community? She was a member of which band?
PARENT: She, it was . . . it's that it comes from the Huard family, it's with the M'ikmaq that I had—
P: And she was a member of which Mi'kmaw group, which band?
PARENT: Well, she wasn't on any reserve.
P: OK, she wasn't on a reserve.
PARENT: No.

P: Was she a status Indian?

PARENT: No, she was Métis.

P: OK, but why did you say—

PARENT: After that, my great—

P: Hold on, hold on a minute. Let's stick with her. Yes, that's it, you're in the middle of talking about her, right? I only want to talk about Miss Huard, OK.

PARENT: That's grandma Huard.

P: Yes.

Under examination by the Crown prosecutor, Parent's story about Mi'kmaw ancestry shifts noticeably. He begins by stating an ancestral connection with the Mi'kmaq, before affirming that the Huard line is "métis," which likely reflects its inclusion in the MNRS's "métis family" database. In its most recent version—updated in September 2014—the MNRS's database "Familles métisses en Gaspésie" lists a remarkable 418 patronyms commonly found in Gaspésie as being "métis families."[30] Upon close inspection, the large majority of the families claim their supposed indigeneity through an ancestral connection to one of the four Caplan sisters (born in the south part of Gaspésie between 1700 and 1704). As Denis Jean explains, "The origins of the historic Gaspésie Métis community reach back to the eighteenth century.... Guillaume Caplan's descendants form what is possibly the oldest clan of the Métis community since he arrived in the Percé region at the very beginning of the eighteenth century."[31]

In the MNRS's own documentation, the Huard line's indigeneity is wrapped up in a mix of aspirational and lateral descent. Essentially, the Huards are directly related to Catherine Caplan, the second of the Caplan sisters born in the region at the very beginning of the eighteenth century. The parents, Guillaume Caplan and an unnamed woman, of the four Caplan sisters—Marguerite, Catherine, Madeleine, and Marie Louise— were married in 1700 in Gaspésie. A great deal of debate has occurred regarding the identity of the unnamed woman, who for a long time was simply known as "unnamed Indian woman" in genealogical circles. As part of the Mothers of Acadia mtDNA project, at least one of the unnamed woman's descendants was tested for their mtDNA, which scientists used to identify a match with haplogroup C (subclade C1c).[32] Genetic scientists have long associated this specific biological substance with people who are indigenous to the Americas. There still remains some controversy over the construction of the four Caplan sisters as the basis of Gaspésian "métis" identity—as I observed on at least two occasions on the genealogy forums—but for the most part, genes associated with Indigenous peoples have emboldened the MNRS in its claims to an Indigenous identity *and* in attendant efforts to oppose the Mi'kmaq. In other words, the Caplan sisters' association with haplogroup C has ensured that the MNRS has normalized the power of Native American DNA in defining the boundaries of Indigenous identity.

Parent's inability to settle on an Indigenous identity for the Huard line appears to arise from his own reliance on Native American DNA. As we know, DNA ancestry testing cannot identify tribal origins, so his original claim that his direct ancestor was Mi'kmaq is not verifiable in the courtroom. The best he can offer is that she is "métis," in the sense of mixed European and (unknown) Indigenous origins. Notably, the reliance on mtDNA to indigenize the Caplans occurs despite the opposite finding in the cases of the Lejeune sisters and of Françoise Grenier. The MNRS also includes Radegonde Lambert, an Acadian woman born around 1621 in present-day Nova Scotia, as an "Indigenous" root ancestor. Lambert is among the twenty or so Acadian ancestors in my genealogy. Little is known about Lambert's mother, but her father was a French colonist.[33] The Mothers of Acadia project confirmed that mtDNA associated with Lambert is of haplogroup X (subclade X2b4), which some scientists first deemed was Native American DNA since it had rarely been encountered beforehand.[34] Ultimately, the discovery of the X2b4 subclade in several dozen European research participants between 2012 and 2014 put to rest speculation of its Native American origins.

The reality is that from its inception, the MNRS has relied on a number of contested ancestors to support race shifting in the region. Evidence, whether documentary or molecular, has not changed the organization's position on these contested ancestors; if anything, the MNRS has proudly stood in defiance of both scholarly and scientific evidence. For MNRS leadership, being "métis" is a matter of faith governed by kinship aspirations and the political capital gained by becoming Indigenous.

In his testimony, the "grand chief" himself evoked the Caplan line while discussing his spouse's membership in the organization. The following exchange between the prosecutor and Lavoie speaks to the strength of lineal descent in his narrative:

P: Excuse me, when you say that she had her Indian [status] card, it was—

LAVOIE: No, she didn't have an Indian [status] card, but she could get it if she wanted.

P: OK, but she's—

LAVOIE: But it was already offered to her.

P: You mean an Indian [status] card—

LAVOIE: She could be an Indian [sic] at Gespeg [third Mi'kmaw community in region] if she wanted to be, but she doesn't want to be, because she's Métis.

P: OK, but she could be a member, what you're saying, she—

LAVOIE: They told me when I verified that if she requested her Indian [status] card, she would get one.

P: Who are the "they"?

LAVOIE: Well, look, her mother, she comes from Gaspé and they, it's ... they're the Caplan line. ... It doesn't mean that they'd get it, but they never applied because they feel Métis [not Mi'kmaq].

In a striking parallel to one of the CMDRSM board members in the previous chapter, Lavoie appears to use proximity to federally recognized Indian status as a way to legitimize the work of the MNRS—proximity that is altogether misapplied in this case. Since the Caplans were all born at the turn of the eighteenth century, the chief's spouse would likely be the eighth generation of Caplan descendants in Gaspésie, which would place her *at least* five generations from obtaining Indian status according to his testimony. Whatever the precise case, an exaggerated proximity to

Indian status is mobilized discursively by both the MNRS and CMDRSM as a strategy to bolster the case for lineal descent, at the same time as the two groups openly denigrate and/or oppose status Indians politically.

In the case of Lavoie's testimony, we see an intense dedication to the reconstruction of the lives of ancestors who lived over 300 years ago. As I explained in the Introduction, the practices of descent that I identify on the forums move thousands of otherwise white French descendants to become "Indigenous" because individual race shifters are willing and able to spend hour upon hour poring over historical records and engaging in debate about whether or not a given woman in the 1600s was French or Indigenous, despite that single ancestor representing less than 1 percent of 1 percent of their ancestry. Their faith in the genealogical origins of their newfound Indigenous identity is unwavering. These practices of descent operate *beyond* descent, into the realm of politics. The fact that "red" and "white" blood are imagined as easy to blend is bound up in the push to depoliticize and racialize Indigenous polities, as the MNRS examples make plain. The repurposing of long-ago ancestry usefully provides the logic for white French descendants to become "Indigenous" in a manner that contributes further to the civilizational efforts to assimilate Indigenous peoples, by, among other means, undermining Indigenous sovereignty and self-determination. It is notable that the emergence of both the CMDRSM and the MNRS in their respective regions nullified land claims and territorial agreements negotiated by Indigenous peoples. Race shifting empowers white settlers to make claims to Indigenous lands and life.

The MNRS eventually turned to molecular science in 2015, when it paid for DNA ancestry testing for twenty of its members, which further emboldened it in its territorial claims.

The Gaspésie "Métis" and the Politics of Native American DNA
In what has been the highest-profile turn to DNA ancestry testing of any of the self-identified métis organizations in Canada, the MNRS publicly announced the results from about twenty DNA ancestry tests that its members had taken earlier in the year at its annual general meeting in mid-September 2015. In the AGM minutes, available on the MNRS website, the organization's "grand chief" explained to the sixty or so members present,

"We did about 20 tests so far, and they all came out positive to show we've been here for 2,000 years."³⁵ A CBC news report on the matter echoed the MNRS president's implausible statement in its headline, claiming that the "métis" presence in Gaspésie dated back two millennia.³⁶ The Canadian Broadcasting Corporation eventually corrected its coverage, explaining that it was actually the *Indigenous ancestors* of today's so-called métis who had lived in the area up to 2,000 years ago. The CBC headline became "Métis in Gaspé Hope DNA Tests Will Grant Them More Rights." The correction at the bottom of the updated story reads: "A previous version of this story said that the Métis people's presence in eastern Quebec dated back 2,000 years. In fact, it was the aboriginal ancestors of today's Métis people who are said to have lived in the area 2,000 years ago. CBC News regrets the error."³⁷ While the differences between these two statements might at first glance seem minute, each expresses a radically different vision that manifests how genes associated with Indigenous peoples facilitate the race-shifting process in the region.

Besides the CBC story, what captured my attention regarding the MNRS's use of Native American DNA to advance its claims was how two of its more prominent board members began identifying themselves as "Beothuk through DNA" on the organization's website after the molecular tests. The Beothuk were the people indigenous to the island of Newfoundland, who were eliminated by genocidal colonial violence. The awkward reference to being Beothuk on the MNRS website led me to the DNA ancestry company that the organization hired to conduct testing of its members. As Kim TallBear has explained, there exists no DNA ancestry test that can identify one's tribal or national origins.³⁸ Yet Accu-metrics, the company hired by the MNRS, has a product that it markets as determining one's precise tribal or First Nations origins. In fact, on its website the company advertises a test that can pinpoint your molecular origins among over 600 tribes or First Nations in the United States and Canada and fifty-six "Native tribes from Mexico."³⁹ It is with this same product that it claims to be able to identify one's Beothuk origins.

On its website, Accu-metrics confidently announces that results from its product "can be used in enrollment, disenrollment, claiming social benefits, or simply for a [*sic*] peace of mind. We understand the impact that this testing service has on the First Nation and Native American community and we try to use our expertise for the community's overall interests."[40] Despite its stated benevolence, the company illustrates what occurs when profit motives and colonial logics about indigeneity combine to mobilize "Native American DNA." The warning written more than a decade ago by fourteen leading scholars of science about the dangers of DNA ancestry testing remains salient: the commercialization of these tests "has led to misleading practices that reinforce misconceptions."[41] It is also instructive to return to TallBear's work on the colonial basis for genomic articulations of indigeneity: "Indigenous peoples' 'ancestry' is not simply genetic ancestry evidenced in 'populations' but biological, cultural, and political groupings constituted in dynamic, long-standing relationships with each other and with living landscapes that define their people-specific identities and, more broadly, their indigeneity."[42] It is clear that Accu-metrics is committed to redefining indigeneity in a manner that suits a primarily white customer base and opposes Indigenous articulations of indigeneity.

First, the MNRS's "grand chief" explicitly used the results of the DNA ancestry tests to *indigenize* an otherwise primarily French-Québécois population. Locating what TallBear calls a "biogeographical pinpoint of originality" to the Gaspé Peninsula up to 2,000 years ago, the so-called métis attempt to territorialize their presence through DNA. Given that the organization itself was only formed in 2006 and that many of its own members are new to this emerging identity, claims to a 2,000-year-old existence are quite remarkable. After all, in a message to members on its website, the MNRS explains the genesis of the Gaspésie "métis" as the result of "interethnic contact" between Europeans and Indigenous peoples in the eighteenth century, or about 300 years ago, just as regional historian Denis Jean did. Anthropologist Duana Fullwiley explains the normative temporal logic used in these types of ancestral claims: "[Genetic ancestry] requires limiting history to two 'depth of time' scales: the twenty-first-century 'present' and the Age of Conquest 'past,' when the populations of the 'New World' encountered each other. That is when the sexual politics of enslavement and conquest resulted in new dynamics of genetic mixing that are imagined not to have taken place before. When present-day people display such mixing, geneticists term this 'admixture.'"[43]

Following the genetic ancestry tests that it ordered in 2015, the MNRS dramatically redefined its origins in the region. How is it possible for the descendants of European settlers to claim a 2,000-year-old bio-geographical origin in Gaspésie when their own origin story places them in the region no more than three centuries ago? Again, the MNRS illustrates the usefulness of Native American DNA, which it mobilizes as a natural resource that makes a difference in its vision of settler-Indigenous relations. Indeed, the incredibly evocative statement by the MNRS "grand chief"—we have been here *as métis* for 2,000 years—moves the depth of time back by a factor of nearly seven in order to instrumentalize Native American DNA in a manner that serves the group's own political interests: to oppose the Mi'kmaq and to stake a legal claim to Aboriginal rights in the region.

Second, these genes then become the property inheritance of Gaspésian settlers, who use them to narrate the history of their presence in the region. DNA is used to significantly alter their relationship to Indigenous peoples currently living in Gaspésie. The 2015 AGM minutes suggest that the results of these DNA ancestry tests have emboldened the community's legal efforts to obtain Aboriginal rights: "[The grand chief] believes that these tests might help Métis community members to defend their rights, for example, when they're arrested for fishing or hunting illegally."[44] It is worth noting that the Mi'kmaq, whom the Gaspésie "métis" claim as ancestors, have their own origin stories in the region that forego any European presence.[45] Fred Metallic, a citizen of Listuguj Mi'gmaq First Nation in the southwestern corner of Gespe'gewa'gi, is one prominent intellectual working on the political history of the Mi'kmaq in the region.[46] In addition, international award–winning filmmaker Alanis Obomsawin wrote, directed, and produced two well-known documentary films about the Gaspésie Mi'kmaw people's resistance to both Québécois and Canadian efforts to intervene in Mi'kmaw lifeways in the region.[47] However, in the MNRS's more recent version of their history, the sustained Mi'kmaw presence in the region known as Gespe'gewa'gi disappears in favour of a "métis" presence—a rather bold statement in favour of Euro-settler primacy, and one that builds on the disappearance thesis promoted by the CMDRSM.

As a matter of fact, the MNRS has long portrayed its members as the only authentic Indigenous people in "their" territory at the same time as it displays a normative white settler sense of national belonging.[48] The Mi'kmaq, it seems, are useful only inasmuch as they provide the MNRS with the genetic basis for political claims that undermine existing Mi'kmaw treaty rights first negotiated at the beginning of the eighteenth century. In this case, the MNRS mobilizes Native American DNA in order to govern settler-Indigenous relations in ways that favour otherwise white, French-descendant claims to Mi'kmaw lands, as evidenced by a recent statement on the organization's website: "This vast and diverse territory, with such breathtaking natural beauty, was never colonized nor ceded to Europeans who arrived on our soil; it has remained the property of the descendants of the original [First Nations] inhabitants ... the Métis."[49] Besides the fact that the MNRS insists on upholding land as a property relation in settler terms, it literally writes the contemporary Mi'kmaq out of place. The thousands of Mi'kmaq in Gespe'gewa'gi who continue to affirm and maintain their relations with their ancestral land are cast aside by the logic of Native American DNA. "Indigenous notions of *peoplehood* as emerging *in relation with* particular lands and waters and their nonhuman actors," TallBear explains, "differ from the concept of a genetic *population*, defined as moving *upon* or *through* landscapes."[50] And so it is with the MNRS, which clearly expresses its Euro-settler relationship to land as property. Even so, since members' own molecular claims to indigeneity are tied to the otherwise insignificant presence of genes associated with Indigenous people in the form of mtDNA haplogroups, they must find a way to account for their belated arrival in the region that gestures toward the Mi'kmaq. In this case, the MNRS cannot erase the Mi'kmaq completely; instead, it reconstitutes the Mi'kmaq as "métis" (just like them), which allows the MNRS to claim Mi'kmaw lands as its own without apparent irony.

In February 2017, another self-declared "métis" organization in a northern region of Quebec (in Cree territory) announced a partnership with Accu-metrics. The organization—the Communauté de Chibougamau-Chapais Eeyou-Istchee—was created on the strength of results from a number of Accu-metrics DNA ancestry tests, after which time it quickly signed up hundreds of members. In a media report on the organization's origins, its elected "chief," Luc Michaud, explained people's reactions to finding out about their Indigenous ancestry: "A lot [of people] were surprised, and a lot were proud when they got their results back.... The majority of the people in Chibougamau are finding out they come from Lac St-Jean. I think Lac St-Jean is one of the places that has the most Métis people around."[51] It is notable here that the "chief" is referring to one of the main regions represented by the CMDRSM. It appears that the CMDRSM's efforts to indigenize French descendants in the Northeast of the province provided Michaud and his organization's membership a narrative through which to locate their own emerging claims to a distinct, rights-bearing "métis" people in Eeyou-Istchee (Cree territory).

A few short months later, "chief" Michaud travelled to Paris as part of a small delegation with three other self-identified "métis chiefs" to present a human rights complaint to the United Nations based in the non-recognition of their "Indigenous" rights by the federal and provincial governments.[52] Again, the legitimacy proffered to genes associated with Indigenous peoples lends itself to the race-shifting process. In a matter of months, Michaud's organization went from receiving the results of a series of DNA ancestry tests and creating a "métis" organization on the strength of those same tests, to affirming its Aboriginal rights to hunt, fish, and trap in Cree territory. At no time—in keeping with the strategy of the MNRS—did the new organization appear to consult with the Indigenous peoples whose territory they now claim as their own for the purpose of Aboriginal rights.

The First Nation, Métis, and Native American DNA Testing Service: DNA Is for the Dogs

In order to verify the MNRS's claims about its molecular origins, I ordered two DNA ancestry testing kits in 2017 from Accu-metrics, the same DNA ancestry testing company that it had hired. On 10 February 2017— a few weeks after ordering the test online—I received the much-awaited package in the mail, containing a buccal swab kit, a biological specimen envelope, and a form on which to provide basic demographic information. I dutifully followed the instructions on the back of the package and gently rubbed the inside of my mouth in a circular motion with a swab for thirty seconds, removing precious cells containing my DNA for later testing. I repeated this process with a second swab and placed both in the envelope provided for that purpose. Once I had completed the test, I sealed it, placed it and the form in the envelope, and hurried to the nearest post office to mail my package to the company's Toronto lab. I received an email with an embedded link about seven weeks later. After several pages explaining the basic logic of mtDNA ancestry testing, my results appeared: Native American ancestry = 9 percent (specifically, 9 percent Mi'kmaq), non-Native American ancestry = 91 percent.

There are two aspects of mtDNA testing that I want to highlight before continuing. First, mtDNA ancestry testing—such as that provided by Accu-metrics—relies on the conventional "depth of time" discussed previously by Fullwiley. In this case, that brings us back *at least* twelve generations to early New France, between 1620 and 1650. At this point in my ancestral genealogy I have over 2,000 ancestors (about 1,200 root ancestors). Through genealogical research, I have identified eighteen Acadian root ancestors in my lineage, none of whom was Mi'kmaq. Only three of my root ancestors are identified as Indigenous at all. I have identified two other ancestors who were captured as children in New England (in 1704) and eventually adopted by Indigenous peoples, though I have not included them here in my calculation because under the logic of molecular testing, their biological material would test as "European." In order for 9 percent of my genome to be "Native American," I would need to count between 150 and 200 Indigenous ancestors at the conventional depth of time (about twelve generations) or dozens of Indigenous (in this case, Mi'kmaq) ancestors at a shallower depth of time. For instance, if at generation five (born in early 1800s) three of my ancestors out of thirty-two were Indigenous, that would correspond to the 9 percent figure. Alternatively, at generation nine the figure would represent about twenty-four ancestors out of 256. Given that I have identified 100 percent of my ancestors in genealogical records going back to generation twelve (or to the early to mid 1600s), and that only three of them were identified as Indigenous at that time, I am confident that Accu-metrics' test grossly miscalculates my ancestral history. Not only do its results misattribute Mi'kmaw origins to me, but they exaggerate the actual extent of my Indigenous ancestry by a factor of more than ten.

Second, in addition to considerations involving "depth of time," it is important to remember that mtDNA testing accounts for only a minute amount of one's genetic ancestry, no more than 1 percent of 1 percent of one's ancestors at generation twelve (see Chapter 2). As such, in order to come up with results in the 10 percent range, Accu-metrics must make a number of calculations based on nothing more than a fraction of one's overall DNA, pointing to Bolnick et al.'s concern that the limitations of DNA ancestry tests "make them less informative than many realize."[53] Remarkably, despite the inclusion in my package of a twenty-two-page document explaining the complex basis for mtDNA testing, Accu-metrics failed to explain the basis for its statistical calculation, which allows it to make its bold claims about a molecular match in the first place. Importantly, Jobling, Rasteiro, and Wetton explain that each direct-to-consumer DNA ancestry company develops its own trademarked statistical model that it protects from its competitors and customers alike; therefore, "ancestry estimates from these [DNA ancestry] tests are always at the mercy of the quality and size of available databases (and, hence, of the company carrying out the tests)."[54] Even with the profound impacts that their product can have on society—or perhaps *because* of those impacts—companies such as Accu-metrics are committed to the "frequent over-interpretation of individual-based data."[55]

As a way to test the reliability of Accu-metrics' testing service, I paid for a second Native American DNA test in April 2017. This time, I sent in my DNA as indicated, but under my friend's name and address in western Canada (this friend also has a common French patronym). The test came back in July 2017. The results varied significantly from the previous test, especially in relation to my so-called tribal origins. In this case, my results were the following: Native American ancestry = 5 percent (2 percent Huron, 2 percent Neutral and Petun, 1 percent Ojibwe), non-Native American ancestry = 95 percent.

TABLE 6. RESULTS FROM NATIVE AMERICAN DNA ANCESTRY TESTS, 2017

	NATIVE AMERICAN DNA	NON-NATIVE AMERICAN DNA
February 2017	9% (Mi'kmaq)	91%
July 2017	5% (Huron, Neutral/Petun, Ojibwe)	95%

Again, according to my ancestral genealogy, Accu-metrics appears to have significantly overestimated my Indigenous ancestry. In light of the extraordinary power of long-ago ancestry, as outlined so far in this study, the company can safely assume that the large majority of people who order its Native American DNA ancestry product are searching for confirmation of their Indigenous ancestry and/or indigeneity. Jobling, Rasteiro, and Wetton explain the impacts of DNA ancestry tests such as Accu-metrics' First Nation, Metis, and Native American DNA testing product:

> Testing reifies race in the minds of many consumers as a biological phenomenon, and supplies apparent links with existing or extinct populations . . . with unwarranted certainty. . . . The companies that apply genetic methods in individual testing . . . fail to explain exactly what the tests are, and how they work; they fail to describe the databases with which they compare their customers' results; they fail to give any measure of the robustness of their conclusions; and in tests of uniparentally inherited lineages, they fail to explain how small a proportion of a customer's ancestry their test reflects.[56]

At no point in the document included with my test results did Accu-metrics address the limits of its database or conclusions, nor did it explain the small proportion of my ancestry that it was testing. Instead, the opening paragraph of the document confidently states, "With the advances of DNA technology, it is now possible to determine Native American ancestry using a simple cheek swab." Combined with the title from the First Nation, Metis, and Native American DNA testing product home page—"The results of this scientific test can be used to receive a status card or tribal enrollment"—it is clear that Accu-metrics is involved in the type of "misleading practices that reinforce misconceptions" that Bolnick et al. warned about more than a decade ago.[57]

Notably, in June 2018, *CBC News* conducted an investigative report on the use of DNA ancestry testing by one of the largest organizations in Canada representing self-identified Indigenous people.[58] As part of its investigation, the CBC reported that members of the organization suspected that Accu-metrics' First Nation, Métis, and Native American

DNA testing service was providing customers with faulty results. One individual, having received quite different results from two separate tests (first 19 percent and then 30.4 percent Native American DNA), sent his dog's DNA to the company claiming it as his own. To his surprise, his French poodle Mollie's results showed that she had 5 percent Indigenous ancestry (2 percent Oji-Cree, 2 percent Saulteaux, 1 percent Mississauga). Remarkably, the CBC discovered a second individual—also a member of the same organization—who had sent his dog's DNA to Accu-metrics. In this case, it turned out that Snoopy, the man's Chihuahua, had 20 percent Native American ancestry (12 percent Abenaki, 8 percent Mohawk). To verify these claims, the CBC sent DNA samples from three of its employees who were born outside of the Americas to Accu-metrics. After a few weeks, the results confirmed the CBC's suspicions: the employees—two of whom were born in India and one in Russia—tested positive for Native American DNA. Specifically, all three received the same results as Snoopy: 20 percent of their genome contained DNA associated by geneticists with peoples who are indigenous to the present-day United States or Canada. Each of the CBC employees' results even presented the same tribal origins as Snoopy: 12 percent Abenaki and 8 percent Mohawk. It seems from both the CBC investigation and my own experience that Accu-metrics capitalizes on general consumer confusion with and/or trust in scientific technologies to market a product that appears at best to be a form of entertainment.

However, instead of reading its results as a form of fabulation, the MNRS used these same tests to redefine relationships between French descendants and the Mi'kmaq in Gespe'gewa'gi in a manner that solidifies white forms of power and control. Remember that the MNRS has used the same results to assert a 2,000-year-old presence in Gespe'gewa'gi that goes against its own origin story. The molecular profile of its membership has emboldened the organization to challenge the very existence of the Mi'kmaq as an Indigenous people with a distinct political relationship with settler governments, illustrating TallBear's analysis that "Native American DNA is a material-semiotic object with power to influence indigenous livelihoods and sovereignties."[59] Between 2004 and 2008, the MNRS was able to mobilize the regional population against a Mi'kmaw project that would have granted the Mi'kmaq of Gesgapegiag limited sovereignty over a small parcel of their ancestral territory. As two of its founders explained above, the MNRS accomplished this task by using practices associated with lineal and aspirational descent to mobilize a significant proportion of the regional French-descendant population to shift into an "Indigenous" identity. Now that the MNRS has discovered the power of DNA to locate it in time (2,000 years ago) and space (Gaspésie), we can expect that its claims will become more audacious.

As a matter of fact, in an interview in November 2017, its "grand chief" announced that the MNRS was accepting members from across North America and was now making a territorial claim to the entirety of eastern North America, including the Atlantic provinces and parts of Quebec and New England. In an open letter published in a local newspaper in June 2018, Lavoie inexplicably claimed that the MNRS "was born more than 10,000 years ago," moving back the depth of time exponentially.[60]

As of early 2019, the MNRS is in court claiming that its members are bearers of constitutionally protected Aboriginal rights in four separate court cases. Most of my analysis in this chapter is of preliminary testimony provided by the so-called grand chief and the accused in the *Parent* case, both of whom were founding members in 2006. First, I illustrated how the organization's founding members were hunters in a specific territory in the heart of Gaspésie that had previously been a wildlife reserve. They were at the forefront of opposition to an agreement signed by the provincial government and the Gesgapegiag Mi'kmaw community in 1999 that provided for the creation of an outfitting territory to be managed by the latter. From its origins as a small hunting rights association, the MNRS catapulted onto the political scene as a so-called métis organization. As the "grand chief" himself explained, the sudden transformation in regional identity took place as a result of the *Powley* decision, in a move that paralleled what had taken place north of the St. Lawrence River just eighteen months prior.

Second, while the movement against the outfitting project was not as outwardly hostile in Gaspésie as it had been in Saguenay and Sept-Îles—the two cities at the centre of the opposition to Innu land claims—MNRS leaders nonetheless participated in stoking anti-Mi'kmaq sentiment in the region. Through analyzing the testimony of the two founding members, it became clear that the movement had as its basis a hypermasculine logic that continues to be displayed today through the disproportionate number of men self-identifying as "métis" in the region. Third, I analyzed the claims made by the founding members and their counsel about several contested ancestors whom I discussed in Chapter 2. Through this analysis, we come to understand that aspirational descent is crucial to the MNRS's recruitment policy, as it proudly accepts members who claim Françoise Grenier, Radegonde Lambert, or Catherine and Edmée Lejeune—all French women —as distant root ancestors. In fact, the MNRS main counsel appeared to weave a fanciful tale about the Lejeune sisters' relationship to Mi'kmaw Grand Chief Membertou, despite the thorough debunking of that story. The case of the MNRS displays the importance of long-ago ancestry to the contemporary race-shifting process among French descendants, through its excessively porous membership policy.

Finally, I explored the MNRS's use of molecular technologies to support its broader political claims. The MNRS illustrates the precise ways that genes associated with Indigenous peoples by genetic scientists (or "Native American DNA") can be used to intervene in the complex politics of Indigenous land claims and self-determination, in the sense that TallBear develops. Moving from a (contested) 300-year-old origin story to one that spans two millennia (and now, 10,000 years), the MNRS capitalizes on the logic of DNA ancestry testing to territorialize its nascent political claims to Mi'kmaw land and life.

Conclusion

White Claims to Indigenous Identity

This study has been concerned with shedding light on a social phenomenon that has been on the rise since the Supreme Court of Canada's *Powley* decision in 2003—white French descendants in the eastern parts of Canada and in New England shifting to an "Indigenous" identity. I have argued that race shifting consolidates contemporary forms of colonialism that oppose actual Indigenous peoples in the present.

This book began by identifying the specific genealogical mechanics that lead French descendants to self-indigenize by analyzing five of the largest French-descendant online genealogy forums. Analyzing genealogy forums has been crucial, since the unique genealogical infrastructure available to French descendants is at the basis of contemporary race shifting. Through my observations, I pinpoint a set of practices that involve claiming an Indigenous identity based on a long-ago ancestor(s), more than ten generations in the past. Together with careful attention to developments in the study of Indigenous citizenship and kinship and contemporary genealogical practice, I focused on the specific ways in which descent is mobilized online. Key to these practices of descent is the development of an obsessive focus on *and* movement beyond descent. In the first instance, specific practices of descent encourage individuals to focus almost exclusively on a few (oftentimes, only one) ancestors out of more than 2,000 at a depth of twelve generations. More to the point, forum participants concentrate primarily on the same handful of (Indigenous) women born before 1650 in their online research. From there, the intense focus on specific seventeenth-century women leads them far beyond a simple story of one's family history into an intervention in contemporary Indigenous life.

The focus on the internal mechanics of race shifting might have led some readers to wonder, "So what?" In fact, the question I was asked most often in presenting different parts of this research in public in 2017 and 2018 was a version of the following: "But *why* are so many white people saying that they're Indigenous today?" My focus in this study has primarily been to explain *how* a large and diverse group of white people is shifting into an Indigenous identity, not so much as a way to avoid the more pernicious question of *why*, but as a way to work toward an understanding of the specific practices at the base of race shifting. My hope is that providing a close examination of *how* race shifting works through (genetic) genealogy will open the door for other scholars to contribute further to our understanding of race shifting and its relation to dominant forms of white social power.

Even so, the last two chapters of this study do explicitly engage with the origins and claims of two of the largest self-identified "métis" organizations in Canada as a way to capture some of the political, social, and legal dynamics that lead to race shifting and how these dynamics impact actual Indigenous peoples on the ground. In three large regions of Quebec, the logic of lineal descent has emboldened individuals to claim an Indigenous identity as a strategy to oppose Indigenous land claims. Building on Circe Sturm's work, I demonstrated that one of the reasons for the success of these two organizations in mobilizing the local population to its political project was in the intimate social contact its leaders had engaged in prior to the *Powley* decision. Whether working closely together in white rights organizations or in hunting rights organizations, race shifters came to know one another in their shared opposition to Indigenous land claims. Much of the social contact occurred in spaces that encouraged dominant displays of masculinity, such as hunting and fishing associations, which explains the disproportionate number of men who self-identify as "métis" in these regions.

These individuals worked closely together mobilizing local residents against the Innu and Mi'kmaq, and once the details of the *Powley* decision were known in the region, race shifting became an attractive political strategy. Because of the ambient support for the practice of lineal descent in Quebec society—based as it is in the "chimera of métissage" in early New France—the organizations' eventual leaders mobilized long-ago ancestry (whether of an actual Indigenous woman or of French women reconstructed as "Indigenous") in order to claim a contemporary "Indigenous" identity. It turns out that the three largest self-identified "métis" organizations in Quebec—the Métis Nation of the Rising Sun (20,000 members), the Communauté métisse autochtone de Maniwaki (6,000 members), and the Communauté métisse du Domaine-du-Roy et de la Segneurie de Mingan (5,000 members)—all empower their members to use a range of French women ancestors as the sole basis for race shifting, ensuring that a large proportion of their membership has absolutely no Indigenous ancestry. Of course, race shifting in these regions has been opposed by both Mi'kmaw, Algonquin, and Innu individuals and institutions respectively, but these self-identified "métis" organizations have been steadfast in their claims to having inherent Aboriginal rights, each eventually taking its legal claim to the Quebec Superior Court.

Looking forward, there are several reasons to believe that race shifting among French descendants will remain ascendant. As of January 2019, there are more self-identified "métis" organizations in provincial courts trying to affirm their Aboriginal rights than at any other time since the *Powley* decision. The CMDRSM, which brought the *Corneau* case to the Quebec Superior Court in 2006 and eventually failed in its appeal at the Quebec Court of Appeal in July 2018, has since filed an application for leave to appeal to the Supreme Court of Canada. In addition, reports by a variety of sources—including the media, the organizations themselves, and various levels of government—seem to confirm that rates of self-indigenization in Ontario, Quebec, New Brunswick, Nova Scotia, Maine, New Hampshire, and Vermont continue to increase.

On that topic, one aspect of this study that warrants further examination involves the political and social relationships among organizations representing French-descendant race shifters in a region covering most of New England and parts of Michigan in the United States and from the Maritimes to south of the Great Lakes in Canada. The unique ancestry of French descendants and the relatively low proportion of Indigenous people in these regions facilitate the race-shifting process. I have encountered a number of alliances, political and otherwise, among a range of organizations that share resources and strategies across the Canada-U.S. border, including "Abenaki tribes" in Vermont and Quebec and "Eastern métis" organizations in New Brunswick and Maine or in Michigan and Ontario, the study of which might inform us further about transformations in white settler colonialism, whiteness, and/or white supremacy. For instance, while the movement itself has attracted the greatest number of self-identified "Indigenous" people in Quebec, Nova Scotia and Vermont have produced the greatest proportion of French-descendant race shifters.

Over 23,000 people in Nova Scotia (or about 2.5 percent of the province's population) identified as Métis in the 2016 Canadian census, while only 830 (or 0.09 percent) did so in 1996. To go along with these skyrocketing figures, the province is now home to no fewer than nine organizations representing so-called "Acadian-métis" individuals who rely principally on 325-to-375-year-old ancestry to claim Aboriginal rights under the Constitution. The two *Powley* cases that have made it to court in Nova Scotia—*Babin* in 2012 and *Hatfield* in 2015—were both dismissed because the plaintiffs were judged not to belong to a Métis community. A public controversy erupted in March 2018 on social media, when several of these provincial organizations were accused of encouraging their members to defraud local businesses of sales tax revenue. Follow-up investigations by the CBC confirmed that the largest "Acadian-métis" organization in the province—the Eastern Woodlands Métis Nation, based in Yarmouth—encouraged its nearly 30,000 members to use their membership cards fraudulently to receive tax breaks on vehicles and fuel, for instance.[1] As a result of the increase in the number of self-identified "Acadian-métis" individuals and organizations in the province, the Mi'kmaq Rights Initiative (MRI), which represents the thirteen Mi'kmaw First Nations in Nova Scotia, as well as a range of Mi'kmaw activists and intellectuals have steadfastly insisted that the Mi'kmaq are the only rights-bearing Indigenous people in Nova Scotia.[2] As part of these efforts, on 27 September 2018, the MRI and the Métis National Council (MNC) signed a memorandum of understanding stating that both "parties are concerned about individuals claiming Métis identity and declaring the presence of Métis Nations in the Province of Nova Scotia."³ As part of their agreement of cooperation, the Mi'kmaq of Nova Scotia and MNC affirmed their resolve to "work collaboratively on the issue of individuals misrepresenting themselves as Métis in Nova Scotia" and to establish "a cultural awareness initiative within each other's territory to educate the public at large with respect to legitimate Métis Nation and Mi'kmaq issues."⁴

Similar numbers have become the norm in Vermont, where a media report in July 2018 stated that nearly 15,000 people (or over 2 percent of the state's population) claimed to be Abenaki.⁵ After a failed attempt at federal recognition in 2007, the St. Francis/Sokoki Band of Abenaki (now the Abenaki Nation at Missisquoi) received state recognition as an "Indian" tribe along with the Koasek Band of the Koas Abenaki Nation in May 2012. A year earlier, in April 2011, the Elnu Abenaki Tribe and the Nulhegan Abenaki Tribe also received state recognition. According to my primary research—based in part in membership records and statements by a range of Abenaki leaders from the two Abenaki communities in Quebec (Odanak and Wolinak)—all four of these state-recognized tribes are comprised primarily of French descendants who have used long-ago ancestry in New France to shift into an "Abenaki" identity. The self-indigenization movement among French descendants appears to have begun earlier in Vermont—as early as the 1970s—though it has picked up speed in recent years, no doubt facilitated by the ready availability of French-descendant genealogy infrastructure in English.

By integrating the work of scholars such as Kim TallBear, Circe Sturm, Joanne Barker, Jill Doerfler, J. Kēhaulani Kauanui, Eva Marie Garroutte, Jennifer Adese, Adam Gaudry, Damien Lee, Pam Palmater, Brenda Macdougall, and Chris Andersen on Indigenous citizenship orders and kinship-making with the work of scholars such as Catherine Nash, Alondra Nelson, Ashley Barnwell, and Marie-Anne Kramer on contemporary (genetic) genealogy practice in Western society, I sought to make a theoretical contribution to our understandings of changing forms of white settler colonialism and whiteness. Race shifting is tricky to study, since race shifters use the language of decolonization—steeped as it can be in discourses of individual empowerment that resemble mainstream self-help narratives based in neoliberalism—to construct their authenticity beyond reproach.

Yet, Sturm reminds us that having a choice about how to identify oneself racially involves a form of social power.[6] Despite the considerable effort that race shifters pour into the denial of their (previous) white identities, white forms of social power cannot but be exposed by centring race in processes of self-indigenization. As I explained in the opening pages, this is above all a twenty-first-century effort to transform the boundaries of whiteness and white identities in a context where Indigenous political claims risk undermining the established (white) order of things. In that sense, race shifting facilitates white futurity in response to conventional reconciliation frameworks.

All in all, this study is my contribution to the complex debates about identity that reverberate in academia, on social media, and in popular culture. I have strived to approach this debate with respect and humility, knowing that my arguments are likely to evoke discomfort in some quarters. I can only hope that readers—especially fellow French descendants—will accept my invitation to reassess the legacy of our forebears in the colonial violence that continues to shape our society. Denying our implication in and responsibility for that same colonial violence through race shifting is but a recent manifestation of that legacy. Many French descendants have approached me with stories of uncles, cousins, and fathers who have shifted into an "Indigenous" identity and encouraged other family members to follow suit, a process that has been repeated by uncles and cousins in my own extended family. Some have confronted their kin; others are too afraid to broach the subject. At times, race shifters insist that they seek only to honour their long-ago Indigenous ancestors or ancestry, which can appear as a legitimate form of recognition or tribute. I encourage those with these seemingly benevolent or benign intentions to understand race shifting as part of societal processes that are much larger than any one individual's motivations. Whatever the case, as French descendants, pushing back against race shifting is ultimately our responsibility. Doing so involves turning to our own communities and families, an intimate form of solidarity that is often avoided. There is no tribute or honour in race shifting, as I have documented in this study.

Besides the necessary work of family and community intervention, the self-indigenization movement among French descendants will remain ascendant until individuals turn their attention to our collective failure to build lasting social and political bonds with Indigenous and racialized peoples. As French descendants, we have been told from a young age that we are the (only) victims of British colonialism, despite the fact that our ancestors colonized significant parts of what we generally call Canada and the United States for a century and a half prior to falling under British dominion. During this time, our forebears not only enslaved African and Indigenous peoples and actively displaced and dispossessed Indigenous peoples across a wide swatch of the continent, but benefited from broader French mercantilist policies that turned the French Antilles into one of the most brutally violent slave societies the world has ever seen. Our belief that we are the only legitimate victims of (British) colonialism continues to be a major stumbling block to building a meaningful social movement dedicated to combatting French-descendant forms of racism and colonialism. French-descendant efforts to claim an Indigenous identity outlined in this study ultimately distort descent in a manner that pushes the boundaries of whiteness and white dominance. These efforts are based in the longstanding belief that white society can claim, appropriate, manipulate, or outright own Indigenous lifeways without consequence. We must heed the voices of Indigenous scholars, activists, and community leaders and turn back the race shifting movement. In the end, there is much more to Indigenous identity than a long-ago ancestor.

ACKNOWLEDGEMENTS

This book would not have been possible without the incredible support of so many family members, friends, and colleagues.

A number of people have helped me navigate through what is ultimately an incredibly complex set of social and political issues. Jennifer Adese, Chris Andersen, Adam Gaudry, Brenda Macdougall, Darren O'Toole, Malinda Smith, and Zoe Todd have all raised ethical and/or political concerns that have shaped my own perspectives in this book. My deepest gratitude to you all.

I had the good fortune of presenting several of the book's main ideas between 2015 and 2019. Included among these visits were invitations to the Indigenous Studies speaker series at the University of Saskatchewan in March 2015; the Political Science speaker series at the University of Alberta in October 2016; the Daniels Symposium hosted by the Rupertsland Centre for Métis Research at the University of Alberta in January 2017; the inaugural Récits autochtones program speaker series at the Université de Montréal in September 2017; the Political Science brown bag series at the Université d'Ottawa in October 2017; the Indigenous Education Week ("Debewin") at Laurentian University in November 2017; the Canada Research Chair in PolEthics speaker series at the Université de Montréal in March 2018; the inaugural Indigenous Joint Policy Conference at McMaster University in March 2018; the Genealogy and Genetics public workshop at the Archives of Ontario in September 2018; the Recognition of the Métis Nation Policy Forum in Winnipeg in November 2018; Carleton University in December 2019; and the University of Manitoba's Indigenous Awareness Month in March 2019. I am grateful to all of those who invited me to their institutions and/or took the time to discuss my work with me at one or more of these events. In addition, Rachel Zellars, Sirma Bilge, Gada Mahrouse,

Leila Benhadjoudja, Nathalie Kermoal, Lisa Gannett, and Pam Palmater each provided me with excellent opportunities to present my ideas to their students between November 2017 and February 2019. Andrea Eidinger and Stephanie Pettigrew built an excellent website and digital storymap (raceshifting.com) that provides a great companion to the book.

Several colleagues read early parts of the draft manuscript in 2018. Pierrot Ross-Tremblay, Corrie Scott, Damien Lee, Stephanie Schwartz, Julie Burelle, Diahara Traoré, and Eve Haque provided me with valuable feedback that strengthened my arguments. Molly Peters and Chelsea Vowel both read the entire manuscript in March 2018, and their comments further pushed the work forward. Finally, the two anonymous external reviewers provided extremely useful feedback that has greatly improved the manuscript.

I wrote this manuscript while on sabbatical during the 2017–18 academic year, the bulk of it spent in Montreal. The Social Sciences and Humanities Research Council provided me with an Insight Grant in 2016 (#435-2016-0869), which made much of the research in Montreal possible. The team at the University of Manitoba Press has been exceptional. From my first encounters with acquisitions editor Jill McConkey at Congress 2016 to editorial and promotion work with their dedicated staff throughout 2018 and 2019, I have had nothing but positive experiences.

My parents, Nicole and Richard, provided me with the space to figure out my path. While I strayed significantly from their own, their support has never wavered. My brother, Shawn, continues to offer sound, careful advice that has often saved me from myself. The rest of his growing family—Amy, Mathieu, and Nicolas—bring me a great deal of joy.

Most importantly, Délice Mugabo is an exceptional partner whose generous and judicious advice I always appreciate. It is a true gift to be able to debate the finer points of one's work and life with such a skilled thinker and caring human. She makes me a better version of myself, and for that I am forever grateful.

APPENDIX

Powley-related "Eastern Métis" Court Cases in Quebec, New Brunswick, and Nova Scotia

The table below includes court decisions in Quebec, New Brunswick, and Nova Scotia that involve individuals charged with a hunting-, fishing-, and/or logging-related offence claiming section 35 constitutional rights as a Métis person or people (under the Supreme Court of Canada's *Powley* test). As of July 2019, I identified seventy-seven individual *Powley* cases, with 104 separate judgments against the claimants, all occurring between 2001 and January 2019. Several of the cases are ongoing, as the defendants have either applied for leave to appeal a lower court decision or have indicated publicly that they intend to do so.

New Brunswick

COURT CASES	DECISION NUMBER	ORGANIZATION	RESULT	ROOT ANCESTOR(S)
R. c. Chiasson	2001 NBPC 5	Nation Indien Métis Acadie; Canadian Métis Coalition; East Coast First Peoples Alliance	Judge ruled against defendant	Not named
Chiasson c. R.	2002 NBBR – Judge Léger	Same as above, plus Ontario Métis Aboriginal Association	Judge upheld lower court ruling	

Case	Citation	Organization	Ruling	Ancestor
R. v. Castonguay	2002 NBPC 26	East Coast First Peoples Alliance/ Rising Sun Community Restigouche West	Judge ruled against defendant	Edmée Lejeune, Catherine Lejeune & Radegonde Lambert, all 12+ generations and French
R. v. Castonguay and Faucher	2002 NBPC 31	Same as above	Judge ruled against defendants	Radegonde Lambert for both, 12th (Faucher) and 9th (Castonguay) generation descendants, French
Castonguay et Faucher c. R.	2003 NBBR 325	Same as above	Judge upheld lower court ruling	
Castonguay and Faucher v. R.	2006 NBCA 43	Same as above	Judges rejected application for leave to appeal	
R. c. Donald Castonguay, Élie Castonguay, Raymond Castonguay, Roger Castonguay et François Faucher	2003 NBCP 16	Same as above	Judge ruled against defendants	Edmée Lejeune for all five defendants, 10+ generations, French
R. v. Daigle	2003 NBPC 4	East Coast First Peoples Alliance	Judge ruled against defendant	Marie Aubois, 10 generations away
Daigle c. R.	2004 NBBR 79	Same as above	Judge upheld lower court ruling	
R. c. Chiasson	2003 NBCP – Judge Finn	Ontario Métis Aboriginal Association	Judge ruled against defendant	Not named
Chiasson c. R.	2004 NBBR 80	Same as above	Judge upheld lower court ruling	
Chiasson c. R.	2005 NBCA 82	Same as above	Judges rejected application for leave to appeal	
R. c. Richard Hopper	2004 NBPC 7	The New Brunswick East Woodland Metis Tribes of Off-Reserve Indians	Judge ruled against defendant	Madokowando, 10 generations away

Hopper c. R.	2005 NBBR 399	Same as above	Judge upheld lower court ruling	
Hopper v. R.	2008 NBCA 42	Same as above	Judges upheld lower court rulings	
R. c. Brideau et Breau	2006 NBCP 74	Communauté métisse de la Grande-Riviere	Judge ruled against defendants	Not named
Brideau et Breau c. R.	2008 NBBR 70	Same as above	Judge upheld lower court ruling	Same as above
R. v. Vautour	2010 NBPC 39	None	Judge ruled against defendants	Madokowando, 11 (Roy) and 10 (Jackie) generations away, others not named (all 10–11 generations away)
Vautour v. R.	2015 NBQB 94	None	Judge upheld lower court ruling	Same as above
Vautour v. R.	2017 NBCA 21	None	Judges upheld lowercourt rulings	Same as above
R. v. Stanley R. Castonguay	2012 NBPC 19	Confederation of Aboriginal People of Canada	Judge ruled against defendant	Not named
R. v. Joseph Cyrille Caissie	2012 NBPC 1	Canadian Métis Council	Judge ruled against defendant	Same as above
R. v. Olive Landry and Fabien Huard	2012 NBPC 18	Conseil autochtone de la Côte-Est	Denial of stay of proceedings	Mi'kmaw mother of Philippe Muis d'Azy, 11 generations away (both)
Attorney General of Canada v. Michelle Landry and Jean-Paul Landry et al.	2014 FCA 197	Same as above	Procedural	Same as above (both)

Michelle Landry and Jean-Paul Landry et al. v. Attorney General of Canada	2015 SCC 17882	Same as above	Judges rejected application for leave to appeal	Same as above
12 cases, 25 decisions (1 procedural) involving 18 individuals overall				18 ancestors for 16 individuals with ancestral information, 10.8 generations average ancestral depth. At least 8 of 16 individuals with ancestral information have no Indigenous ancestry.

Quebec

COURT CASES	DECISION NUMBER	ORGANIZATION	RESULT	ROOT ANCESTOR(S)
Québec (Procureure générale) c. Marchand	2007 QCCQ 11711	Communauté métisse de l'est du Canada	Judge rejected request for public funds	Jeanne-Marie Kagigconiac, 11 generations away (both)
Directeur des poursuites criminelles et pénales c. Marchand	2014 QCCQ 13157	Métis Nation of the Rising Sun	Judge upheld previous ruling	Same as above
Marchand c. Directeur des poursuites criminelles et pénales	2018 QCCS 82	Same as above	Judge upheld lower court rulings	Same as above
Marchand c. Directeur des poursuites criminelles et pénales	2019 QCCA 32	Same as above	Judges upheld lower court rulings	Same as above
Québec (Procureure générale) c. Côté	2009 QCCS 244	Coopérative de solidarité économique autochtone Kitchisaga/l'Assemblée des communautés autochtones de Saguenay-Nitassinan	Judge ruled against defendant	Not named

Directeur des poursuites criminelles et pénales c. Québec (Procureur général) [Claude Gauthier]	2011 QCCQ 12296	Alliance autochtone du Québec/Ontario Metis and Aboriginal Association	Judge ruled against Gauthier	Not named
Directeur des poursuites criminelles et pénales c. Ghislain Gagnon	2013 QCCQ 13081	Communauté métisse du Domaine-du-Roy et de la Seigneurie de Mingan	Procedural	Marie Sylvestre, 11 generations away
Gagnon c. Procureur général du Québec	2017 QCCS 2465	Same as above	Judge rejected request for public funds	Same as above
Directeur des poursuites criminelles et pénales c. Gagnon	2018 QCCQ 4214	Same as above	Judge ruled against defendant	Same as above
Directeur des poursuites criminelles et pénales c. Paul	2014 QCCQ 4012	Communauté Wikanis Mamiwinnik	Judge ruled against defendants	Marie Pinesi Okijikokwe, 6 generations away (all five)
Directeur des poursuites criminelles et pénales c. Paul	2016 QCCQ 2030	Same as above	Judge upheld previous ruling	Same as above
Paul c. Directeur des poursuites criminelles et pénales	2017 QCCA 1691	Same as above	Judge upheld lower court rulings	Same as above
Paul c. Directeur des poursuites criminelles et pénales	2017 QCCS 4163	Same as above	Judge upheld lower court rulings	Same as above
Québec (Procureure générale) c. Vallée	2014 QCCS 5468	Métis Nation of the Rising Sun	Judge ruled against defendant	Not named
Procureure générale du Québec c. Vallée	2017 QCCS 3974	Same as above	Procedural	Same as above
Procureure générale du Québec c. Vallée	2018 QCCS 2017	Same as above	Procedural	Same as above

Case	Citation	Plaintiff/Defendant	Ruling	Ancestry
Québec (Procureure générale) c. Corneau	2008 QCCS 1133	Communauté métisse du Domaine-du-Roy et de la Seigneurie de Mingan	Judge ruled against defendant's counterclaim	Christine Kichera, 6 generations away
Tremblay c. Première Nation de Pessamit	2008 QCCS 1536	Same as above	Judge ruled against request for injunction against land claim negotiations	Marie Sylvestre (J-R Tremblay), 12 generations away
Québec (Procureure générale) c. Corneau	2009 QCCS 6301	Same as above	Judge ruled against three Innu First Nations (Mashteuiatsh, Essipit, and Nutashkuan) requesting to be intervenors	Christine Kichera, 6 generations away
Québec (Procureure générale) c. Corneau	2010 QCCS 463	Same as above	Judge accepted request for public funds	There were 22 defendants at this time, of whom 17 continued on to the 2015 decisions below. I include the ancestral information here for the 5 defendants who dropped out between 2010 and 2015: #1. Catherine Lejeune, 12 generations away (Emond). #2. Catherine Lejeune, 12 generations away and Jean Abenaki, 6 generations away (C. Tremblay). #3. Catherine Lejeune, 12 generations away (C. Simard). #4. Catherine Lejeune, 12 generations away and Françoise Ouebechinokwe, 10 generations back (Martel). #5. Catherine Lejeune, 12 generations away and Jean Abenaki, 6 generations away (R. Tremblay).

Québec (Procureure générale) (Ministère des Ressources naturelles) c. Corneau	2015 QCCS 482	Same as above		Judge ruled against defendant	Christine Kichera, 6 generations away
Corneau c. Procureure générale du Québec	2018 QCCA 1172	Same as above		Judges upheld lower court ruling.	Same as above
Québec (Procureure générale) (Ministère des Ressources naturelles) c. Simard	2015 QCCS 452	Same as above		Judge ruled against defendant	Christine Kichera, 7 generations away.
Québec (Procureure générale) (Ministère des Ressources naturelles) c. Duchesne	2015 QCCS 453	Same as above		Judge ruled against defendant	Catherine Lejeune, 12 generations away, French
Québec (Procureure générale) (Ministère des Ressources naturelles) c. Lalancette	2015 QCCS 454	Same as above		Judge ruled against defendant	Madokowando, 11 generations away
Québec (Procureure générale) (Ministère des Ressources naturelles) c. Lalancette	2015 QCCS 455	Same as above		Judge ruled against defendant	Madokowando, 11 generations away

Québec (Procureure générale) (Ministère des Ressources naturelles) c. Perron	2015 QCCS 456	Same as above	Judge ruled against defendant	Christine Kichera, 7 generations away and Françoise Ouebechinokwe, 10 generations back (Piché, co-defendant), and not named (Bouchard, co-defendant)
Québec (Procureure générale) (Ministère des Ressources naturelles) c. Lavoie	2015 QCCS 457	Same as above	Judge ruled against defendant	Marie Sylvestre, 13 generations away and Catherine Lejeune, 11 generations away, French
Québec (Procureure générale) (Ministère des Ressources naturelles) c. Minier	2015 QCCS 458	Same as above	Judge ruled against defendant	Catherine Lejeune, 11 generations away, French
Québec (Procureure générale) (Ministère des Ressources naturelles) c. Jean	2015 QCCS 459	Same as above	Judge ruled against defendant	Christine Kichera, 6 generations away
Québec (Procureure générale) (Ministère des Ressources naturelles) c. Riverin	2015 QCCS 460	Same as above	Judge ruled against defendant	Catherine Lejeune, 12 generations away, French and Françoise Ouebechinokwe, 10 generations away (twice)
Québec (Procureure générale) (Ministère des Ressources naturelles) c. Gagné	2015 QCCS 461	Same as above	Judge ruled against defendant	Unnamed Nipissing woman, 12 generations away (Gagné, co-defendant) and Catherine Lejeune 12 generations away (Simard, co-defendant)

Québec (Procureure générale) (Ministère des Ressources naturelles) c. Pelletier	2015 QCCS 462	Same as above	Judge ruled against defendant	Marie Sylvestre, 12 generations away
Québec (Procureure générale) (Ministère des Ressources naturelles) c. Corneau (fils)	2015 QCCS 463	Same as above	Judge ruled against defendant	Christine Kichera, 7 generations away, and Catherine Lejeune, 14 generations away, French
Québec (Procureure générale) (Ministère des Ressources naturelles) c. Corneau (frère)	2015 QCCS 464	Same as above	Judge ruled against defendant	Christine Kichera, 6 generations away
Québec (Procureur général) c. Côté	2014 QCCS 5469	Métis Nation of the Rising Sun	Judge ruled against defendant	Not named
Québec (Procureure générale) c. Gobeil	2015 QCCS 1698	Communauté métisse du Domaine-du-Roy et de la Seigneurie de Mingan	Judge put off ruling until Corneau decision	Not named
Procureure générale du Québec c. Gobeil	2019 QCCS 3050	Same as above	Judge ruled against defendant (Corneau 2018)	Same as above
Québec (Procureure générale) c. Gagnon	2015 QCCS 6225	Communauté métisse du Domaine-du-Roy et de la Seigneurie de Mingan	Judge put off ruling until Corneau decision	Not named
Procureure générale du Québec c. Gagnon	2019 QCCS 3051	Same as above	Judge ruled against defendant (Corneau 2018)	Same as above
Procureure générale du Québec c. Chiquette	2019 QCCS 3049	Communauté métisse du Domaine-du-Roy et de la Seigneurie de Mingan	Judge ruled against defendant (Corneau 2018)	Not named

Procureure générale du Québec c. Girard	2019 QCCS 3048	Communauté métisse du Domaine-du-Roy et de la Seigneurie de Mingan	Judge ruled against defendant (Corneau 2018)	Not named
Procureure générale du Québec c. Lalancette	2019 QCCS 3047	Communauté métisse du Domaine-du-Roy et de la Seigneurie de Mingan	Judge ruled against defendant (Corneau 2018)	Not named
Procureure générale du Québec c. Doucet	2019 QCCS 3046	Communauté métisse du Domaine-du-Roy et de la Seigneurie de Mingan	Judge ruled against defendant (Corneau 2018)	Not named
Procureure générale du Québec c. Dufour	2019 QCCS 3045	Communauté métisse du Domaine-du-Roy et de la Seigneurie de Mingan	Judge ruled against defendant (Corneau 2018)	Not named
Procureure générale du Québec c. Chiquette	2019 QCCS 3044	Communauté métisse du Domaine-du-Roy et de la Seigneurie de Mingan	Judge ruled against defendant (Corneau 2018)	Not named
Procureure générale du Québec c. Rousseau	2019 QCCS 3043	Communauté métisse du Domaine-du-Roy et de la Seigneurie de Mingan	Judge ruled against defendant (Corneau 2018)	Not named
Procureure générale du Québec c. Mailhot	2019 QCCS 3042	Communauté métisse du Domaine-du-Roy et de la Seigneurie de Mingan	Judge ruled against defendant (Corneau 2018)	Not named
Procureure générale du Québec c. Simard	2019 QCCS 3041	Communauté métisse du Domaine-du-Roy et de la Seigneurie de Mingan	Judge ruled against defendant (Corneau 2018)	Not named
Procureure générale du Québec c. Samuelson	2019 QCCS 3040	Communauté métisse du Domaine-du-Roy et de la Seigneurie de Mingan	Judge ruled against defendant (Corneau 2018)	Not named
Procureure générale du Québec c. Maltais	2019 QCCS 3039	Communauté métisse du Domaine-du-Roy et de la Seigneurie de Mingan	Judge ruled against defendant (Corneau 2018)	Not named

Procureure générale du Québec c. Gravel	2019 QCCS 3038	Communauté métisse du Domaine-du-Roy et de la Seigneurie de Mingan	Judge ruled against defendant (Corneau 2018)	Not named
Procureure générale du Québec c. Lapointe	2019 QCCS 3037	Communauté métisse du Domaine-du-Roy et de la Seigneurie de Mingan	Judge ruled against defendant (Corneau 2018)	Not named
Procureure générale du Québec c. Tremblay	2019 QCCS 3036	Communauté métisse du Domaine-du-Roy et de la Seigneurie de Mingan	Judge ruled against defendant (Corneau 2018)	Not named
Procureure générale du Québec c. Larouche	2019 QCCS 3035	Communauté métisse du Domaine-du-Roy et de la Seigneurie de Mingan	Judge ruled against defendant (Corneau 2018)	Not named
Procureure générale du Québec c. Bouchard	2019 QCCS 3034	Communauté métisse du Domaine-du-Roy et de la Seigneurie de Mingan	Judge ruled against defendant (Corneau 2018)	Not named
Procureure générale du Québec c. Bouchard	2019 QCCS 3033	Communauté métisse du Domaine-du-Roy et de la Seigneurie de Mingan	Judge ruled against defendant (Corneau 2018)	Not named
Procureure générale du Québec c. Sirois	2019 QCCS 3032	Communauté métisse du Domaine-du-Roy et de la Seigneurie de Mingan	Judge ruled against defendant (Corneau 2018)	Not named
Procureure générale du Québec c. Otis	2019 QCCS 3031	Communauté métisse du Domaine-du-Roy et de la Seigneurie de Mingan	Judge ruled against defendant (Corneau 2018)	Not named
Procureure générale du Québec c. Duchesne	2019 QCCS 3030	Communauté métisse du Domaine-du-Roy et de la Seigneurie de Mingan	Judge ruled against defendant (Corneau 2018)	Not named
Procureure générale du Québec c. Girard	2019 QCCS 3029	Communauté métisse du Domaine-du-Roy et de la Seigneurie de Mingan	Judge ruled against defendant (Corneau 2018)	Not named

Procureure générale du Québec c. Grenon	2019 QCCS 3028	Communauté métisse du Domaine-du-Roy et de la Seigneurie de Mingan	Judge ruled against defendant (Corneau 2018)	Not named
Procureure générale du Québec c. Girard	2019 QCCS 3027	Communauté métisse du Domaine-du-Roy et de la Seigneurie de Mingan	Judge ruled against defendant (Corneau 2018)	Not named
Procureure générale du Québec c. Verville	2019 QCCS 3026	Communauté métisse du Domaine-du-Roy et de la Seigneurie de Mingan	Judge ruled against defendant (Corneau 2018)	Not named
Procureure générale du Québec c. Rousseau	2019 QCCS 3025	Communauté métisse du Domaine-du-Roy et de la Seigneurie de Mingan	Judge ruled against defendant (Corneau 2018)	Not named
Fédération des producteurs acéricoles du Québec c. Bolduc	2011 QCRM-AAQ 61	Nation algonquine abénakise Antaya	Judge ruled against defendant (Bolduc)	Madokowando, 11 generations away, and Unnamed Nipissing woman, 12 generations away
Fédération des producteurs acéricoles du Québec c. Bolduc	2016 QCCQ 489	Alliance autochtone du Québec/Native Alliance of Quebec	Judge ruled against defendant (Bolduc)	Same as above
Dominique Côté v. Attorney General of Canada	2016 CF 296	Nation algonquine abénakise Antaya	Procedural	Not named
Directeur des poursuites criminelles et pénales c. Noël	2016 QCCQ 16459	East Coast First Peoples Alliance	Judge ruled against defendants	Magdeleine Micmac, 9 generations away, and Marie Micmac, 12 generations away, the latter is likely French (Martine)
Québec (Procureure générale) c. Tremblay	2016 QCCS 340	Communauté métisse du Domaine-du-Roy et de la Seigneurie de Mingan	Judge put off ruling until Corneau decision	Not named
Procureure générale du Québec c. Tremblay	2019 QCCS 3053	Same as above	Judge ruled against defendant (Corneau 2018)	Same as above

Québec (Procureure générale) c. Savard	2016 QCCS 4391	Communauté métisse du Domaine-du-Roy et de la Seigneurie de Mingan	Judge put off ruling until Corneau decision	Not named
Procureure générale du Québec c. Savard	2019 QCCS 3060	Same as above	Judge ruled against defendant (Corneau 2018)	Same as above
Québec (Procureure générale) c. Bouchard	2016 QCCS 4392	Communauté métisse du Domaine-du-Roy et de la Seigneurie de Mingan	Judge put off ruling until Corneau decision	Not named
Procureure générale du Québec c. Bouchard	2019 QCCS 3061	Same as above	Judge ruled against defendant (Corneau 2018)	Same as above
Québec (Procureure générale) c. Desbiens	2016 QCCS 4393	Communauté métisse du Domaine-du-Roy et de la Seigneurie de Mingan	Judge put off ruling until Corneau decision	Not named
Procureure générale du Québec c. Desbiens	2019 QCCS 3062	Same as above	Judge ruled against defendant (Corneau 2018)	Same as above
Québec (Procureure générale) c. Séguin	2016 QCCS 1881	Communauté métis autochtone de Maniwaki	Judge rejected request for public funds	Mother of Marie Minoéwé, 7 generations away
Procureure générale du Québec c. Pelletier	2017 QCCS 4342	Communauté métisse du Domaine-du-Roy et de la Seigneurie de Mingan	Judge put off ruling until Corneau decision	Not named
Procureure générale du Québec c. Pelletier	2019 QCCS 3063	Same as above	Judge ruled against defendant (Corneau 2018)	Same as above
Directeur des poursuites pénales du Canada c. Éric Parent	2013 QCCQ 5173	Métis Nation of the Rising	Procedural	Unnamed woman, mother of Catherine Caplan, 10 generations away, possibly French

Parent c. R	2017 QCCS 6292	Same as above	Judge rejected request for public funds	Same as above
Parent c. R	2018 QCCA 1146	Same as above	Procedural	Same as above
Parent c. R	2019 QCCA 442	Same as above	Judges upheld lower court decision and rejected request for public funds	Same as above
Procureure générale du Québec c. De Launière	2018 QCCS 1111	Communauté métisse du Domaine-du-Roy et de la Seigneurie de Mingan	Judge ruled against defendant (Corneau 2018)	Not named
Directeur des poursuites criminelles et pénales c. Donat Delarosbil et Pascal Delarosbil	2018 QCCB	Métis Nation of the Rising Sun	Judge ruled against defendants	Unnamed woman, mother of Catherine Caplan, 10 generations away, possibly French (both)
Directeur des poursuites criminelles et pénales c. Michel J. Tremblay	2018 QCCQ	Méts Nation Ontario	Judge ruled against defendant	Not named
Procureure générale du Québec c. Tremblay	2018 QCCS 2209	Communauté métisse du Domaine-du-Roy et de la Seigneurie de Mingan	Judge put off ruling until Corneau decision	Not named
Procureure générale du Québec c. Tremblay	2019 QCCS 3064	Same as above	Judge ruled against defendant (Corneau 2018)	Same as above
Directeur des poursuites criminelles et pénales c. Lehoux	2019 QCCQ 1089	Alliance autochtone du Québec/Native Alliance of Quebec	Judge ruled against defendant	Radegonde Lambert, 12 generations away, French

Appendix | 237

62 cases, 76 decisions (14 procedural), involving 72 individuals

46 ancestors for 36 individuals with ancestral information, 10 generations average ancestral depth. At least 6 of 36 individuals have no Indigenous ancestry. At least 7 others list a French woman as an "Indigenous" root ancestor.

Nova Scotia

COURT CASES	DECISION NUMBER	ORGANIZATION	RESULT	ROOT ANCESTOR(S)
R. v. Smith	2012 NSPC 84	None	Judge ruled against defendant	Not named
R. v. Babin	2013 NSSC 434	Kespu'kwitk Métis Council	Judge ruled against defendant	Not named
R. v. Hatfield	2015 NSSC 77		Judge ruled against defendant	Not named

3 cases, 5 decisions (2 trial judge decisions not included above) involving 3 individuals

Overall ancestral depth of 64 root ancestors named by 52 individuals = 10.25 generations or born about 1680–1700. *At least* 28 percent of individuals whose ancestry is known have zero Indigenous ancestry. They rely on well-known French women as their "Indigenous" root ancestor (e.g., Catherine and Edmée Lejeune and Radegonde Lambert).

NOTES

Introduction
SELF-INDIGENIZATION IN THE TWENTY-FIRST CENTURY

1. Beauregard, "Mythe ou réalité."
2. Charbonneau, "Le caractère français"; Charbonneau, "Et pourtant français à 95 pour cent"; Charbonneau, *Vie et mort de nos ancêtres*; Charbonneau, *Tourouvre-au-Perche*; Charbonneau et al., *Naissance d'une population*; Desjardins, "La contribution différentielle"; Desjardins, "Homogénéité ethnique."
3. For an overview, see Bibeau, *Le Québec transgénique*; Leroux, "'We've Been Here for 2,000 Years.'"
4. Statistics Canada, "Aboriginal Peoples in Canada."
5. Boulle, "François Bernier," 12.
6. Aubert, "'Blood of France,'" 444.
7. Ibid., 452, emphasis in original.
8. Stuurman, "François Bernier," 1.
9. Bernier cited in Boulle, "François Bernier," 13.
10. See also Roberts, *Fatal Invention*, 29.
11. Saada, "Race and Sociological Reason," 362.
12. Ibid.
13. Groulx, *Pièges de la mémoire*, 13, my translation. Unless otherwise noted, the author has translated all French-language text into English.
14. Chrétien, Delâge, and Vincent, *Au croisement de nos destins*; D'Avignon and Girard, *A-t-on-oublié que jadis nous étions 'frères'?*; Karahasan, *Métissage in New France and Canada*; Bouchard, Foxcurran, and Malette, *Songs upon the Rivers*.
15. For a critique, see Cornellier, *La "chose indienne"*; Cornellier, "The 'Indian Thing'"; Burelle, *Encounters on Contested Lands*.
16. Salée, "Les peuples autochtones," 155.
17. Gaudry and Leroux, "White Settler Revisionism."
18. Hodson and Rushforth, "Absolutely Atlantic," 107.

19 Havard, "'Nous ne ferons plus,'" 98.
20 Deslandres, "'... alors nos garçons se marieront à vos filles," 29, emphasis in original.
21 Anderson, *Chain Her by One Foot*.
22 Cook, "Onontio Gives Birth," 178.
23 Ibid.
24 Havard, "Nous ne ferons plus," 98.
25 Havard, "Nous ne ferons plus"; Belmessous, "Assimilation and Racialism"; Cook, "Onontio Gives Birth"; Cowan, "Education, Francisation, and Shifting Colonial Priorities."
26 Pouliot-Thisdale, "Unions Métis et reclamations au Québec," 12–13.
27 For a critique, see Salée, "Les peuples autochtones."
28 Havard, "Nous ne ferons plus," 101. See also Lozier, "In Each Other's Arms."
29 Belmessous, "Assimilation and Racialism," 54.
30 Cooper, *Hanging of Angélique*; Rushforth, *Bonds of Alliance*; Rushforth, "Slavery."
31 See Basu, *Highland Homecomings*.
32 Choquette, *Frenchmen into Peasants*, 5.
33 Jetté, "Les pionniers de la généalogie au Québec," 16, emphasis in original.
34 See Leroux, "'A Genealogist's Paradise.'"
35 Desjardins, "Homogénéité ethnique."
36 Charbonneau, "Le caractère français."
37 Desjardins, "Homogénéité ethnique," 72.
38 Kemper, "'Geronimo!'"; Peweardy, "So You Think You Hired"; Yellow Bird, "Cowboys and Indians."
39 Adese, "Colluding with the Enemy?"; O'Bonsawin, "'No Olympics on Stolen Native Land.'"; O'Bonsawin, "'There Will Be No Law.'"
40 Deloria, *Playing Indian*.
41 Ruffo, *Grey Owl*.
42 See, for instance, Gaudry, "Communing with the Dead"; Lee and Horn-Miller, "Wild Card."; Lindberg, "Imaginary Passports."
43 Cook-Lynn, "Meeting of Indian Professors"; Redsteer, "An Open Epistle"; Tsosie, "The New Challenge to Native Identity."
44 Peweardy, "So You Think You Hired," 201.
45 Brings Plenty, "Pretend Indian Exegesis"; Corbiere, "Identity, Appropriation, and Imposters"; Lewis, "A Story of Identity."
46 In the Australian white settler context, see Kowal and Paradies, "Indigeneity and the Refusal of Whiteness"; Watt and Kowal, "To Be or Not To Be Indigenous."

See also Junka-Aikio, "Can the Sámi Speak Now?" for an example of self-indigenization from Finland.
47 Pearson, "'The Last Bastion of Colonialism,'" 166.
48 Ibid., 169–71.
49 Ibid., 168.
50 Ibid., 178.
51 Schrift, *Becoming Melungeon*.
52 Haley and Wilcoxon, "How Spaniards Became Chumash"; Haley and Wilcoxon, "Anthropology and the Making of Chumash Tradition."
53 Haley and Wilcoxon, "How Spaniards Became Chumash," 435.
54 Ibid., 440.
55 Ibid., 441.
56 Ibid.
57 Ibid., 432.
58 Ibid., 441.
59 Sturm, *Becoming Indian*, 15.
60 Ibid., 6.
61 Ibid., 60.
62 Ibid., 136, emphasis in original.
63 Andersen, *Métis*.
64 See, for example, Gaudry and Leroux, "White Settler Revisionism."
65 See Daniels and Chartrand, "Unravelling the Riddles"; Devine, *People Who Own Themselves*; Macdougall, *One of the Family*; Macdougall, "Wahkootowin"; O'Toole, "Thomas Flanagan on the Stand."
66 *R. v. Powley*, [2003] 2 SCR 207, 2003 SCC 43.
67 Vowel and Leroux, "White Settler Antipathy," 39.
68 Adese, "A Tale of Two Constitutions"; Gaudry and Andersen, "Daniels v. Canada"; Todd, "From a Fishy Place"; Vowel and Leroux, "White Settler Antipathy."
69 Gaudry and Andersen, "Daniels v. Canada," 28.
70 Gaudry, "Communing with the Dead," 163.
71 Ibid., 172.
72 Ibid., 175.
73 Macdougall, "Wahkootowin," 433.
74 See also Kolopenuk, "'Pop-Up' Métis."
75 Sturm, *Becoming Indian*, 42.
76 Jordan, "Historical Origins."

77 Kauanui, *Hawaiian Blood*, 50.
78 See also Mihesuah, "American Indian Identities."
79 Ibid., 199–200.
80 Gómez, *Manifest Destinies*.
81 Allen, "Investigating the Cultural Conception," 203.
82 Ibid.
83 Gullickson and Morning, "Choosing Race," 499.
84 Moreton-Robinson, *The White Possessive*, xviii.
85 Nash, "Genealogical Relatedness," 3.
86 Ibid., 4.
87 Ibid., 4, 5.
88 Garroutte, *Real Indians*, 82.
89 Ibid., 6.
90 Ibid., 129.
91 Barker, *Native Acts*, 94; see also recent work by Horn-Miller, "How Did Adoption"; Lindberg, "Imaginary Passports"; Raven, "Ka oopihikihtamashook.'"
92 Palmater, *Beyond Blood*, 202–8.
93 Doerfler, *Those Who Belong*.
94 Meyer, "American Indian Blood"; Simpson, "Land as Pedagogy"; Lee, "Because Our Law Is Our Law."
95 According to the Smith-Francis orthography, "Mi'kmaw" is the adjectival form of "Mi'kmaq" (thus, the Mi'kmaq, but the Mi'kmaw people).
96 Nelson, "Bio Science," 761.
97 TallBear, *Native American DNA*, 6.
98 Ibid., 17.
99 Nelson, "Bio Science," 763.
100 Kramer, "Genomic Imaginary."
101 Barnwell, "Genealogy Craze," 263.
102 Ibid., 271.
103 Nelson, "Bio Science," 762.
104 Ibid.
105 TallBear, *Native American DNA*.
106 Devine, *The People Who Own Themselves*, 13.
107 Pelta, "La judiciarisation de l'identité métisse," 132.

Chapter One
LINEAL DESCENT AND THE POLITICAL USE OF INDIGENOUS WOMEN ANCESTORS

1   Manuel and Derrickson, *Reconciliation Manifesto*.
2   Gaudry, "Communing with the Dead," 164–65.
3   Sturm, *Becoming Indian*, 82.
4   Ibid., 133.
5   Kramer, "Genomic Imaginary."
6   Alliance autochtone du Québec, "Qui peut devenir membre."
7   "Re: Le métissage au Québec: un phénomène de faible ampleur," Vos origines (hereafter, VO forum), 8 September 2013, 7:49 p.m., https://www.vosoriginesyourroots.org/t1019-le-metissage-au-quebec-un-phenomene-de-faible-ampleur (accessed 5 January 2017). All excerpts from the GQAF, VO, and NAQ forums are translated from French to English by the author, except where a posting was originally in English (less than 1 percent of the time). All excerpts from the Ancestry and Rootsweb forums are quoted in their original English-language version, except those originally posted in French (less than 1 percent), which the author has translated.
8   Ibid., 8 September 2013, 7:53 p.m.
9   Ibid., 8 September 2013, 7:54 p.m.
10 Ibid., 8 September 2013, 7:54 p.m.
11 TallBear, *Native American DNA*, 5.
12 Arbour, "Re: Le métissage au Québec," 8 September 2013, 8:02 p.m.
13 *Enquête*, Radio-Canada.
14 See Hunt, "Representing Colonial Violence"; Pamela Palmater, "Shining Light."
15 Simpson, "The State Is a Man," 17.
16 See Macdougall, "Wahkootowin."
17 Adese, Todd, and Stevenson, "Mediating Métis Identity," 10–11.
18 "Re: Le métissage au Québec," VO forum, 8 September 2013, 8:02 p.m.
19 Sturm, *Becoming Indian*, 40–41.
20 Henripin, "De la fécondité naturelle"; Fournier, "Pourquoi la revanche des berceaux?"
21 Nash, "Genealogical Relatedness," 3.
22 Ibid.
23 "Re: manitouabeouich/outchibahabanoukoueou," Metis – Family History & Genealogy Message Board, Ancestry (hereafter, Ancestry forum), 28 September 2011, 9:53 a.m., https://www.ancestry.co.uk/boards/topics.ethnic.natam.nations.metis.metisgen/2622/mb.ashx (accessed 10 February 2017).

24 Ibid., 23 February 2013, 7:14 p.m.
25 Ibid., 6 January 2016, 1:49 p.m.
26 "Canadian Metis Organizations," Ancestry forum, 3 September 2005, 11:37 a.m., https://www.ancestry.com/boards/thread.aspx?mv=flat&m=804&p=topics.ethnic.natam.nations.metis.metisgen (accessed 10 February 2017).
27 Gaudry, "Communing with the Dead," 168.
28 Macdougall, "Wahkootowin," 433.
29 "Re: manitouabeouich," Ancestry forum, 30 December 2008, 11:22 a.m.
30 Ibid., 28 September 2011, 8:17 p.m.
31 "Re: Canadian Metis Organizations," Ancestry forum, 23 May 2008, 6:00 p.m., https://www.ancestry.co.uk/boards/topics.ethnic.natam.nations.metis.metisgen/804.2.1/mb.ashx (accessed 10 February 2017).
32 To read more about the political struggle of non-status Algonquins in the territory covered by the AOO land claim process, see Lawrence, *Fractured Homeland*; Gehl, *The Truth That Wampum Tells*.
33 Algonquin Nation Secretariat, "Review of AOO Voter's List."
34 Anishinabek is used in central and northern Ontario, and Anishnaabeg is used by Algonquins in Quebec and eastern Ontario. I follow the term used in the given region.
35 Barnwell, "Genealogy Craze," 265.
36 Algonquins of Ontario, "Master Schedule of Algonquin Ancestors."
37 Algonquins of Ontario, "Thomas Laguarde Decision."
38 Barrera, "Key Algonquin Chief."
39 APTN National News, "Algonquins of Pikwakanagan."
40 Sturm, *Becoming Indian*, 153.
41 Watso, "Vermont Senate."
42 Roy, "Abenaki Sociality," 5.
43 Standing Committee, "Testimony by Gilles O'Bomsawin."
44 Simpson, "Land as Pedagogy." See also Doerfler, Stark, and Sinclair, *Centering Anishinaabeg Studies*.
45 "Re: Le métissage au Québec," Ancestry forum, 8 September 2013, 8:04 p.m.
46 Ibid., 8 September 2013 8:07 p.m.
47 Ibid., 8 September 2013 8:07 p.m.
48 Barker, *Native Acts*, 94.
49 Gaudry, "Communing with the Dead," 163.
50 "Descendance Métis," Généalogie du Québec et d'Amérique française (hereafter, GQAF forum), 28 March 2016, 3:42 p.m., https://www.nosorigines.qc.ca/genealogie_forum_famille.aspx?question=5067 (accessed 14 February 2017).

51 Ibid., 28 March 2016, 6:06 p.m.; 28 March 2016, 6:12 p.m.; 28 March 2016, 6:20 p.m.; 28 March 2016, 6:42 p.m.; 28 March 2016, 6:44 p.m.; 28 March 2016, 6:46 p.m.
52 Ibid., 30 March 2016, 9:26 a.m.
53 Ibid., 30 March 2016, 1:39 p.m.
54 Garroutte, *Real Indians*, 82, emphasis in original.
55 Ibid., 85.
56 Cook-Lynn, "Meeting of Indian Professors," 58.
57 Native American and Indigenous Studies Association, "NAISA Statement on Indigenous Identity Fraud."
58 "Re: Descendance Métis," GQAF forum, 30 March 2016, 9:26 p.m.
59 Ibid.
60 Desjardins, "Homogénéité ethnique."

Chapter Two
ASPIRATIONAL DESCENT: CREATING INDIGENOUS WOMEN ANCESTORS

1 Haley and Wilcoxon, "How Spaniards Became Chumash."
2 Barnwell, "Genealogy Craze," 263.
3 "Descendance Métis," GQAF forum, 7 July 2017, 2:12 p.m., https://www.nosorigines.qc.ca/genealogie_forum_famille.aspx?question=5790 (accessed 12 March 2017).
4 Ibid., 7 July 2017, 5:20 p.m.
5 "Descendance autochtone," Vos origins (hereafter, VO forum), 28 March 2016, 4:35 p.m., https://www.vosoriginesyourroots.org/t16853-descendance-autochtone (accessed 5 January 2017).
6 Ibid., 28 March 2016, 6:10 p.m.
7 Ibid., 29 March 2016, 12:41 p.m.
8 Ibid., 2 April 2016, 10:03 a.m.
9 "Opinion sur cette nation Métis," VO forum, 28 April 2016, 3:56 p.m., https://www.vosoriginesyourroots.org/t17150-demandes-de-cartes-metisses-et-informations (accessed 5 January 2017).
10 "Re: Demandes de cartes Métisses et informations," VO forum, 29 April 2016, 2:53 p.m., https://www.vosoriginesyourroots.org/t17150-demandes-de-cartes-metisses-et-informations (accessed 5 January 2017).
11 "Arrière-arrière-grand-mère Ojibwé?," Forum de discussions, Nation autochtone du Québec (hereafter, NAQ forum), 4 May 2017, 11:01 a.m., http://forum.autochtones.ca/viewtopic.php?t=9182 (accessed 25 March 2017).
12 Ibid., 6 May 2017, 6:50 p.m.

13 Ibid.
14 "Re: ancêtre améridiens," NAQ forum, 26 April 2017, 9:37 a.m., http://forum.autochtones.ca/viewtopic.php?t=9180 (accessed 25 March 2017).
15 Ibid., 28 April 2017, 11:14 a.m.
16 "Re: Françoise Morel – une autochtone ??," NAQ forum, 17 December 2012, 1:08 p.m., http://forum.autochtones.ca/viewtopic.php?t=8708 (accessed 25 March 2017).
17 Ibid.
18 "Re: Les meilleures sources pour la recherche généalogique," NAQ forum, 31 Dec. 2012, 12:28 a.m., http://forum.autochtones.ca/viewtopic.php?f=17&t=4253 (accessed 25 March 2017).
19 Ibid., 1 January 2012, 12:05 p.m., emphasis in original.
20 Ibid.
21 Sturm, *Becoming Indian*, 42.
22 Gaudry, "Communing with the Dead," 168.
23 Nelson, "Bio Science," 761.
24 Nash, "Genealogical Relatedness," 4.
25 Kramer, "Genomic Imaginary," 80.
26 TallBear, *Native American DNA*, 17.
27 Bolnick et al., "Science and Business," 399.
28 Jobling, Rasteiro, and Wetton, "In the Blood," 143.
29 "Descendance autochtone," VO forum, March 29, 2016. 12:41a.m.
30 Ibid., 29 March 2016, 12:51 p.m.
31 "Re: Indiens Algonquins de Trois-Rivières," Ancestry forum, 18 March 2011, 7:32 p.m., https://www.ancestry.ca/boards/thread.aspx?mv=flat&m=2668&p=topics.ethnic.natam.nations.metis.metisgen (accessed 10 February 2017).
32 Ibid., 19 March 2011, 8:28 a.m.
33 Ibid., 19 March 2011, 11:06 p.m.
34 "Re: Le métissage au Québec: un phénomène de faible ampleur," VO forum, 24 February 2014, 8:59 p.m., https://www.vosoriginesyourroots.org/t1019-le-metissage-au-quebec-un-phenomene-de-faible-ampleur (accessed 5 January 2017), emphasis added.
35 Ibid., 24 February 2014, 10:52 p.m.
36 Ibid., 25 February 2014, 12:34 p.m.
37 Algonquins of Greater Golden Lake First Nation, "Françoise Grenier Decision," 6.
38 "Re: Descendance Métis," GQAF forum, 31 March 2016, 10:26 a.m., https://www.nosorigines.qc.ca/genealogie_forum_famille.aspx?question=5067 (accessed 14 February 2017).

39 Duster, "Post-genomic Surprise." See also Emery et al., "Estimates of Continental Ancestry"; Jobling, Rasteiro, and Wetton, "In the Blood."
40 Lussier, King-McMahon, and Robitaille, "Catherine Pillard."
41 Ibid., 53.
42 Smith, "In Canada, Feeling 'Robbed.'"
43 Lussier, King-McMahon, and Robitaille, "Catherine Pillard," 53.
44 Nelson, "Bio Science," 763.
45 Lussier, King-McMahon, and Robitaille, "Catherine Pillard," 53.
46 "Re: Charles Ouellette born 1867-02-06 Oka, Qc.," Ancestry forum, 24 May 2008 9:32 a.m., https://www.ancestry.com/boards/thread.aspx?mv=flat&m=804&p=topics.ethnic.natam.nations.metis.metisgen (accessed 10 February 2017).
47 Ibid.
48 "Re: Indiens Algonquins de Trois-Rivières," Ancestry forum, 27 March 2016, 6:00 p.m., https://www.ancestry.com/boards/topics.ethnic.natam.nations.metis.metisgen/2668.3.1.3.1/mb.ashx (accessed 10 February 2017).
49 Beaugrand, "L'ADN mitochondrial de Catherine Pillard," 8–9.
50 Ibid., 5.
51 Viel, "Sur les traces de Catherine Pillard"; Moreau-DesHarnais, "Timeline on Catherine Pillard."
52 Colby, "DNA Update–Catherine Pillard."
53 Barnwell, "Genealogy Craze," 263.
54 Association des Charron et Ducharme, "Catherine Pillard's Origins."
55 White, *Dictionnaire généalogique des familles acadiennes*.
56 Scherer et al., "The History."
57 "Ascendance Micmac et/ou Malécite," GQAF forum, 22 February 2017, 2:51 p.m., https://www.nosorigines.qc.ca/genealogie_forum_famille.aspx?question=5572 (accessed 10 March 2017).
58 Ibid., 23 February 2017, 3:40 p.m.
59 Ibid., 25 February 2017, 8:35 a.m.
60 Savard, "Racines acadiennes."
61 "RE: Ascendance Micmac," 26 February 2017, 1:01 p.m.
62 Ibid., 26 February 2017, 4:06 p.m.
63 Nelson, "Bio Science," 764.
64 "Questionable record Lejeune," MetisGen Mailing List, Rootsweb (hereafter, Rootsweb forum), 7 March 2015, 3:52 a.m., https://lists.rootsweb.com/hyperkitty/list/metisgen@rootsweb.com/thread/227853/ (accessed 10 June 2017).

65 Ibid., 7 March 2015, 5:39 a.m.

66 Ibid.

67 See Vachon, *L'histoire de la famille acadienne*.

68 "Racine indienne/métis provenant d'Acadie," VO forum, 30 October 2013, 12:28 a.m., https://www.vosoriginesyourroots.org/t5645-racine-indienne-metis-provenant-d-acadie (accessed 5 January 2017).

69 Ibid., 30 October 2013, 12:29 a.m.

70 Ibid., 21 April 2014, 11:58 p.m.

71 Sturm, *Becoming Indian*, 112.

72 Palmater, *Beyond Blood*, 203.

73 Sturm, *Becoming Indian*, 17.

Chapter Three
LATERAL DESCENT: REMAKING FAMILY IN THE PAST

1 "Re: Canadian Metis Organizations," Ancestry forum, 15 September 2005, 1:43 p.m., https://www.ancestry.com/boards/thread.aspx?m=804&p=topics.ethnic.natam.nations.metis.metisgen (accessed 10 February 2017).

2 Ibid., 15 September 2005, 3:14 p.m.

3 Stanley, *Louis Riel*.

4 Pelta, "La judiciarisation de l'identité métisse," 146.

5 Canada, Parliament, Senate, Le comité sénatorial permanent des peuples autochtones [Standing committee on Aboriginal peoples], *Témoignages*, 41st Parl., 1st sess. (2012).

6 "J'aimerais savoir si j'ai des ancêtres amérindiens?," GQAF forum, 25 August 2015, 11:36 a.m., https://www.nosorigines.qc.ca/genealogie_forum_famille.aspx?question=4650 (accessed 10 January 2017).

7 Ibid., 30 August 2015, 12:30 p.m.

8 The book's full title is *The Redeemed Captive, Returning to Zion. A Faithful History of Remarkable Occurrences, in the Captivity and the Deliverance of Mr. John Williams ... Who ... Was ... Carried Away, with His Family, and His Neighbourhood, unto Canada*.

9 Haefeli and Sweeney, *Captive Histories*, 341.

10 Simpson, "Captivating Eunice," 109.

11 See also Parmenter, "After the Mourning Wars."

12 Simpson, "Captivating Eunice," 116.

13 Ibid., 114.

14 Demos, *Unredeemed Captive*.

15 Garroutte, *Real Indians*, 131.

Notes to Pages 109 – 122 | 249

16 Pouliot-Thisdale, "Unions Métis et réclamations au Québec," 4, my translation.
17 Adese, "Anxious States," 6.
18 Gaudry, "Métis-ization of Canada," 66.
19 "Re: Indiens Algonquins de Trois-Rivières," Ancestry forum, 7 August 2011, 7:32 p.m., https://www.ancestry.ca/boards/thread.aspx?mv=flat&m=2668&p=topics.ethnic.natam.nations.metis.metisgen (accessed 10 February 2017).
20 Ibid.
21 Ibid., 8 August 2011, 11:19 p.m.
22 See Andersen, *Métis*; Adese, Todd, and Stevenson, "Mediating Métis Identity."
23 Devine, *The People Who Own Themselves*, 4.
24 Lavoie, *L'émigration des Québécois*.
25 See Thistle, "Puzzle of the Morrissette-Arcand Clan," 73.
26 Ibid., 52.
27 McKay, "History of the McKay Family."
28 Devine, *The People Who Own Themselves*, 134–35.
29 Thistle, "Puzzle of the Morrissette-Arcand Clan," 74.
30 Ibid., 87.
31 Bumsted, *Red River Rebellion*, 137.
32 Thistle, "Puzzle of the Morrissette-Arcand Clan," 100.
33 Barkwell, "Veterans and Families."
34 Podruchny and Thistle, "Geography of Blood."
35 Thistle, "Puzzle of the Morrissette-Arcand Clan," 118.
36 Macdougall, "Wahkootowin," 433.
37 See Innes, *Elder Brother*, 99.
38 Devine, *The People Who Own Themselves*, 169–72.
39 Thistle, "Puzzle of the Morrissette-Arcand Clan."
40 Innes, *Elder Brother*, 57.
41 Morin, *First Metis Families of Quebec*.
42 Devine, *The People Who Own Themselves*, 136.
43 Canada, Parliament, *Sessional Papers, 1886*, Paper no. 45a, p. 3.
44 Macdougall and St-Onge, "Métis in the Borderlands," 259.
45 Ibid., 261.
46 As cited in Graybill, *Policing the Great Plains*, 44.
47 Barkwell, "Metis Petition of September 2, 1880."
48 Barkwell, "Métis Petition of August 29, 1882."

49 Morin, *First Metis Families of Quebec*.
50 See Innes, *Elder Brother*, 60–63; Vrooman, *Whole Country*.
51 See Morin, *First Metis Families of Quebec*.
52 Innes, *Elder Brother*, 61.
53 Morin, *First Metis Families of Quebec*.
54 Macdougall, "Wahkootowin," 449.
55 Foster, *We Know Who We Are*; Hogue, *Metis and the Medicine Line*.
56 Macdougall and St-Onge, "Métis in the Borderlands."
57 Martel, *Collected Writings of Louis Riel*, 223–26.
58 See Morin, *First Metis Families of Quebec*.
59 Innes, *Elder Brother*, 63–65, 83.
60 Macdougall and St-Onge, "Métis in the Borderlands," 260.
61 Ibid., 261.
62 Marmon, "Last Card Played."
63 Vrooman, *Whole Country*.
64 Nash, "Genealogical Relatedness," 4.
65 Ens, "Battle of Seven Oaks." See also Andersen, *Métis*.
66 Nash, "Genealogical Relatedness," 4.
67 Innes, *Elder Brother*, 38.
68 Gaudry, "Communing with the Dead."

Chapter Four
AFTER POWLEY: ANTI-INDIGENOUS ACTIVISM AND BECOMING MÉTIS IN TWO REGIONS OF QUEBEC

1 Ross-Tremblay and Hamidi, "Les écueils de l'extinction," 53.
2 Sturm, *Becoming Indian*, 82.
3 In what may be a first instance for self-identified métis plaintiffs, the Vautour group whose *Powley* claims were ultimately rejected by the New Brunswick courts filed a land claim to a vast expanse of territory in Mi'kma'ki (in this case, central-east New Brunswick) in July 2018. Their claim overlaps with that filed by the Elsipogtog First Nation, the largest Mi'kmaw community in New Brunswick.
4 Gélinas and Duceppe-Lamarre, "Chamanisme et définition identitaire"; Michaux, "Ni Amérindiens ni Eurocanadiens."
5 Andersen, *Métis*, 73–74.
6 Pelta, "La judiciarisation de l'identité métisse," 126–27.
7 Statistics Canada, "2006 Aboriginal Population Profile: Quebec."

8   Andersen, "From Nation to Population," 359. Sociologist C. Matthew Snipp's much earlier study of the 1980 U.S. Census explained how the large majority of individuals (six out of seven million) claiming "Indian" ancestry did not claim to be "American Indian." He went on to conclude that socioeconomic factors accounted for one's choice in the census; that is, people move to an "American Indian" identity when it is economically and socially desirable. Snipp, "Who are American Indians?"
9   Statistics Canada, "2006 Aboriginal Population Profile: Quebec."
10 Statistics Canada, "2006 Census Topic-Based Tabulations."
11 Statistics Canada, "Aboriginal Peoples in Canada."
12 See Gélinas, *Indiens et Eurocanadiens*.
13 I refer to each interview participant by a number that corresponds to the order in which they were interviewed.
14 Tremblay, "André Forbes."
15 Statistics Canada, "2006 Census Topic-Based Tabulations."
16 Sturm, *Becoming Indian*, 82.
17 "Charte des valeurs," *Huffington Post Québec*.
18 Duchaine, "Côte-Nord."
19 Sturm, *Becoming Indian*, 82–83.
20 Ibid., 82.
21 Charest, "Qui a peur des Innus?"
22 Charest, "Les relations entre les Innus et les non-Innus."
23 For instance, in the last years of her life, Jeanne-Mance Charlish along with other Innu women elders founded the Coalition Ukauimau aimu (Mothers organize) to oppose the treaty negotiations. See "Décès de Jeanne-Mance Charlish," CMAQ.
24 Ross-Tremblay and Hamidi, "Les écueils de l'extinction," 52.
25 Sturm, *Becoming Indian*, 54.
26 Pelta, "La judiciarisation de l'identité métisse," 117.
27 Leydet, "Autochtones et non-autochtones," 63.
28 See, for example, Charest, "Qui a peur des Innus?"; Cook, "Les droits ancestraux."
29 Philosopher Dominique Leydet has outlined many examples of sustained Innu resistance to these efforts, including in numerous briefs presented to the government commission charged with investigating the "controversy" in 2003. See Leydet, "Autochtones et non-autochtones," 61, 65.
30 Sturm, *Becoming Indian*, 50.
31 Charest, "Qui a peur des Innus?," 203.
32 Ibid., 190.
33 Charest, "Les relations entre les Innus et les non-Innus," 17.

34 Bouchard et al., *Le pays trahi*, 23, emphasis mine.
35 Rousseau, "Critique en matière d'ethnogenèse," 119.
36 Charest, "Qui a peur des Innus?"; Leydet, "Autochtones et non-autochtones"; Cook, "Les droits ancestraux."
37 See, for example, Cleary, *L'enfant de 7 000 ans*.
38 Charest, "Qui a peur des Innus?"
39 Cook, "Les droits ancestraux."
40 Bouchard, "Don't Think of Self-Government," 101.
41 "L'Association du droit des blancs," *Le Soleil*, A5.
42 Loranger-Saindon, "Médias, innus et allochtones."
43 Bouchard, "Don't Think of Self-Government," 84.
44 Ibid., 100.
45 Charest, "Qui a peur des Innus?," 204.
46 Cliche, "Ignatieff congédie un candidat."
47 Cook, "Les droits ancestraux."
48 Ibid.
49 McKenzie and Vincent, "La 'guerre du saumon,'" 108–9.
50 Cleary, *L'enfant de 7 000 ans*, 202.
51 Ibid., 203.
52 Capitaine, "Le Québec n'est pas raciste, mais . . . ," 47.
53 Statistics Canada, *Aboriginal Languages*.
54 Sturm, *Becoming Indian*, 60. See also Gaudry and Leroux, "White Settler Revisionism."
55 Charest, "Qui a peur des Innus?"; Charest, "Les relations entre les Innus et les non-Innus"; Cook, "Les droits ancestraux."
56 Côté, "Un constat d'une extrême brutalité"; Charest, "La supposée disparition"; Cleary, "Autochtones." For Innu commentators embedded in articles, see Saint-Pierre, "Dans 'Le dernier des Montagnais'"; Saint-Pierre, "La disparition d'une race"; Tremblay, "Les Montagnais."
57 Cook, "Les droits ancestraux," 200–201.
58 Rousseau, "Ni tout l'un, ni tout l'autre," 116.
59 See also Charest, "La disparition des Montagnais."
60 Bouchard, *Le dernier des Montagnais*, 201.
61 Bouchard was also one of the editors and the principal author of *Le pays trahi* (2000).
62 Bouchard, *Mémoire adressé à la commission parlementaire*.

63   Minutes, CMDRSM annual general meeting, 28 October 2006, 5.
64   Ibid., 6.
65   Alleman, *Nomenclature des Métis*.
66   Rousseau, "Critique en matière d'ethnogenèse," 43.
67   Charest, "Les relations entre les Innus et les non-Innus," 12.

Chapter Five
THE LARGEST SELF-IDENTIFIED MÉTIS ORGANIZATION IN QUEBEC: THE MÉTIS NATION OF THE RISING SUN

1   Minutes, Métis Nation of the Rising Sun (MNRS) special general meeting, 10 September 2016.
2   Courtemanche, "Le nombre de métis gaspésiens."
3   Gaudry and Leroux, "Making Métis Everywhere"; Leroux, "'We've Been Here for 2,000 Years.'"
4   Statistics Canada, "Aboriginal Peoples in Canada."
5   Ibid.
6   Statistics Canada, *Focus on Geography Series*.
7   Page, "More Quebecers Identifying as Indigenous."
8   Statistics Canada, *Focus on Geography Series*.
9   Les pourvoiries du Québec, "La pourvoirie statistique/économique," 2.
10 Tremblay, "Politique de la mémoire," 131.
11 Ibid., 136.
12 Ibid., 137.
13 Sturm, *Becoming Indian*, 82.
14 Statistics Canada, "Aboriginal Peoples in Canada"; Sturm, *Becoming Indian*, 18.
15 "Pourvoirie autochtone," Radio-Canada.
16 Jean cited in Michaux, "Ni Amérindiens ni Eurocanadiens," 209.
17 Tremblay, "Politique de la mémoire," 142.
18 Lavoie, "La pourvoirie autochtone."
19 Ibid.
20 Quoted in "Re: Pourvoirie: les Métis s'opposent," NAQ forum, 8 November 2006, 1:12 p.m., http://forum.autochtones.ca/viewtopic.php?f=2&t=1802&start=15 (accessed 15 January 2018).
21 Ibid.
22 Lavoie, "La pourvoirie autochtone."

23 Quoted in "voici réponse à m.leblanc," NAQ forum, 16 December 2006, 8:10 p.m., http://forum.autochtones.ca/viewtopic.php?f=2&t=1802&start=15 (accessed 15 January 2018).

24 Ibid.

25 Communauté métisse de la Gaspésie and Communauté métisse de l'Estrie, "Un peuple 'oublié.'"

26 Ibid.

27 Lavoie, "90% des Gaspésiens."

28 Ibid.

29 Nelson, "Bio Science."

30 MNRS, "Familles métisses en Gaspésie."

31 Jean, "Ethnogenèse des premiers métis canadiens," 225.

32 Mothers of Acadia, "Mothers of Acadia mtDNA Project."

33 MNRS, "Familles métisses en Gaspésie."

34 Mothers of Acadia, "Mothers of Acadia mtDNA Project."

35 Minutes, MNRS annual general meeting, 12 September 2015, http://www.metisgaspesie.com/files/AGA-Métis-12-septembre-2015.pdf (accessed 29 September 2017).

36 "Métis in Gaspé," *CBC News*.

37 Ibid.

38 TallBear, *Native American DNA*.

39 This product has been taken off the Accu-metrics website after the dog controversy discussed on page 211.

40 Accu-metrics, "First Nation, Metis & Native American DNA Testing Service."

41 Bolnick et al., "Science and Business," 399.

42 TallBear, "Genomic Articulations of Indigeneity," 510.

43 Fullwiley, "'Contemporary Synthesis,'" 805.

44 MNRS, *Procès-verbal*.

45 Gespe'gewa'gi Mi'gmawei Mawiomi, *Nta'tugwaqanminen, Our story*.

46 Metallic, "Ta'n teligji'tegen"; Metallic, "Strengthening Our Relations."

47 Obomsawin, *Incident at Restigouche*; Obomsawin, *Our Nationhood*.

48 See, for example, Gaudry and Leroux, "Making Métis Everywhere"; Leroux, "'We've Been Here for 2,000 Years.'"

49 Minutes, MNRS special general meeting, 10 September 2016.

50 TallBear, *Native American DNA*, 6, emphasis in original.

51 Isaac, "Métis Movement in Chibougamau?"

52 Tremblay, "La communauté de Chibougamau-Chapais."
53 Bolnick et al., "Science and Business," 399.
54 Jobling, Rasteiro, and Wetton, "In the Blood," 147.
55 Ibid., 155.
56 Ibid., 157.
57 Bolnick et al., "Science and Business."
58 Barrera and Foxcroft, "Heredity or Hoax?"
59 TallBear, *Native American DNA*, 17.
60 Lavoie, "Les Paspéyas sont Autochtones."

Conclusion
WHITE CLAIMS TO INDIGENOUS IDENTITY

1 Chiu, "Probe Launched."
2 Mi'kmaq Rights Initiative, "Challenge with Self-Identification"; Mi'kmaq Rights Initiative, "Mi'kmaq Chiefs Respond"; Mi'kmaq Rights Initiative, "Understanding Métis Rights."
3 Métis National Council and Mi'kmaq of Nova Scotia, "Memorandum of Understanding," 1.
4 Ibid, 2.
5 Marcus, "Northfield's Day of History."
6 Sturm, *Becoming Indian*, 51–55.

BIBLIOGRAPHY

GENEALOGY FORUMS CONSULTED

Ancestry.co.uk Metis/First Nations Family History & Genealogy Message Board. https://www.ancestry.co.uk/boards/topics.ethnic.metis/mb.ashx.

Généalogie du Québec et d'Amérique française (GQAF) forum. https://www.nosorigines.qc.ca/genealogie_forum.aspx.

Nation autochtone du Québec (NAQ) forum. http://forum.autochtones.ca/viewforum.php?f=17.

Rootsweb MetisGen-L list. https://mailinglists.rootsweb.com/listindexes/details?list_name=metisgen.

Vos origines (VO) forum. https://www.vosoriginesyourroots.org/.

SIGNIFICANT LEGAL CASES AND STATUTES

Calder et al. v. Attorney-General of British Columbia, [1973] SCR 313.

The Constitution Act, 1982, Schedule B to the Canada Act 1982 (UK), 1982, c 11.

Corneau c Québec (Procureure générale), 2016 QCCA 1835.

Game and Fish Act, RSO 1990, c G.1.

Indian Act, RSC 1985, c I-5.

Parent c R, 2016 QCCA 271.

R v Powley, [2003] 2 SCR 207, 2003 SCC 43.

Séguin c Québec (Procureure générale), 2016 QCCS 1881.

SCHOLARLY AND OTHER SOURCES

Aboriginal Peoples Television Network. "Algonquins of Pikwakanagan Reject AOO Modern Treaty." 17 March 2016. https://aptnnews.ca/2016/03/17/algonquins-of-pikwakanagan-reject-aoo-modern-treaty/ (accessed 25 August 2017).

Accu-metrics. "First Nation, Metis & Native American DNA Testing Service." http://www.accu-metrics.com/first-nation.php (accessed 10 January 2017).

Adese, Jennifer. "Anxious States and the Co-optation of Métisness." *Nomorepotlucks*, no. 24 (November–December 2012). http://nomorepotlucks.org/site/anxious-states-and-the-co-optation-of-metisness-jennifer-adese/ (accessed 15 January 2017).

———. "A Tale of Two Constitutions: Métis Nationhood and Section 35(2)'s Impact on Interpretations of Daniels," *TOPIA: Canadian Journal of Cultural Studies* 36 (2016): 7–19.

Adese, Jennifer, Zoe Todd, and Shaun Stevenson. "Mediating Métis Identity: An Interview with Jennifer Adese and Zoe Todd," *MediaTropes* 7, no. 1 (2017): 1–25.

Algonquin Nation Secretariat. "Review of AOO Voter's List of December 2, 2015." https://www.scribd.com/doc/300528995/Algonquin-Nation-Secretariat-Analysis-of-AOO-Voters-List-Feb-25-2016 (accessed 25 July 2017).

Algonquins of Greater Golden Lake First Nation. "Françoise Grenier Decision." 12 May 2013. http://www.greatergoldenlake.com/adob/FrancoisGrenierDecisionMay14.pdf (accessed 21 March 2017).

Algonquins of Ontario. "Master Schedule of Algonquin Ancestors – DRAFT," 2 October 2013.

———. "Thomas Laguarde Decision," 31 March 2013.

Alleman, Alexandre. *Nomenclature des Métis du Domaine du Roy et la Seigneurie de Mingan*. Chicoutimi, self-pub., 2005.

Allen, Reuben. "Investigating the Cultural Conception of Race in Puerto Rico: Residents' Thoughts on the U.S. Census, Discrimination, and Interventionist Policies." *Latin American and Caribbean Ethnic Studies* 12, no. 3 (2016): 201–26.

Alliance autochtone du Québec. "Qui peut devenir membre." http://www.aaqnaq.com/accueil/membership/qui-peut-devenir-membre/ (accessed 21 December 2018).

Andersen, Chris. "From Nation to Population: The Racialisation of 'Métis' in the Canadian Census." *Nations and Nationalism* 14, no. 2 (2008): 347–68.

———. *Métis: Race, Recognition, and the Struggle for Indigenous Peoplehood*. Vancouver: University of British Columbia Press, 2014.

Anderson, Karen. *Chain Her by One Foot: The Subjugation of Women in Seventeenth-Century New France*. London: Cambridge University Press, 1991.

Association des Charron et Ducharme. "Catherine Pillard's Origins." http://www.charron-ducharme.org/index.php/en/catherine-pillard-en/87-catherine-pillard-s-origin (accessed 3 December 2017).

Aubert, Guillaume. "'The Blood of France': Race and Purity of Blood in the French Atlantic World." *William and Mary Quarterly* 61, no. 3 (2004): 439–78.

Barker, Joanne. *Native Acts: Law, Recognition, and Cultural Authenticity*. Durham, NC: Duke University Press, 2011.

Barkwell, Lawrence. "Métis Petition of August 29, 1882." Saskatoon: Gabriel Dumont Institute, 2009.

———. "Metis Petition of September 2, 1880." Saskatoon: Gabriel Dumont Institute, 2014.

———. "Veterans and Families of the 1885 Northwest Resistance." Saskatoon: Gabriel Dumont Institute, 2011.

Barnwell, Ashley. "The Genealogy Craze: Authoring an Authentic Identity through Family History Research." *Life Writing* 10, no. 3 (2013): 261–75.

Barrera, Jorge. "Key Algonquin Chief Wants Tighter Rules on Who Can Be Part of Massive Ontario Modern Treaty." *APTN National News*, 27 February 2016. http://aptnnews.ca /2016/02/27/key-algonquin-chief-wants-tighter-rules-on-who-can-be-part-of-massive-ontario-modern-treaty/ (accessed 25 August 2017).

Barrera, Jorge, and Tiffany Foxcroft. "Heredity or Hoax? How Dog DNA Helped Uncover a Suspected Indian Status Scam." *CBC News*, 13 June 2018. https://newsinteractives.cbc. ca/longform/dna-ancestry-test (accessed 13 June 2018).

Basu, Paul. *Highland Homecomings: Genealogy and Heritage Tourism in the Scottish Diaspora*. London: Routledge, 2007.

Beaugrand, Jacques. "L'ADN mitochondrial de Catherine Pillard." *Traits d'union* 16, no. 3 (2009). http://www.charron-ducharme.org/images/PDF/Vol_16No3.pdf (accessed 28 October 2017).

Beauregard, Yves. "Mythe ou réalité. Les origines amérindiennes des Québécois: Entrevue avec Hubert Charbonneau." *Cap-aux-Diamants: La revue d'histoire du Québec*, no. 34 (1993): 38–42.

Belmessous, Saliha. "Assimilation and Racialism in Seventeenth- and Eighteenth-Century French Colonial Policy." *American Historical Review* 110, no. 2 (2005): 322–49.

Bibeau, Gilles. *Le Québec transgénique: Science, marché, humanité*. Montreal: Boréal, 2004.

Bolnick, Deborah A., Duana Fullwiley, Troy Duster, Richard S. Cooper, Joan H. Fujimura, Jonathan Kahn, Jay S. Kaufman, et al. "The Science and Business of Ancestry Testing." *Science*, no. 318 (2007): 399–400.

Bouchard, Michel, Robert Foxcurran, and Sébastien Malette, eds. *Songs upon the Rivers: The Buried History of the French-Speaking Canadiens and Metis from the Great Lakes and the Mississippi across the Pacific*. Montreal: Baraka, 2016.

Bouchard, Nancy. "Don't Think of Self-Government: The Debate over Which Language Should Govern Aboriginal Peoples' Relationship with the State." Master's thesis, Concordia University, 2010.

Bouchard, Russel. *Le dernier des Montagnais: Vie et mort de la nation ilnu*. Chicoutimi, self-pub., 1995.

———. "Mémoire adressé à la commission parlementaire siégeant sur l'Approche commune en janvier 2003," 2003.

Bouchard, Russel, Charles Côté, Charles-Julien Gauvin, Richard Harvey, Daniel Larouche, and Mario Tremblay. *Le pays trahi*. Saguenay–Lac-Saint-Jean: La société du 14 juillet, 2001.

Boulle, Pierre. "François Bernier and the Origins of the Modern Concept of Race." In *The Color of Liberty: Histories of Race in France*, edited by Tyler Stovall and Sue Peabody, 11–27. Durham, NC: Duke University Press, 2003.

Brings Plenty, Trevino L. "Pretend Indian Exegesis: The Pretend Indian Uncanny Valley Hypothesis in Literature and Beyond." *Transmotion* 4, no. 2 (2018): 142–52.

Bumsted, John M. *The Red River Rebellion*. Winnipeg: Watson and Dwyer, 1996.

Burelle, Julie. *Encounters on Contested Lands: Indigenous Performances of Sovereignty and Nationhood in Québec*. Chicago: Northwestern University Press, 2018.

Canada. Parliament. Senate. Le comité senatorial permanent des peuples autochtones [Standing committee on Aboriginal peoples]. *Témoignages*, 41st Parl., 1st sess. (2012). https://sencanada.ca/en/Content/Sen/committee/411/appa/49826-f (accessed 10 August 2017).

Canada. Parliament. *Sessional Papers, 1886*. Paper no. 45a, 3–4.

Capitaine, Brieg. "Le Québec n'est pas raciste, mais . . . : Conflictualités réelles et imaginaires sur la Côte-Nord." *Nouveaux Cahiers du socialisme* 18 (2017): 46–50.

Charbonneau, Hubert. "Le caractère français des pionniers de la vallée laurentienne." *Cahiers québécois de démographie* 19, no. 1 (1990): 49–62.

———. "Et pourtant français à 95 pour cent." *Mémoires de la Société généalogique canadienne-française* 40, no. 1 (1989): 11–17.

———. *Tourouvre-au-Perche aux XVIIe et XVIIIe siècles: Étude de démographie historique*. Paris: Presses universitaires de France, 1970.

———. *Vie et mort de nos ancêtres: Étude démographique*. Montreal: Presses de l'Université de Montréal, 1975.

Charbonneau, Hubert, André Guillemette, Jacques Légaré, Bertrand Desjardins, Yves Landry, and François Nault, eds. *Naissance d'une population: Les Français établis au Canada au XVIIe siècle*. Montreal: Presses de l'Université de Montréal, 1987.

Charest, Paul. "La disparition des Montagnais et la négation des droits aborigènes: Commentaires critiques sur le livre de Nelson-Martin Dawson, *Feu, fourrures, fléaux et foi foudroyèrent les Montagnais* (2005)." *Recherches amérindiennes au Québec* 39, no. 3 (2009): 81–95.

———. "La supposée disparition des Attikamekw et des Montagnais." *Le Soleil*, 25 March 1996, B7.

———. "Les relations entre les Innus et les non-Innus en Sagamie: Une double analyse 'impressionniste' et discursive." *Recherches amérindiennes au Québec* 43, no. 1 (2013): 9–24.

———. "Qui a peur des Innus? Reflexions sur les debats au sujet du projet d'entente de principe entre les Innus de Mashteuiatsh, Essipit, Betsiamites et Nutashkuan et les gouvernements du Quebec et du Canada." *Anthropologie et sociétés* 27, no. 2 (2003): 185–207.

"Charte des valeurs: le surprenant témoignage des Pineault-Caron aux audiences publiques." *Huffington Post Québec*, 17 January 2014. http://quebec.huffington post.ca/ 2014/ 01/ 17/temoignage-famille-pineault-caron-audiences-charte-des-valeurs_n_4618477.html (accessed 2 February 2017).

Chiu, Elizabeth. "Probe Launched into Allegations N.S. 'Métis Cards' Used to Buy Cars and Gas." *CBC News*, 26 June 2018. https://www.cbc.ca/news/canad a/nova-scotia/probe-launched-into-n-s-métis-card-tax-free-1.4716468 (accessed 26 June 2018).

Choquette, Leslie. *Frenchmen into Peasants*. Cambridge, MA: Harvard University Press, 1997.

Chrétien, Yves, Denys Delâge, and Sylvie Vincent, eds. *Au croisement de nos destins: Quand Uepishtikueiau devint Québec*. Montreal: Recherches amérindiennes au Québec, 2009.

Cleary, Bernard. "Autochtones: la 'job-de-bras' des 'historiens-politiciens.'" *La Presse*, 8 May 1996, B3.

———. *L'enfant de 7 000 ans: Le long portage vers la délivrance*. Quebec City: Septentrion, 1989.

Cliche, Jean-François. "Ignatieff congédie un candidat pour propos racistes." *Le Soleil*, 7 April 2011.

Colby, Susan. "DNA Update–Catherine Pillard." *Michigan's Habitant Heritage* 36, no. 3 (2015): 116–17.

Communauté métisse de la Gaspésie and Communauté métisse de l'Estrie. "Un peuple 'oublié' depuis des siècles." Brief presented to La Commission de consultation sur les pratiques d'accommodement reliées aux differences culturelles [Bouchard-Taylor Commission], October 2007. http://www.autochtones.ca/portal/fr/ArticleView.php?article_id=469 (accessed 16 July 2016).

Cook, Mathieu. "Les droits ancestraux autochtones: Reconnaissance et contestation: La controverse entourant 'l'Approche commune.'" *Recherches amérindiennes au Québec* 43, no. 1 (2013): 59–68.

———. "Les droits ancestraux des Innus: Reconnaissance et analyse des discours sur l'altérité déployés lors d'une controverse à propos de négociations territoriales." PhD diss., Université Laval, 2016.

Cook, Peter. "Onontio Gives Birth: How the French in Canada Became Fathers to Their Indigenous Allies, 1645–73." *Canadian Historical Review* 96, no. 2 (2015): 165–93.

Cook-Lynn, Elizabeth. "Meeting of Indian Professors Takes Up Issues of 'Ethnic Fraud,' Sovereignty and Research Needs." *Wicazo Sa Review* 9, no. 1 (1993): 57–59.

Cooper, Afua. *The Hanging of Angélique: The Untold Story of Canadian Slavery and the Burning of Old Montréal*. Athens: University of Georgia Press, 2006.

Corbiere, Alan. "Identity, Appropriation, and Imposters: What Do Our Aadizookaanag (Sacred Stories) Tell Us?" *Shekon Neechie: An Indigenous History Site*, 21 June 2018.

Cornellier, Bruno. *La "chose indienne": Cinéma et politiques de la représentation autochtone au Québec et au Canada*. Montreal: Nota Bene, 2014.

———. "The 'Indian Thing': On Representation and Reality in the Liberal Settler Colony." *Settler Colonial Studies* 3, no. 1 (2013): 49–64.

Côté, Daniel. "Un constat d'une extrême brutalité." *Le Progrès-Dimanche*, 1 October 1995, A4.

Courtemanche, Alexandre. "Le nombre de métis gaspésiens double en six mois." *CHAU TVA Nouvelles*, 5 October 2016. http://chau.teleinterrives.com/nouvelle-alaune_Le_nombre_de_metis_gaspesiens_double_en_six_mois-29700 (accessed 12 October 2016).

Cowan, Mairi. "Education, Francisation, and Shifting Colonial Priorities at the Ursuline Convent in Seventeenth-Century Québec." *Canadian Historical Review* 99, no. 1 (2018): 1–29.

Daniels, Harry, and Paul L.A.H. Chartrand. "Unravelling the Riddles of Metis Definition." Unpublished Policy Paper, 2001, 60p.

D'Avignon, Mathieu, and Camil Girard, eds. *A-t-on-oublié que jadis nous étions 'frères'? Alliances fondatrices et reconnaisances des peuples autochtones dans l'histoire du Québec*. Quebec City: Les Presses de l'Université Laval, 2009.

"Décès de Jeanne-Mance Charlish, fondatrice de la Coalition Ukaimau aimu." Centre des médias alternatifs du Québec (CMAQ), 8 October 2004. http://archives-2001-2012.cmaq.net/fr/node/18407.html (accessed 29 January 2018).

Deloria, Philip J. *Playing Indian*. New Haven, CT: Yale University Press, 1998.

Demos, John. *The Unredeemed Captive: A Family Story from Early America*. New York: Vintage, 1995.

Desjardins, Bertrand. "Homogénéité ethnique de la population québécoise sous le Régime français." *Cahiers québécois de démographie* 19, no. 1 (1990): 63–76.

———. "La contribution différentielle des immigrants français à la souche canadienne-française." *Annales de Normandie* 58, no. 3–4 (2008): 69–79.

Deslandres, Dominique. "'... alors nos garçons se marieront à vos filles, & nous ne ferons plus qu'un seul peuple': Religion, genre et déploiement de la souveraineté française en Amérique aux XVIe-XVIIIe siècles – une problématique." *Revue d'histoire de l'Amérique française* 66, no. 1 (2012): 5–35.

Devine, Heather. *The People Who Own Themselves: Aboriginal Ethnogenesis in a Canadian Family, 1660–1900*. Calgary: University of Calgary Press, 2004.

Doerfler, Jill. *Those Who Belong: Identity, Family, Blood, and Citizenship among the White Earth Anishinaabeg*. Winnipeg: University of Manitoba Press, 2015.

Doerfler, Jill, Heidi Kiiwetinepinesiik Stark, and Niigaanwewidam James Sinclair, eds. *Centering Anishinaabeg Studies: Understanding the World through Stories*. East Lansing: Michigan State University Press, 2013.

Duchaine, Gabrielle. "Côte-Nord: Retour chez les Pineault-Caron." *La Presse*, 17 March 2014. http://www.lapresse.ca/actualites/dossiers/le-quebec-au-temps-de-la-charte/201403/15/ 01-4748084-cote-nrd-retour-chez-les-pineault-caron.php (accessed 2 February 2017).

Duster, Troy. "A Post-genomic Surprise: The Molecular Re-inscription of Race in Science, Law and Medicine." *British Journal of Sociology* 66, no. 1 (2015): 1–27.

Emery, Leslie S., Kevin M. Magnaye, Abigail W. Bigham, Joshua M. Akey, and Michael J. Bamshad. "Estimates of Continental Ancestry Vary Widely among Individuals with the Same mtDNA Haplogroup." *American Journal of Human Genetics* 96, no. 2 (2015): 183–93.

Enquête. Radio-Canada, 22 October 2015. http://ici.radio-canada.ca/tele/enquete/2015-2016/episodes/360817/femmes-autochtones-surete-du-quebec-sq (accessed 17 January 2017).

Ens, Gerhard J. "The Battle of Seven Oaks and the Articulation of a Metis National Tradition, 1811–1849." In *Contours of a People: Metis Family, Mobility, and History*, edited by Carolyn Podruchny, Nicole St-Onge, and Brenda Macdougall, 93–119. Norman: University of Oklahoma Press, 2012.

Foster, Martha H. *We Know Who We Are: Métis Identity in a Montana Community*. Norman: University of Oklahoma Press, 2006.

Fournier, Daniel. "Pourquoi la revanche des berceaux? L'hypothèse de la sociabilité." *Recherches sociographiques* 30, no. 2 (1990): 171–98.

Fullwiley, Duana. "The 'Contemporary Synthesis': When Politically Inclusive Genomic Science Relies on Biological Notions of Race." *Isis* 105, no. 4 (2014): 803–14.

Garroutte, Eva Marie. *Real Indians: Identity and the Survival of Native America*. Oakland: University of California Press, 2003.

Gaudry, Adam. "Communing with the Dead: The 'New Métis,' Métis Identity Appropriation, and the Displacement of Living Métis Culture." *American Indian Quarterly* 42, no. 2 (2018): 162–90.

———. "The Métis-ization of Canada: The Process of Claiming Louis Riel, Métissage and the Métis People as Canada's Mythological Origin." *aboriginal policy studies* 2, no. 2 (2013): 64–87.

Gaudry, Adam, and Chris Andersen. "Daniels v. Canada: Racialized Legacies, Settler Self-Indigenization and the Denial of Indigenous Peoplehood." *TOPIA: Canadian Journal of Cultural Studies*, no. 36 (2016): 19–30.

Gaudry, Adam, and Darryl Leroux. "White Settler Revisionism and Making Métis Everywhere: The Contemporary Evocation of Métissage in Québec and Nova Scotia." *Journal of Critical Ethnic Studies* 3, no. 1 (2017): 116–42.

Gehl, Lynn. *The Truth That Wampum Tells: My Debwewin on the Algonquin Land Claims Proces*. Halifax, NS: Fernwood Publishing, 2014.

Gélinas, Claude. *Indiens et Eurocanadiens et le cadre social du métissage au Saguenay-Lac-Saint-Jean, XVIIe–XXe siècles*. Quebec City: Septentrion, 2011.

Gélinas, Claude, and Virginie Duceppe-Lamarre. "Chamanisme et définition identitaire parmi les Métis du Québec." *Anthropologica* 57, no. 2 (2015): 341–52.

Gespe'gewa'gi Mi'gmawei Mawiomi. *Nta'tugwaqanminen, Our Story: Evolution of the Gespege'wa'gi Mi'gmaq*. Halifax: Fernwood, 2016.

Gómez, Laura E. *Manifest Destinies: The Making of the Mexican American Race*. New York: New York University Press, 2007.

Graybill, Andrew. R. *Policing the Great Plains: Rangers, Mounties, and the North American Frontier, 1875–1910*. Lincoln: University of Nebraska Press, 2007.

Groulx, Patrice. *Pièges de la mémoire: Dollard des Ormeaux, les Amérindiens et nous*. Hull, QC: Vents d'Ouest, 1998.

Gullickson, Aaron, and Ann Morning. "Choosing Race: Multiracial Ancestry and Identification." *Social Science Research* 40, no. 2 (2011): 498–512.

Haefeli, Evan, and Kevin Sweeney. *Captive Histories: English, French and Native Narratives of the 1704 Deerfield Raid*. Amherst: University of Massachusetts Press, 2004.

Haley, Brian D., and Larry R. Wilcoxon. "Anthropology and the Making of Chumash Tradition." *Current Anthropology* 38, no. 5 (1997): 761–94.

———. "How Spaniards Became Chumash and Other Tales of Ethnogenesis." *American Anthropologist* 107, no. 3 (2005): 432–45.

Havard, Gilles. "'Nous ne ferons plus qu'un peuple': Le métissage en Nouvelle-France à l'époque de Champlain." In *Le nouveau monde et Champlain*, edited by Guy Martinière and Didier Poton, 85–107. Paris: Les Indes savants, 2008.

Henripin, Jacques. "De la fécondité naturelle à la prévention des naissances: L'évolution démographique au Canada français depuis le XVIIe siècle." In *La société canadienne française*, edited by Marcel Rioux and Yves Martin, 215–26. Montreal: Les Éditions Hurtubise HMH, 1971.

Hodson, Christopher, and Brett Rushforth. "Absolutely Atlantic: Colonialism and the Early Modern French State in Recent Historiography." *History Compass* 8, no. 1 (2010): 101–17.

Hogue, Michael. *Metis and the Medicine Line: Creating a Border and Dividing a People*. Chapel Hill: University of North Carolina Press, 2015.

Horn-Miller, Kahente. "How Did Adoption Become a Dirty Word? Indigenous Citizenship Orders as Irreconcilable Spaces of Aboriginality." *AlterNative: An International Journal of Indigenous Peoples* 14, no. 4 (2018): 354–64.

Hunt, Sarah. "Representing Colonial Violence: Trafficking, Sex Work, and the Violence of Law." *Atlantis: Critical Studies in Gender, Culture and Social Justice* 37, no. 2 (2016): 25–39.

Innes, Robert A. *Elder Brother and the Law of the People: Contemporary Kinship and Cowessess First Nation*. Winnipeg: University of Manitoba Press, 2013.

Isaac, Dan. "Métis Movement in Chibougamau?" *Nation*, 16 February 2016.

Jean, Denis. "Ethnogenèse des premiers métis canadiens (1603–1763)." Master's thesis, Université de Moncton, 2011.

Jetté, René. "Les pionniers de la généalogie au Québec." *Cap-aux-Diamants: La revue d'histoire du Québec*, no. 34 (1993): 14–17.

Jobling, Mark A., Rita Rasteiro, and Jon H. Wetton. "In the Blood: The Myth and Reality of Genetic Markers of Identity." *Ethnic and Racial Studies* 39, no. 2 (2016): 142–61.

Jordan, Winthrop D. "Historical Origins of the One-Drop Racial Rule in the United States." *Journal of Critical Mixed Race Studies* 1, no. 1 (2014): 98–132.

Junka-Aikio, Laura. "Can the Sámi Speak Now?" *Cultural Studies* 30, no 2 (2016): 205–33

Karahasan, Devrim. *Métissage in New France and Canada: 1508 to 1886*. New York: Peter Lang, 2009.

Kauanui, J. Kēhaulani. *Hawaiian Blood: Colonialism and the Politics of Sovereignty and Indigeneity*. Durham, NC: Duke University Press, 2008.

Kemper, Kevin R. "'Geronimo!' The Ideologies of Colonial and Indigenous Masculinities in Historical and Contemporary Representations about Apache Men." *Wicazo Sa Review* 29, no. 2 (2014): 39–62.

Kolopenuk, Jessica. "'Pop-Up' Métis and the Rise of Canada's Post-Indigenous Formation." *American Anthropologist* 120, no. 2 (2018): 333–37.

Kowal, Emma, and Yin Paradies. "Indigeneity and the Refusal of Whiteness." *Postcolonial Studies* 20, no. 1 (2017): 101–117.

Kramer, Anne-Marie. "The Genomic Imaginary: Genealogical Heritage and the Shaping of Bioconvergent Identities." *MediaTropes* 5, no. 1 (2015): 80–104.

"L'Association du droit des blancs menace de bloquer les routes." *Le Soleil*, 1 May 2002, A5.

Lavoie, Alain. "90% des Gaspésiens seraient des Métis!" *L'Écho de la Baie*, 30 July 2006.

———. "La pourvoirie autochtone sera un puissant outil de développement." *L'Écho de la Baie*, 2 October 2006.

———. "Les Paspéyas sont Autochtones de mère en fils et de mère en fille." *L'Écho de la Baie*, 12 July 2018.

———. "Pourvoirie: Les Métis s'opposent." *L'Écho de la Baie*, 30 July 2006. http://forum.autochtones.ca/viewtopic.phpf=2&t=1802&sid=2d1db1c7039d6eb904c978ca9594a1b (accessed 21 March 2017).

Lavoie, Yolande. *L'émigration des Québécois aux États-Unis de 1840 à 1930*. Quebec City: L'éditeur officiel du Québec, 1981.

Lawrence, Bonita. *Fractured Homeland: Federal Recognition and Algonquin Identity in Ontario*. Vancouver: University of British Columbia Press.

Lee, Damien. "Because Our Law Is Our Law": Considering Anishinaabe Citizenship Orders through Adoption Narratives at Fort William First Nation." PhD diss., University of Manitoba, 2017.

Lee, Damien, and Kahente Horn-Miller. "Wild Card: Making Sense of Adoption and Indigenous Citizenship Orders in Settler Colonial Contexts. *AlterNative: An International Journal of Indigenous Peoples* 14, no. 4 (2018): 293–99.

Leroux, Darryl. "'A Genealogist's Paradise': France, Québec and the Genealogics of Race." *Ethnic and Racial Studies* 38, no. 5 (2015): 718–33.

———. "'We've Been Here for 2,000 Years': White Settlers, Native American DNA, and the Phenomenon of Indigenization." *Social Studies of Science* 48, no. 1 (2018): 80–100.

Les pourvoiries du Québec. "La pouvoirie statistique/La pouvoirie économique." Fact sheet. 2012. https://www.pourvoiries.com/wp-content/uploads/2012/12/Les-pourvoiries-du-Qu%C3%A9bec-Statistiques-Final.pdf (accessed 23 June 2018).

Lewis, Patrick. J. "A Story of Identity: A Cautionary Tale." *AlterNative: An International Journal of Indigenous Peoples* 13, no. 2 (2017): 114–21.

Leydet, Dominique. "Autochtones et non-autochtones dans la négociation de nouveaux traités: Enjeux et problèmes d'une politique de la reconnaissance." *Négociations* 2, no. 8 (2007): 55–71.

Lindberg, Darcy. "Imaginary Passports or the Wealth of Obligations: Seeking the Limits of Adoption into Indigenous Societies." *AlterNative: An International Journal of Indigenous Peoples* 14, no. 4 (2018): 326–32.

Loranger-Saindon, Arianne. "Médias, innus et allochtones: L'image des Premières Nations dans les journaux de la Côte-Nord et des effets sur les rapports interethniques." Master's thesis, Université Laval, 2007.

Lozier, Jean-François. "In Each Other's Arms: France and the St. Lawrence Mission Villages in War and Peace, 1630-1730." PhD diss., University of Toronto, 2012.

Lussier, Raymond F., Thomas King-McMahon, and Johan Robitaille. "Catherine Pillard, A King's Daughter of Algonquin-Siberian Origin, Born in France in 1651 . . . What Is Wrong with This Picture." *Michigan's Habitant Heritage* (2008): 53–65.

Macdougall, Brenda. *One of the Family: Metis Culture in Nineteenth-Century Northwestern Saskatchewan*. Vancouver: University of British of Columbia Press, 2011.

———. "Wahkootowin: Family and Cultural Identity in Northwestern Saskatchewan Metis Communities." *Canadian Historical Review* 86, no. 3 (2006): 431–62.

Macdougall, Brenda, and Nicole St-Onge. "Métis in the Borderlands of the Northern Plains in the Nineteenth Century." In *Sources and Methods in Indigenous Studies*, edited by Chris Andersen and Jean M. O'Brien, 257–65. London: Taylor and Francis, 2016.

Manuel, Arthur, and Ronald Derrickson. *The Reconciliation Manifesto: Recovering the Land, Rebuilding the Economy*. Toronto: Lorimer, 2017.

Marcus, Max. "Northfield's Day of History Presents 'Living Archaeology,'" *Recorder*, 15 July 2018.

Marmon, Roland E. "Last Card Played: A History of the Turtle Mountain Chippewa and the Ten Cent Treaty of 1892." PhD diss., University of Arizona, 2009.

Martel, Gilles. *The Collected Writings of Louis Riel*. Vol. 2. Edmonton: University of Alberta Press, 1985.

McKay, Raoul. "A History of the McKay Family of St-Eustache, Manitoba, 1846 to the Present." Report to the Royal Commission of Aboriginal Peoples, 1994.

McKenzie, Gérald, and Thierry Vincent. "La 'guerre du saumon' des années 1970–1980: Entrevue avec Pierre Lepage." *Recherches amérindiennes au Québec* 40, no. 1–2 (2010): 103–11.

Metallic, Fred. "Strengthening Our Relations in Gespe'gewa'gi, the Seventh District of Mi'gma'gi." In *Lighting the Eighth Fire: The Liberation, Resurgence, and Protection of Indigenous Nations*, edited by Leanne Simpson, 59–71. Winnipeg: Arbeiter Ring, 2008.

———. "Ta'n teligji'tegen 'nnuigtug aq ta'n goqwei wejgu'aqamulti'gw." PhD diss., York University, 2010.

"Métis in Gaspé Hope DNA Tests Will Grant Them More Rights." *CBC News*, 14 September 2015. http://www.cbc.ca/news/canada/montreal/dna-tests-metis-in-gaspe-1.3227589 (accessed 24 March 2016).

Métis National Council and Mi'kmaq of Nova Scotia. 2018. "Memorandum of Understanding."

Métis Nation of the Rising Sun (MNRS). "Familles métisses en Gaspésie." 2014. https://vigile.quebec/IMG/pdf/familles_metisses_autochtones_de_la_gaspesie.pdf (accessed 10 July 2017).

Meyer, Melissa. L. "American Indian Blood Quantum Requirements: Blood Is Thicker Than Family." In *Over the Edge: Remapping the American West*, edited by Valerie J. Matsumoto and Blake Allmendinger, 231–44. Berkeley: University of California Press, 1999.

Michaux, Emmanuel. "Ni Amérindiens ni Eurocanadiens: Une approche néomoderne du culturalisme métis au Canada." PhD diss., Université Laval, 2014.

Mihesuah, Devon A. "American Indian Identities: Issues of Individual Choices and Development. *American Indian Culture & Research Journal* 22, no. 2 (1998): 193–226.

Mi'kmaq Rights Initiative. "Mi'kmaq Chiefs Respond to the Daniels Decision." Press release. 21 April 2016. http://mikmaqrights.com/wp-content/uploads/2014/01/Press-Release_Daniels-Decision_21April16.pdf (accessed 10 June 2018).

———. "The Challenge with Self-Identification and Recent Court Decisions." 24 August 2018. http://mikmaqrights.com/the-challenge-with-self-identification-and-recent-court-decisions/ (accessed 27 August 2018).

———. "Understanding Métis Rights within Mi'kma'ki." 1 October 2013. http://mikmaqrights.com/understanding-metis-rights-within-mikmaki/ (accessed 1 June 2017).

Moreau-DesHarnais, Gail. "Timeline on Catherine Pillard: circa 1647, 1649, 1651, 1654–1717." *Traits d'union* 18, no. 1 (2010): n.p.

Moreton-Robinson, Aileen. *The White Possessive: Property, Power, and Indigenous Sovereignty*. Minneapolis: University of Minnesota Press, 2015.

Morin, Gail. *First Metis Families of Quebec*. Vol. 6, *Pierre Lamoureux and Marguerite Pigarouiche*. Self-published, CreateSpace, 2016.

Mothers of Acadia. "Mothers of Acadia mtDNA Project – mtDNA Test Results for Members." https://www.familytreedna.com/public/mothersofacadia?iframe=mtresults (accessed 17 December 2017).

Nash, Catherine. "Genealogical Relatedness: Geographies of Shared Descent and Difference." *Genealogy* 1, no. 2 (2017). doi:10.3390/genealogy1020007.

Native American and Indigenous Studies Association. "NAISA Statement on Indigenous Identity Fraud." 15 September 2015. https://www.naisa.org/about/documents-archive/previous-council-statements/ (accessed 28 January 2018).

Nelson, Alondra. "Bio Science: Genetic Genealogy Testing and the Pursuit of African Ancestry." *Social Studies of Science* 38, no. 5 (2008): 759–83.

Obomsawin, Alanis, dir. *Incident at Restigouche*. Canada: National Film Board, 1984.

———, dir. *Our Nationhood*. Canada: National Film Board, 2003.

O'Bonsawin, Christine M. "'No Olympics on Stolen Native Land'": Contesting Olympic Narratives and Asserting Indigenous Rights within the Discourse of the 2010 Vancouver Games." *Sport in Society* 13, no. 1 (2010): 143–56.

———. 2012 "'There Will Be No Law that Will Come Against Us': An Important Episode of Indigenous Resistance and Activism in Olympic History." In *The Palgrave Handbook of Olympic Studies*, edited by Helen J. Lenskyj and Stephen Wagg, 474–86. London: Palgrave Macmillan, 2012.

O'Toole, Darren. "Thomas Flanagan on the Stand: Revisiting Métis Land Claims and the Lists of Rights in Manitoba." *International Journal of Canadian Studies/Revue internationale d'études canadiennes*, no. 41 (2010): 137–77.

Page, Julia. "More Quebecers Identifying as Indigenous, 2016 Census Figures Show." *CBC News*, 25 October 2017. http://www.cbc.ca/news/canada/montre al/census-report-2016-quebec-indigenous-population-1.4370938 (accessed 25 October 2017).

Palmater, Pamela. *Beyond Blood: Rethinking Indigenous Identity*. Vancouver: University of British Columbia Press, 2011.

———. "Shining Light on the Dark Places: Addressing Police Racism and Sexualized Violence against Indigenous Women and Girls in the National Inquiry." *Canadian Journal of Women and the Law* 28, no. 2 (2016): 253–84.

Parmenter, Jon. "After the Mourning Wars: The Iroquois as Allies in Colonial North American Campaigns, 1676–1760." *William and Mary Quarterly* 64, no.1 (2007): 39–76.

Pearson, Stephen. "'The Last Bastion of Colonialism': Appalachian Settler Colonialism and Self-Indigenization." *American Indian Culture and Research Journal* 37, no. 2 (2013): 165–84.

Pelta, Anne. "La judiciarisation de l'identité métisse ou l'éveil des Métis au Québec: Communauté Métisse du Domaine du Roi et de la Seigneurie de Mingan." PhD diss., Université Laval, 2015.

Pewewardy, Cornel D. "So You Think You Hired an 'Indian' Faculty Member?" In *Indigenizing the Academy*, edited by Devon A. Mihesuah and Angela Cavender Wilson, 200–217. Lincoln: University of Nebraska Press, 2004.

Podruchny, Carolyn, and Jesse Thistle. "A Geography of Blood: Uncovering the Hidden Histories of Metis Peoples in Canada." In *Spaces of Difference: Conflicts and Cohabitation*, edited by Ursula Lehmkuhl, Hans-Jürgen Lüsebrink, and Laurence McFalls, 61–82. New York: Waxmann, 2016.

Pouliot-Thisdale, Éric. "Unions Métis et reclamations au Québec." Ottawa: Library and Archives Canada, 2016.

"Pourvoirie autochtone: résistance en Haute-Gaspésie." Radio-Canada, 28 April 2008. http://ici.radio-canada.ca/regions/est-quebec/2008/04/25/007-pourvoirie-autochtone_n.asp (accessed 19 December 2017).

Raven, Krystl. "Ka oopikihtamashook': Becoming Family." *AlterNative: An International Journal of Indigenous Peoples* 14, no. 4 (2018): 319–25.

Redsteer, Robert W. "An Open Epistle to Dr. Traditional Cherokee of the Nonexistent Bear Clan. *American Indian Quarterly* 27, no. 1/2 (2003): 376–380.

Roberts, Dorothy. *Fatal Invention: How Science, Politics, and Big Business Re-create Race in the Twenty-First Century*. New York: The New Press, 2011.

Ross-Tremblay, Pierrot, and Nawel Hamidi. "Les écueils de l'extinction: Les Premiers peuples, les négociations territoriales et l'esquisse d'une ère postcoloniale." *Recherches amérindiennes au Québec* 43, no. 1 (2013): 51–57.

Rousseau, Louis-Pascal. "Critique en matière d'ethnogenèse: Rapport sur la portée scientifique des travaux de Russel Bouchard et d'Alexandre Alleman à propos de l'existence d'une communauté ou d'un people métis dans la région du Saguenay-Lac-Saint-Jean," 2009.

———. "Ni tout l'un, ni tout l'autre: Rencontres, métissages et ethnogenèse au Saguenay-Lac-Saint-Jean aux 16e et 17e siècle." PhD diss., Université Laval, 2012.

Roy, Christopher A. "Abenaki Sociality and the Work of Family History." PhD diss., Princeton University, 2012.

Ruffo, Armand G. *Grey Owl: The Mystery of Archie Belaney*. Regina, SK: Coteau Books, 1996.

Rushforth, Brett. *Bonds of Alliance: Indigenous and Atlantic Slaveries in New France*. Chapel Hill: University of North Carolina Press, 2012.

———. "Slavery, the Fox Wars, and the Limits of Alliance." *William and Mary Quarterly* 63, no. 1 (2006): 53–80.

Saada, Émmanuelle. "Race and Sociological Reason in the Republic: Inquiries on the Métis in the French Empire (1908–37)." *International Sociology* 17, no. 3 (2002): 361–91.

Saint-Pierre, Jean-Claude. "Dans 'Le dernier des Montagnais' les autochtones se sentent 'agressés.'" *Journal de Québec*, 13 October 1995, 23.

———. "La disparition d'une race/'Les folies à Russel Bouchard font la manchette,'" *Journal de Québec*, 20 June 1996.

Salée, Daniel. "Les peuples autochtones et la naissance du Québec: Pour une réécriture de l'histoire?" *Recherches sociographiques* 51, no. 1–2 (2010): 151–59.

Savard, Denis. "Racines acadiennes—la famille Lejeune." *Acadie nouvelle*, 3 March 2016. https://www.acadienouvelle.com/chroniques/2016/03/20/la-famille-lejeune/ (accessed 25 January 2017).

Scherer, Bernard, Rosa Fregel, José M. Larruga, Vicente M. Cabrera, Phillip Endicott, José J. Pestano, and Ana M. González. "The History of the North African Mitochondrial DNA Haplogroup U6 Gene Flow into the African, Eurasian and American Continents." *BMC Evolutionary Biology* 14, no. 1 (2014): 109–125.

Schrift, Melissa. *Becoming Melungeon: Making an Ethnic Identity in the Appalachian South*. Lincoln: University of Nebraska Press, 2013.

Simpson, Audra. "Captivating Eunice: Membership, Colonialism, and Gendered Citizenships of Grief." *Wicazo Sa Review* 24, no. 2 (2009): 105–29.

———. "The State Is a Man: Theresa Spence, Loretta Saunders and the Gender of Settler Sovereignty." *Theory and Event* 19, no. 4 (2016). https://muse.jhu.edu/article/633280/.

Simpson, Leanne. "Land as Pedagogy: Nishnaabeg Intelligence and Rebellious Transformation." *Decolonization: Indigeneity, Education and Society* 3, no. 3 (2014): 1–25.

Smith, Craig S. "In Canada, Feeling 'Robbed' of Indian Identity, and Benefits." *New York Times*, 1 December 2016.

Snipp, C. Matthew. "Who are American Indians? Some Observations about the Perils and Pitfalls of Data for Race and Ethnicity." *Population Research and Policy Review* 5, no. 3 (1986): 237–52.

Standing Committee on Aboriginal Affairs, Northern Development, and Natural Resources. "Testimony by Gilles O'Bomsawin, Chief of Odanak," 26 March 2003. http://www.ourcommons.ca/DocumentViewer/en/37-2/AANR/meeting-55/evidence#Int-476244 (accessed 21 December 2018).

Stanley, George F.G. *Louis Riel*. Toronto: Ryerson Press, 1963.

Statistics Canada. "2006 Aboriginal Population Profile: Quebec." http://www12.statcan.ca/census-recensement/2006/dp-pd/prof/92-594/search-recherche/lst/page.cfm?Lang=E&GeoCode=24 (accessed 12 January 2018).

———. "2006 Census Topic-Based Tabulations." http://www12.statcan.gc.ca/census-recensement/index-eng.cfm (accessed 10 August 2017).

———. "Aboriginal Peoples in Canada: Key Results from the 2016 Census." *The Daily*, 25 October 2017. http://www.statcan.gc.ca/daily-quotidien/171025/dq171025a-eng.htm (accessed 16 December 2018).

———. *Census in Brief: The Aboriginal Languages of First Nations People, Métis and Inuit.* Catalogue no. 98-200-X201602. Ottawa: Minister of Industry, 2017. http://www12.statcan.gc.ca/census-recensement/2016/as-sa/98-200-x/2016022/98-200-x2016022-eng.cfm (accessed 23 March 2018).

———. "Focus on Geography Series, 2016 Census: Census Divisions (CDs) Grouped by Provinces and Territories." http://www12.statcan.ca/census-recensement/2016/as-sa/fogs-spg/select-Geo-Choix.cfm?Lang=Eng&GK=CD&TOPIC=10 (accessed 15 March 2018).

Sturm, Circe. *Becoming Indian: The Struggle over Cherokee Identity in the Twenty-First Century.* Santa Fe, NM: School for Advanced Research Press, 2011.

Stuurman, Siep. "François Bernier and the Invention of Racial Classification." *History Workshop Journal*, no. 50 (2000): 1–21.

TallBear, Kim. "Genomic Articulations of Indigeneity." *Social Studies of Science* 43, no. 4 (2013): 509–33.

———. *Native American DNA: Tribal Belonging and the False Promise of Genetic Science.* Minneapolis: University of Minnesota Press, 2013.

Thistle, Jesse. "The Puzzle of the Morrissette-Arcand Clan: A History of Metis Historic and Intergenerational Trauma." Master's thesis, University of Waterloo, 2016.

Todd, Zoe. "From a Fishy Place: Examining Canadian State Law Applied in the Daniels Decision from the Perspective of Métis Legal Orders." *TOPIA: Canadian Journal of Cultural Studies*, no. 36 (2016): 43–57.

Tremblay, Bertrand. "Les Montagnais en état de choc profond." *Le Quotidien*, 13 March 1995.

Tremblay, Fabien. "Politique de la mémoire chez les Métis de la Gaspésie." In *L'identité métisse en question: strategies identitaires et dynamismes culturels*, edited by Denis Gagnon and Hélène Giguère, 129–53. Quebec City: Presses de l'Université Laval, 2012.

Tremblay, Guy. "La communauté de Chibougamau-Chapais Eeyou-Istchee se rend à Paris." *La Sentinelle/Le Jamésien*, 13 July 2017.

Tremblay, Stéphane. "André Forbes, le premier des défenseurs des droits des Blancs." *Le Soleil*, 24 January 2002, A17.

Tsosie, Rebecca. "The New Challenge to Native Identity: An Essay on Indigeneity and Whiteness." *Washington University Journal of Law & Policy* 18, (2005): 55–98.

Vachon, André-Carl. *L'histoire de la famille acadienne des Lejeune dit Briard: Les sept premières générations et plus.* Sainte-Adèle, QC: KLEMT, 2014.

Viel, Jean-François. "Sur les traces de Catherine Pillard." *Traits d'union* 18, no. 2 (2010): n.p.
Vowel, Chelsea, and Darryl Leroux. "White Settler Antipathy and the Daniels Decision." *TOPIA: Canadian Journal of Cultural Studies*, no. 36 (2016): 30–42.
Vrooman, Nicholas C.P. *"The Whole Country Was... 'One Robe'": The Little Shell Tribe's America*. Helena, MT: Drumlummon Institute, 2013.
Watso, Denise L. "Vermont Senate Attempts to Silence Abenaki Voices." Press release. *Denise Watso's Abenaki Journal* (blog), 3 February 2011. http://abenakinews.blogspot.ca/2011/02/vermont-senate-attempts-to-silence.html (accessed 2 February 2018).
Watt, Elizabeth, and Emma Kowal. "To Be or Not To Be Indigenous? Understanding the Rise of Australia's Indigenous Population since 1971. *Ethnic and Racial Studies* (2018): 1–20.
White, Stephen. *Dictionnaire généalogique des familles acadiennes: Première partie, 1636 à 1714*. Moncton, NB: Centre d'études acadiennes, 1999.
Yellow Bird, Michael. "Cowboys and Indians: Toys of Genocide, Icons of Colonialism." *Wicazo Sa Review* 19, no. 2 (2004): 33–48.

INDEX

A

Abenaki, 54–55, 58–63, 72, 89, 92, 143, 194, 211, 217–18

Abénaki, Marie, 96

Abitawis (NAQ forum), 76–79

Aboriginal rights, 3, 21, 35–37, 60, 78, 93, 140–42, 149, 159, 177–78, 181–83, 191, 195, 205, 207, 212, 216–17

Acadia, 77, 80, 82, 93–97, 159, 195–96, 199–200; people, 70, 83, 97, 101, 159, 195, 200

Acadian-métis, 101, 138, 217

Acadian: Amerindian Ancestry Project, 80; ancestry, 159, 195; Deportation, 195; genealogical circles, 95; genealogy, 45, 97; history, 196; migration, 159, 195; origins, 94, 97; root ancestors, 208; sisters, 93; woman, 94, 200

Acadian(s)

Acadie-nouvelle, 94

Accu-metrics, 203–204, 206–211, 254n39

Adese, Jennifer, 22, 49, 110, 218

Alberta, 7, 20, 115, 123

Algonquin: ancestry, 59; Nation Secretariat (ANS), 55–58, 61, 63; people, 8, 50, 54–59, 61–63, 65, 72, 194, 216; territory, 57; woman/women, 50, 56, 98–99

Alleman, Alexandre, 172

Alliance autochtone du Québec (AAQ)/Native Alliance of Quebec, 45, 52, 76, 79, 98, 145

Alliance laurentienne des Métis et Indiens hors reserve, 45

American Metis Aboriginal Association Lodge, 52

Amoratio (NAQ forum), 75–76

ancestral: claims, 180, 204; connection(s), 21, 29, 62, 64, 66, 86, 89, 98, 101, 108–109, 112, 118, 129, 150, 199; DNA, 85; genealogy, 71, 75, 86, 139, 145, 208, 210; history, 27, 32, 34, 56, 70, 196, 198, 208; lineage, 34, 196; origins, 93, 100, 102; substance, 2, 24, 28, 64; rights, 164, 170

ancestry: Chumash, 18; Indigenous, 2, 4, 14, 17, 19, 23, 26, 33–34, 37, 41–42, 44–45, 47, 57, 61, 68, 70, 74–76, 78, 95, 105, 112–13, 129, 142–45, 147–50, 158, 182, 188, 206, 208, 210–11, 216, 226, 237; Acadian, 159, 195

Ancestry (Métis) genealogy forum, 89

Andersen, Chris, 20, 22, 30, 70, 138, 140, 218

Anishinaabe(g), 29–30, 49, 54, 57, 70, 194, 209

Anne-Marie (VO forum), 45, 47, 66

anti-black(ness), 24, 28, 100, 147–48, 175

A-pis-chas-koos (Little Bear), 117

Appalachian: people, 16–17; Reservation, 16; settlers, 16; studies, 16

Aral Sea, 90, 99

Arcand, Alexandre, 114, 116

Arcand, François Régis, 116

Arcand, Jean-Baptiste, 114, 116

Arcand, Jr., Jean-Baptiste, 116

Arcand, Joseph, 114, 116

Arcand, Marie, 116

Arcand, Marie-Joseph-Laviolette, 116

Arcand, Pierre, 113

Arcand, St-Pierre, 116

Arcand, Thérèse, 114, 116

Arcand Métis family, 112–13, 116–18, 122–23, 130

Arosen, François-Xavier, 109

aspirational descent, 34, 36, 73–75, 80, 84–86, 92–93, 95, 98, 101–2, 105, 112, 139, 143, 149, 150, 159, 175, 195–99, 212–13

Assiniboine: kin, 7, 116–17, 128; people, 20, 117, 122; River, 114, 122

Association des Charron et Ducharme, 90–92

Association for White Rights (AWR), 142, 160–61, 165

Association Métis Côte-Nord, 161

Athabasca (region), 115

Aubert, Guillaume, 4

B

Babin case, 138, 217, 237

Baldwin affair, 189, 191

BALSAC, 13

Barker, Joanne, 29, 67, 78, 126, 218

Barnwell, Ashley, 31, 58, 73, 91, 102, 218

Batoche, Saskatchewan, 114–15, 117, 122, 125

Battle of Long Sault, 8

Battle of Seven Oaks, 127

Beaugrand, Jacques, 90–91

Belaney, Archibald (Archie). *See* Grey Owl

Bercier, Josephte, 114

Bernard (VO forum), 46–47, 65–66

Bernier, François, 5

Bing, 89

Black Sea, 90, 99

black: blood, 25; majority under apartheid, 160; subjectivity, 25; women, 24

Blackfeet Reservation, 124–25

blanqueamiento, 25

blood: "black", 25; Indian, 19, 33, 143–45, 149, 186; logic(s), 30, 63, 197; memory, 22, 67; quantum, 29; "red", 25–26, 28, 65, 202; "white", 25–26, 28, 65, 202

Bolduc case, 137, 234

Bolnick, Deborah, 81, 209–10

Bonnechere Algonquin First Nation, 54

Bouchard case, 137, 235

Bouchard, Gérard, 13

Bouchard, Russel-Aurore, 169–74, 252n61

Bouchard-Taylor Commission, 193

Boulle, Pierre, 4

Brabant Métis, 119–20, 122–28, 130

Brabant, Augustin, 119

Brabant Jr., Augustin, 120

Brabant, Charlotte, 119

Brabant, Élisabeth, 120

Brabant, Geneviève, 119

Brabant, Sylvestre, 119

Briard II, Pierre Lejeune, 94, 96

Brideau and Breau case, 138, 225

British Columbia, 7, 20

British: authorities, 159; colonial control, 169; colonialism, 220; Conquest, 14; dominion, 220

C

Caissie case, 138, 225

Cajun, 95

Canada: Government of, 61, 68, 117, 120, 122, 127, 151, 190; Dominion of, 115; Liberal Party of, 161; Statistics, 140; -U.S. border, 123, 125–26, 217; Department of Indian and Northern Affairs, 66

Caplan, Guillaume, 98, 199

Caplan sisters, 198–200

Carlton, Saskatchewan, 116

Castonguay case (2002), 137, 224

Castonguay case (2012), 138, 225

Castonguay and Faucher case, 138, 224

Castonguay et al. and Faucher case, 137, 224

Champlain, Samuel de, 50, 135

Charbonneau, Hubert, 2, 13–14, 45, 67

Charest, Paul, 155, 160–61, 174

Charlish, Jeanne-Mance, 251n23

Charron, François, 89

Charron, Jean, 89

Charron, Pierre, 86, 90, 92

Cherokee (people), 19–20, 23–24, 42–43, 51, 64, 79, 149

Chiasson case (2001–2002), 137, 223

Chiasson case (2003–2005), 137, 224

Chic-Choc Mountains, 181

Chicoutimi, Québec, 35, 136, 160, 171

Chumash (people), 17–18, 73

Cleary, Bernard, 151, 164

colonialism: British, 220; contemporary forms of, 214; French, 11–12, 100; settler, 4–5, 9–10, 41, 65, 67, 217–18;

Communauté Métis autochtone de Maniwaki (CMAM), 52, 86, 216, 235, 227–28, 231–36

Communauté métisse de la Gaspésie. *See* Métis Nation of the Rising Sun

Communauté métisse de la Gaspésie, des Îles-de-la-Madeleine et du Bas-St-Laurent. *See* Métis Nation of the Rising Sun

Communauté métisse du Domaine-du-roi et la Seigneurie de Mingan (CMDRSM), 35, 37, 93, 136–39, 141, 143–50, 152–56, 158–62, 165–77, 179, 181–82, 188, 190, 201–202, 205, 207, 216 communities: Abenaki, 218; African-American, 24; Chumash, 17; Indigenous, 11, 15, 108, 180, 191; Innu, 136, 139, 151, 172; Métis, 22, 53, 67, 116, 119, 121, 125; Mi'kmaw, 87, 179; Mohawk, 71, 109; self-identified, 68

Connecticut, 60, 106

consanguinity, 2, 12, 106, 109, 130

Conseil des Abénakis d'Odanak, 59, 61

Conseil des Abénakis de Wolinak, 59

Cook, Mathieu, 161, 163, 170

Cook, Peter, 10

Corneau case, 35, 137–39, 143, 145, 159, 164, 216, 228–29, 231–36, 257

Corneau, Ghislain, 137

Côté case, 234

Côte-Nord, Québec, 37, 137, 149–50, 160–61, 164, 172, 180

Council of the First Métis People of Canada, 161

Cowasuck Band of the Pennacook Abenaki, 62–63, 97

Cowessess First Nation, 128

Cree: -based practices, 23; kin, 7, 116–17, 128; Muskeg Lake Nation, 114; people, 20, 117, 122, 128, 194; -speaking, 104; territory, 206–207

Cypress Hills, 116, 123–24

Cyr, Raymond, 181–82, 184, 186

D

Daigle case, 137, 224

Dakar, Sénégal, 6

decolonization, 16, 218

Deerfield raid (1704), 106–7, 129

De Launière case, 137, 236

Delarosbil case, 137, 178, 236

Dene, 7, 104

Denise (VO forum), 46–47, 66, 68–69, 75, 82

Desbiens case, 137, 235

desire-for-indigeneity, 74, 101–102, 105

descent: beyond, 32, 65, 102, 202, 214; blood, 101; practice(s) of, 28–29, 32–34, 36, 64–65, 73, 79–80, 102, 110, 180, 202, 214; mechanics of, 24, 27, 39, 42, 131; European and Russian, 85; French, 89; obsessed with, 32; theorizing, 24; use(s) of, 128, 130, 176

Desjardins, Bertrand, 13–14, 71

Desjarlais Métis, 113, 120

Deslandres, Dominique, 9

Desportes, Hélène, 44

Devine, Heather, 34, 113–14, 120

Dion, Céline, 106

"disappearance" thesis, 47, 166, 169–70, 174, 193, 205

DNA ancestry testing, 30–31, 73, 76, 80–81, 85–87, 90, 96, 98, 101, 200, 202–10, 213

Doerfler, Jill, 29–30, 70, 78, 126, 218

Dominique (GQAF forum), 68, 70–71, 84, 94–95

Duchesne case, 137, 233

Duck Lake, Saskatchewan, 116

Dumont, Gabriel, 116

Duster, Troy, 85

E

Eastern métis, 7, 22, 43, 47, 49, 53, 60, 104, 113, 118, 130, 138, 140, 161, 189, 217

Eastern Woodlands Métis Nation, 217

eighteenth century, 5, 11, 18, 71, 76, 106, 170, 172, 175, 195, 199, 201, 204, 206

Elnu Abenaki tribe, 218

England, 57, 71

English: Canada, 115; (ethnicity), 14, 70, 106–107, 110; 173; (language), 5–7, 33, 43, 45, 52, 64, 91–92, 111, 167, 218, 239n13, 243n7; settlers, 107

ethnic fraud, 15, 69

F

filles du roi (King's daughters), 11

fishing: club, 163; commercial, 167; guide, 191; history, 164; hunting and, 120, 141, 159, 163, 165, 180–83, 187, 190–91, 215; organization(s), 181–83, 187, 215; rights, 141, 165, 181; salmon, 163; territories, 190

Fondation équité territoriale, 153–55, 160–61

Forbes, André, 160–61

Fort Belknap Reservation, 124

Fort-de-France, Martinique, 6

Fort Qu'Appelle, Saskatchewan, 121

France, 4–6, 11, 13–14, 56–57, 71, 75, 77, 82–83, 87–88, 90–92, 94, 96, 100, 108, 111–12, 119, 172

French-Canadian: ancestry, 85; community, 108, 156; family, 127; genealogical circles, 106; historiography, 4, 8; men, 113; population, 170; settlers, 55, 126–27; society, 126; stepmother, 46; town, 56; woman, 56, 126

French: administrators, 11; ancestor(s), 73, 77, 106; ancestry, 52; Atlantic, 9; Canada, 9, 12, 104, 135; colonial policy, 9–10; colonialism, 11–12, 100; colonist(s), 8, 11, 44, 46–48, 56, 62, 200; descendant(s) (people), 1–3, 7–8, 12, 20–22, 27–28, 31–32, 37, 42–44, 49, 52, 55–59, 62, 64, 67, 71–73, 77, 79, 81, 86, 90, 92, 95, 101–102, 106, 108–110, 119, 130–31, 136, 143, 147, 150–51, 183, 187, 202, 207, 211, 213–14, 216, 218–20; descent, 89; father, 9, 104; gender norms, 9; genealogist, 91; Heritage DNA, 85; identity, 3; man/men, 9–12, 14, 47–50, 51, 98; (language), 5–7, 33, 43, 45, 52, 64–65, 89, 94, 101, 115, 167; mercantilist policies, 220; missions, 49; origins, 67, 77, 87; parents, 119; patronym, 209; poodle, 211; Québécois, 47, 51, 156; regime, 2, 8, 10, 13–14, 46; settler(s), 2, 8, 11–12, 14–15, 46, 106, 135; settler colonialism, 4, 9–10; woman/women, 3, 11, 26, 36, 46, 51, 73, 75, 77, 82–83, 86, 88, 99, 101, 106, 150, 198, 213, 216, 237

French-descendant: ancestry, 64, 71; colonialism, 220; desires, 65; efforts to redefine indigeneity, 29; genealogical claims, 35; genealogists, 45; genealogical circles, 62, 98; genealogy, 44, 80, 85–86, 100, 106; genealogy infrastructure, 218; indigeneity, 48; men, 37, 47; men, 37, 47; mobility away from settler identity, 28; online genealogy forums, 33, 214; population, 65, 156, 160, 163, 165–66, 212; race shifters, 27, 62, 74, 77, 79, 102, 216–17; research, 101, 106; settlers, 195

French-Québécois: activists, 157; ancestors, 67; ancestry, 159; historiography, 8; men, 156; opposition to land claim, 136; patronym, 103; (people), 35, 154; population, 168–69, 204; woman, 143

Frenchification, 10

G

Gagné case, 137, 230

Gagnon case (2013–2018), 137, 227

Gagnon case (2015–2019), 137, 231

Gagnon, Denis, 138, 181

Garroutte, Eva Marie, 28–29, 69, 108, 218

Gaspésie, Québec, 37, 98, 178–80, 185–86, 189–95, 198–99, 201–205, 212

Gaspésie National Park, 181

Gaudry, Adam, 8, 22–23, 30, 42, 53, 67, 79, 110, 129, 218

genealogical: connection(s), 29, 106, 118, 130; database(s), 49–50, 74, 82; distance, 79; evidence, 46, 51, 84, 88, 91; infrastructure, 13, 32, 214; inheritance, 51; link(s), 27, 62, 126; mechanics, 2; model of identity, 51, 53, 56, 58, 65; practice(s), 3, 31, 36, 64, 129, 214; reconstruction, 34–35, 70, 95, 103, 113; records, 12, 14, 71, 77, 81, 208; relatedness, 27, 128; research, 24, 27, 31, 58, 71, 86, 92, 143, 145, 149, 183, 208; sources of indigeneity, 66; technologies, 81; transformation, 93

Généalogie du Québec et d'Amérique française (GQAF) genealogy forum, 44, 67, 74, 84, 94, 105, 112, 241n7

genealogist(s), 12–13, 17–18, 34–35, 44–45, 51, 54, 58, 68, 76–81, 84–85, 87, 90–91, 93–94, 96, 98, 100, 102, 105, 172

genealogy: Acadian, 45, 97; ancestral, 71, 75, 86, 210; author's own, vii, 35, 62, 71, 82, 99, 103, 106, 109, 118, 126, 130, 198, 200, 208, 210; critical studies of, 24; database(s), 94; as family, 27; forums, 2, 28, 31–33, 36–37, 41–44, 48, 50, 63–64, 71–73, 77–78, 80–82, 86–87, 92–94, 96, 98, 101–103, 111, 118, 143, 149, 159, 197–98, 200, 204; French-descendant, 44, 71, 85–86, 100–101, 218; genetic, 30–32, 73, 80–81, 88, 92, 95, 97, 100–102; practice of, 43; as a technology of belonging, 31, 43; as technology of self-making, 74; use of, 32, 102

Gespe'gewa'gi, Mi'kma'ki, 193, 205–206, 211

Gobeil case, 137, 231

Grand Council of the Waban-Aki
  Nation, 61
Great Lakes, 88, 216
Grenier (Garnier), Françoise, 77,
  82–87, 92–93, 98–101, 111,
  197–98, 200, 213
Grey Owl, 15

H
Haley, Brian, 17–19, 73
Hamidi, Nawel, 135, 152
Hanmer, Ontario, 127
haplogroup: A, 88–91, 99; C, 200; J,
  85, 99, 198; U, 93, 100; X, 200
Hartford, Connecticut, 106
Hatfield case, 138, 217, 237
Havard, Gilles, 9–10
Hodson, Christopher, 9
Hopper case, 138, 224–25
Hudson's Bay Company, 114
hunting: association, 179; camp, 137;
  charges, 144, 223; and fishing, 120,
  141, 159, 163, 165, 180–83, 187,
  190–91, 215; and fishing dispute,
  159; and fishing rights, 141, 165,
  181; moose, 21, 192; rights, 175,
  182–83, 187, 212, 215; territory,
  183, 186–87, 189
Huron-Wendat, 8, 92, 99, 194, 209
hyperdescent, 25–27
hypodescent, 24–25, 27, 86

I
Indian Act, 1, 22, 29, 41, 57, 125, 128,
  144, 151, 163, 166, 168, 175–76,
  194

indigeneity: blurring the lines between
  whiteness and, 8; claim(s) to,
  15, 18, 28, 43, 49, 78, 95, 102,
  130, 139, 150, 197, 206; form
  of, 53, 149; French-descendant,
  48; genomic articulations of,
  204; politics of, 77; pushing the
  boundaries between whiteness and,
  26; reconstruction of, 22, 31, 36,
  64, 66; redefine, 28–29, 62, 204;
  through genealogy, 58
Indigenous: ancestry, 2, 4, 14, 17, 19,
  23, 26, 33–34, 37, 41–42, 45, 47,
  57, 61, 68, 70, 74–76, 78, 95, 105,
  112–13, 129, 142–45, 147–50,
  158, 182, 188, 206, 208, 210–11,
  216, 226, 237; citizenship orders,
  24, 78, 218; communities, 11, 15,
  108, 180, 191; forms of belonging,
  27, 65; identity, 46, 49, 51, 59,
  65–70, 73, 76–77, 79–80, 87, 89,
  101, 103, 111, 129, 138, 140, 144,
  146–48, 159, 165–66, 175, 188,
  200, 202, 214–15, 220; kinship-
  making practices, 24; scholars, 42,
  69–70, 220; self-determination,
  12, 28, 30, 53, 72, 78–79, 104, 113,
  131, 136, 157, 168, 177, 202, 213;
  sovereignty, 20, 22, 28, 31, 53, 60,
  72, 82, 114, 126, 131, 135, 152,
  202
Innu, 35, 49, 76, 135–37, 139, 142–45,
  147–48, 150–55, 157–58, 160–76,
  191, 193–94, 213, 215–16, 228
international: border(s), 26, 126; law,
  78; political economy, 5
Irene (Ancestry forum), 54–55, 58
Ireland, 71, 106, 110
Iron Alliance. *See* Nêhiyaw Pwat
  Confederacy
Islamophobia, 100, 148, 160, 175
Itka (Crooked Leg), 117

J

Jean case, 137, 230

Jetté, René, 13

Jim Crow, 25, 31

Johan (Ancestry forum), 54–55, 104

K

Kahnawake, 107, 109

Kah-paypamhchukwao (Wandering Spirit), 117

Kauanui, J. Kēhaulani, 25–26, 28, 65, 218

Kichi Sibi, 99. *See also* Ottawa River

kin: adoptive, 107; Arcand, 116–17; Assiniboine and Cree, 116–17; Brabant, 120, 129, 131; Cree/Métis, 117; First Nation(s), 23, 116–17; groupings, 34; Indigenous, 1, 41, 122, 129, 176; Métis 122; Plains Cree, Assiniboine, and Saulteaux, 7, 128

King-McMahon, Thomas, 87–88, 90

kinscapes, 121–22, 125

kinship: aspirations, 31, 88, 102, 105, 196, 201; belonging and, 29, 67; and citizenship, 43, 188, 214; family and, 27; Indigenous, 29; Indigenous conventions about citizenship and, 28; -based political alliances, 20; -making practice(s), 24, 27, 106; networks, 49; patterns, 128; practices, 79; obligations, 107–108; racial, 79; relations, 62, 79–80, 118, 125, 128, 130, 174, 176, 194; ties, 81, 150

Kit-ahwah-ke-ni (Miserable Man), 117

Koas Abenaki Tribe, 218

Kramer, Anne-Marie, 31, 43, 80–81, 218

L

L'Hirondelle, Marguerite (Geneviève), 119, 124, 126

La Rochelle, France, 87–88, 91–92, 106

Lac des Deux-Montagnes (Oka), Québec, 56, 108–109, 129

Lafond, Jean-Baptiste, 114

Lafond, Jean-Baptiste Tchehasaso, 114, 116

Laguarde dit St-Jean, Thomas, 58–59

Lake Winnipeg, 122–23, 127

Lake Superior, 115

Lalancette (A.) case, 137, 229

Lalancette (C.) case, 137, 229

Lambert, Radegonde, 200, 213, 224, 236–37

Lanaudière, Quebec, 108, 119

Landry and Landry case, 225–26

Laval, Quebec, 127

Lavoie, Benoît, 98, 181–85, 190, 197–98, 201–202, 212

Lavoie case, 137, 230

lateral descent, 34, 37, 95, 103–105, 110–12, 118–119, 129–30, 149, 199

Le Chaînon, 87

Le dernier des Montagnais, 169–70

Leblanc, Marc, 181, 183–85, 190–92

Lebret, Saskatchewan, 120–21

Lee, Damien, 218

Lehoux case, 137, 236

Lejeune, Edmée, 93–101, 196, 200, 213, 224, 237

Lejeune, Catherine, 77, 93–101, 150, 159, 196, 200, 213, 224, 228–31, 237

LeTardif, Olivier, 46

Limerick, Ireland, 106

Linda (Ancestry forum), 111–13, 118

Linda (GQAF forum), 105, 109–10

lineage, 4–5, 20, 33, 54, 57, 72, 88, 102, 118–19, 193–94, 196, 208, 210

lineal descent, 22, 34, 36, 64–65, 67, 69–70, 72–73, 78, 80, 82, 98, 105, 118, 139, 143, 149, 196, 201–202, 215–16

Lise (Ancestry forum), 52

Listuguj Mi'gmaq First Nation, 179, 205

Little Bras d'Or Indian Association, 87

Little Shell Tribe of Chippewa Indians of Montana, 125

Lory (VO forum), 46–47, 49, 84, 98

Louis XIV, King of France, 11, 90

Lowell, Massachusetts, 114

Lower Canada (Québec), 57, 170

Lussier, Raymond, 87–88, 90, 92

M

Macdonald, John A. (Prime Minister), 115

Macdougall, Brenda, 23, 30, 53, 117, 121–25, 218

Madokawando, Marie-Mathilde, 196

Maine, 43, 60, 196, 216–17

Maine Franco-American Genealogical Society, 111

Manchoose (Bad Arrow), 117

Manitoba, 7, 20, 53, 104, 115, 119

Manitoba Act, 115, 120

Marchand case, 137, 226

Marco (VO forum), 47–49, 66

masculinity, 37, 141, 179, 185, 215

Mashteuiatsh, 151, 155, 172, 228

Massachusetts, 60, 106, 114

Master Schedule of Algonquin Ancestors, 56, 58, 62, 84

Mattawa/North Bay Algonquin First Nation, 54, 57

McKay, Ignace, 114

McKay, Josephte, 114

McKay, Marguerite, 114

McKay, Nancy Anne, 114

Melungeon, 17

Membertou, 96–97, 99, 195–96, 213

man/men: 57, 140–41, 147, 151, 213, 215; Acadian, 195; Brabant, 56; French, 9–12, 14, 47–51, 98; French-Canadian, 113; French-descendant, 37, 47; French settler, 2, 8; Métis, 97, 120, 124; white, 24

mésalliance, 4

métis: "clans," 138, 141, 147, 161; explaining terminology, 5–7; meaning mixed-race, 5–12, 22, 42, 47, 53, 78, 140, 173, 200; Eastern, 7, 22, 43, 47, 49, 53, 60, 104, 113, 118, 130, 138, 140, 161, 189, 217; Federation of Canada, 89, 161; Nation of the Rising Sun (MNRS), 36–37, 85, 93, 177–83, 185–207, 211–13, 216; self-identified, 3; self-identified organization(s), 22, 35, 37, 63, 72, 75, 79, 84–86, 93, 96, 98, 101, 104, 137, 140; Quebec, 7, 45, 47, 68, 104–105, 111–113, 118, 130, 138, 193–94

282 | DISTORTED DESCENT

Métis: ancestors, 66; Arcand, 112–13, 116–18, 122–23, 130; Brabant, 119–20, 122–28, 130–31; communities, 22, 53, 67, 116, 119, 121, 125; ethnogenesis, 49, 120; families, 23, 114–15, 118, 120, 124; history, 34; identity, 105, 138, 143, 150; National Council (MNC), 53, 217; Nation of Ontario, 52; patronyms, 37, 112, 123; peoplehood, 20–23, 53, 70, 140, 144, 149–50; petition(s), 120–22, 124, 127; Qu'Appelle River, 122; Red River, 111, 120; Resistance (1870), 127, 130; Resistance (1885), 116, 125, 127, 130; rights, 21, 120; scholars, 22–23, 49, 53, 63; scrip, 125; self-determination, 113, 177; sovereignty, 31, 82; territories, 123, 126; traders, 114; women, 119

métissage: fiction of, 9–10; chimera of, 8, 11–12, 14, 135, 216; trope of, 4; policy of, 9; myth of, 8; self-indigenization and, 20

Mexican: Americans, 25; settlers, 18

Mexico, 17, 203

Michel (GQAF forum), 94–95

Michigan, 216–17

Michigan's Habitant Heritage, 87, 91

Micmacs of Gesgapegiag First Nation, 179–82, 185–86, 190–92, 211

migration, 34, 57, 90, 100, 113, 120, 159, 195

Mi'kma'ki, 94

Mi'kmaq of Nova Scotia. *See* Mi'kmaq Rights Initiative

Mi'kmaq Rights Initiative (MRI), 217

Mi'kmaw: identity, 101; communities, 87, 179

Milk River (Montana), 116, 124

Minier case, 137, 230

Missouri River (Montana), 116

Miteouamegoukwe, Marie, 50, 56, 62–64, 99

Mohawk (people), 56, 71, 106–110, 129, 194, 211

Mollie (French poodle), 211

Monet dit Belhumeur, Marguerite, 116

Montana, 7, 20, 116–17, 119, 122–25, 131

Montreal, Quebec, 6–8, 12–13, 49, 56, 87, 89, 104, 106–109, 113, 119, 126–27, 147

moose: season, 181–82; hunters, 183; hunting, 21, 191–92

Mothers of Acadia mtDNA research project, 80, 93–94, 196, 199–200

mtDNA haplogroup, 85, 88, 99–100, 206

Mystery (Ancestry forum), 83, 112–13, 118

N

Nahpase (Iron Body), 117

Nash, Catherine, 27, 51, 80, 126, 128, 218

Nathalie (GQAF forum), 67–68, 71

Nation autochtone du Québec (NAQ) forum, 45, 75–78, 191–92

Nation Métis Contemporaine, 75

Nation Métis Québec, 105

national: belonging, 206; boundaries, 12; census figures, 141; "Eastern métis" organizations, 161; debate about Métis and Aboriginal rights, 21; increase in Métis self-identification in census, 3; origins, 203

nationalism: French-descendant, 9; Puerto Rican, 26; Québécois, 8, 136, 167

Native American: DNA, 30–31, 81, 88, 90, 102, 177, 180, 200, 202–207, 210–11, 213; and Indigenous Studies Association, 69

neo-Chumash, 17–18, 20, 73

Nêhiyaw Pwat Confederacy, 122–24

Nelson, Alondra, 30–32, 71, 80, 88, 95–96, 101, 196, 218

New Brunswick, 3, 7, 22, 43, 60, 75, 94, 96, 137, 159, 216–17, 223–24, 250n3

New England, 2, 7, 35, 60–62, 90, 106–107, 114, 129, 179, 208, 212, 214, 216

New France, 2, 7–14, 35, 47–49, 51, 55–57, 61–62, 84, 90–91, 106, 109, 113, 119, 130, 139, 155, 174, 208, 216, 218

New Hampshire, 36, 43, 59–60, 62–63, 89, 92, 143, 216

New Richmond, Quebec, 36

New York, 60, 109

Nicolet, Euphrosine-Madeleine, 46, 50–51, 64, 99

Nicolet, Jean, 46, 50

Nims, Marie-Élisabeth Touatogouach, 107–108

nineteenth century, 17, 25, 51, 60, 73, 95, 104, 113–14, 119–20, 124–25, 130, 168

"Nipissing woman," 46, 50, 63, 230, 234

Noël case, 137, 234

North Dakota, 7, 20, 113, 119, 122–23, 125, 131

North West Company, 113

Northwest Resistance, 116–17

Northwest Territories, 7, 20

Nouvelle division de la terre, 5

Nova Scotia, 3, 7, 22, 36, 43, 60, 82–83, 87, 138, 159, 178, 195, 200, 216–18, 223, 237

Nulhegan Abenaki Tribe, 218

O

O'Bomsawin, Gilles, 61

Obomsawin, Alanis, 205

Odanak Abenaki First Nation, 59–61, 63, 218

Ojibwe. *See* Anishinaabe(g)

Oji-Cree, 211

"Oka Crisis," 162

one-drop rule. *See* hypodescent

Ontario: 2–3, 7, 21–22, 54–57, 60, 62–63, 84, 119, 121, 126–27, 130, 142–43, 216–17; Superior Court, 21, 58–59; Court of Appeal, 21; Legislative Assembly of, 57; Free Grants and Homestead Act (1868), 57, 119, 129; and Qu'Appelle Land Company (OQLC), 122; Game and Fish Act (1990), 21

Ottawa River, 8, 57, 108, 126–27

Ouechipichinokoue, Françoise, 49

P

Pahpah-me-kee-sick (Round the Sky), 117

Palmater, Pamela, 29–30, 70, 101, 126, 218

Parent case, 36, 137, 178–79, 181–87, 195–201, 212, 235–36, 257

Parent, Éric, 178, 181, 183

Paris, France, 5–6, 14, 46, 106, 119, 207

patronyms, 37, 106, 123–24, 199

Paul case, 137, 227

Paul (Rootsweb forum), 96

Pearson, Stephen, 16–17, 19

Pelletier case, 137, 235

Pelletier, François, 49, 83, 144

Pembina, North Dakota, 113, 122, 125

Penobscot, 196

Perron case, 137, 230

Pessamit, 151, 172

Piétacho, Philippe, 163

Pigarouiche, Marguerite, 56–57, 63–64, 99

Pillard, Catherine, 86–93, 97–101

Plains Cree, 7, 128

Podruchny, Carolyn, 116

Pouliot-Thisdale, Éric, 108–109

Powley decision, 21–22, 37, 45–46, 53–54, 93, 135–38, 140–43, 145–48, 150–53, 163, 171, 175, 178–79, 181–83, 188, 190, 195, 212, 214–17, 223, 241, 257

Powley test, 21, 37, 136–38, 143, 150, 175, 178, 223

Prévost, Martin, 46, 50, 52

Prince Albert, Saskatchewan, 117

Project de recherche démographique historique (PRDH), 13

Puritan(s), 106–107

Q

Qu'Appelle River, Saskatchewan, 120–23, 128

Quebec: Court of Appeal 137–38, 178, 216, 223; Government of, 180–81, 189, 195; Human Rights Commission, 163; nationalism, 8; Superior Court, 86, 136–37, 144, 159, 177–78, 216; métis, 7, 45, 47, 68, 104–105, 111–113, 118, 130, 138, 193–94

Quebec City, Quebec, 12, 44, 46, 50, 82, 113, 173

Québécois: -as-Euro, 14; descendants, 193; genealogy, 91; historiography, 4, 14; identity, 8, 156; nationalism, 8; (people), 2, 64, 70, 155, 159, 192; settlements, 108; white, 152, 154, 156, 159

R

race shifting: dynamics of, 143, 156; mechanics of, 43, 215; movement, 220; process, 72, 79, 82, 129

racial: background, 30, 80; category, 26; classification, 5; divisions, 11; dynamics, 9, 35; frame, 26; group(s), 5, 27; hierarchy/ies, 24–25; homeopathy, 24, 64; homogeneity, 13; kinship, 79; logics, 24; mixedness, 67; mixing, 149; origins, 80, 92; politics, 158; science, 30; slavery, 25; racialization, 26, 42, 72, 75, 79, 126, 140 racism: anti-black, 28, 100, 147–48, 175; anti-Indigenous, 162; anti-Innu, 164; biological, 101, 194

Raizenne, Josiah-Ignace Shoentakouani, 108–109, 129

Raymond (Ancestry forum), 104

Recherches amérindiennes du Québec, 163

Redeemed Captive Returning to Zion, The, 106–107, 248n8

Red River: Settlement, 53, 104, 114–15, 19, 119–20, 122, 126, 128, 130; Métis, 111, 120; Expeditionary Force (RREF), 115

Renée (GQAF forum), 68, 74

Regina, Saskatchewan, 117

residential schools, 1, 22, 41, 128, 166, 176, 194

Restigouche (River or Region), 184, 224

Richer, Mr. (NAQ forum), 78

Riel, Jean-Baptiste, 106, 110

Riel, Louis, 53, 103–105, 110, 115–17, 124, 126, 129–30

Riel, Rosalie, 105–106, 108–110

Riverin case, 137, 230

Robert (Ancestry forum), 52

Robinson-Huron Treaty (1850), 57, 129

Robitaille, Johan, 87–88, 90

Rocky's Boy Reservation, 124–25, 131

Rods (VO forum), 97–98

Rollet, Marie, 46, 50

root ancestors, 14, 55–56, 58–59, 63, 71, 86, 89, 93, 96, 106, 110, 139, 143–44, 159, 194, 197–98, 208, 213, 237

Rootsweb MetisGen-L genealogy forum, 45, 96, 243n23

Ross-Tremblay, Pierrot, 135, 152

Rouen, France, 106

Roy, Chistopher A., 60–61

Rupert's Land, 115

Rushforth, Brett, 9

S

Saada, Émanuelle, 5–6

Saguenay–Lac-Saint-Jean, Québec, 37, 137, 140, 149–50, 170–71, 174, 180

Saint-Pierre, Rameau de, 95

"salmon war(s)," 163–64

Santa Barbara, California, 17–18

Sarcelle (GQAF forum), 74–75, 82

Saskatoon, Saskatchewan, 48

Saskatchewan, 7, 20, 104, 112–13, 115–17, 119–20, 122–24

Saulteaux, 7, 20, 122, 128, 211

Savard case, 137, 235

Sayer, Guillaume, 114

section 35(1) of the Constitution Act, 1982, 21, 140, 142–43

Séguin case, 86, 137, 235, 257

self-identification, 15, 28, 42–43, 46, 52–53, 69–70, 74, 78–79, 139–41, 158, 179

self-identified "Cherokee", 19–20, 23–24, 42–43, 79, 149

self-indigenization, 1, 3, 5–6, 12, 15–16, 19–20, 22, 26–27, 42, 65, 67, 161, 216, 218–219

Sept-Îles, Quebec, 149, 160, 212

seventeenth century, 2–3, 5, 8–10, 36, 43, 48–49, 58, 60–61, 63–66, 69, 71–72, 77, 79–80, 82, 85, 94, 98–99, 101–102, 106, 109–110, 130, 135, 170, 174, 195, 214

Silverrose (Ancestry forum), 52

Simard case, 137, 232

Simpson, Audra, 48, 107

Simpson, Leanne Betasamosake, 62

Sixties Scoop, 1, 22, 41, 166, 176

Snoopy (Chihuahua), 211

Sophie (GQAF forum), 74

South Saskatchewan River, 115–16, 122

Spanish: ancestry, 26; blood, 25; Santa Barbara, 18

St. Boniface, Manitoba, 104, 114, 119, 122

St. François Xavier, Manitoba, 114, 122

St. Francis/Sokoki Band of Abenaki (Abenaki Nation at Missisquoi), 218

St. Laurent de Grandin, Saskatchewan, 116

St. Regis Reservation, 109

St-Onge, Nicole, 121–22, 124–25

Sturm, Circe, 19–20, 23–24, 42–43, 50–51, 54, 60, 64, 68, 77, 79, 99, 136, 149–52, 154, 161, 169, 188, 195, 215, 218–19

symbolic inversion, 19, 169

St. Lawrence River, 37, 76, 82, 89, 108–109, 113, 135, 163, 193, 198, 212

Stuurman, Siep, 5

Sudbury, Ontario, 56–57, 119, 127

Supreme Court of Canada, 21, 37, 140, 150, 179, 214, 216, 223

Sylvestre, Marie Olivier, 46–47, 50–55, 58–59, 61–64, 66, 112–13, 118–19, 126–27, 143–44, 159

T

Tadoussac, Quebec, 49, 135

TallBear, Kim, 30–32, 47, 71, 81, 90, 102, 203–204, 206, 211, 213, 218

Tanguay, Cyprien, 12

Thistle, Jesse, 114–17

Thunder Bay, Ontario, 48

Tremblay case (QCCQ), 137, 236

Tremblay case (QCCS), 137, 234

Trois-Rivières, Quebec, 12, 49, 56, 62, 113

Turtle Mountain Chippewa, 131

twentieth century, 8, 13, 44, 67, 124, 167

twenty-first century, 1, 22–23, 32, 82, 110, 128, 204, 219

U

United States: Bureau of Indian Affairs (BIA), 17–18; census, 19, 26, 251n8; imperialism, 25; -Mexican War, 17

Ursulines, 11

V

Val d'Or, Quebec, 48

Vallée case, 137, 227

Vancouver, British Columbia, 48

Vautour case, 138, 223

Vautour, Jackie, 248n3

Vermont, 36, 43, 59–61, 143, 216–18

Vestro (Jeannot), Marie, 114

virtual ethnography, 32, 34, 71, 96, 103

Vos origines (VO) genealogy forum, 44–45, 65, 74, 82–83, 97

W

wahkootowin, 23, 53, 117, 125–26, 128

Waywahnitch (Man Without Blood), 117

White, Stephen, 93

white: blood, 202; Canadians, 110, 113; citizens, 125; fishermen, 164; French descendants, 136, 151, 156, 160, 163–66, 170, 183, 202, 206, 214; hunters, 183; masculinity, 179; men, 24; Québécois, 152–54, 156, 159; (people), 76, 139, 152–53, 162, 164–65, 193, 215; rights organization(s), 139, 142, 152, 155, 161–62, 215; rights movement, 136, 142, 150–51, 153–54, 158–61, 165, 174–75; settler(s), 115–17, 121, 123, 125, 127, 131, 136, 148, 158, 160, 163, 166, 189–90, 192, 202, 206, 217–18; society, 220; supremacy, 4, 26, 176, 217; women, 195

whiteness, 4, 8, 17, 26–28, 151–52, 154, 162, 217–20

Wilcoxon, Larry, 17–19, 73

Winnipeg, Manitoba, 48, 53, 104, 115–16

Williams, Eunice (a.k.a. Marguerite Kanenstenhawi Arosen), 107, 109

Williams, Thomas (Théoragwanegon), 109

Wolinak Abenaki First Nation, 59, 61, 63, 218

woman/women: Acadian, 94, 200; ancestor(s), 18, 34, 80, 95; Algonquin, 50, 56, 98–99; Algonquin-Siberian, 87, 92; Anishinaabe, 49; black, 24; European, 34, 86, 196–98; French, 3, 11, 36, 46, 51, 56, 73, 75, 77, 82–83, 86, 88, 99, 101, 106, 150, 198, 213, 216, 237; French-Canadian, 56, 126; French-Québécois, 143; Indigenous, 2–3, 8–12, 14–15, 25, 28, 31, 34, 36, 41, 43, 46–52, 54, 59, 61–66, 69, 72–73, 75, 77, 80, 82, 84, 98, 101, 112, 118, 126, 143, 145, 165, 214–16; McKay, 114; Innu, 144–45; Métis, 49, 97, 114, 116, 119, 126; Mi'kmaw, 94–95, 101, 196; Nipissing, 46, 50, 63, 230, 231; Parisian, 46; seventeenth-century, 65, 82, 85, 98, 102; white, 195

Y

Yarmouth, Nova Scotia, 217

Yves (GQAF forum), 74, 94, 98

www.ingramcontent.com/pod-product-compliance
Lightning Source LLC
Chambersburg PA
CBHW031333230426
43670CB00006B/333